the family cookbook: **dessert**

the family cookbook:

by Charlotte Adams
& Doris McFerran Townsend
Special Consultant: Alvin Kerr

Illustrations
by Helen Federico
Photography
by Arie deZanger

dessert

A Ridge Press Book | Holt, Rinehart and Winston | New York

RIDGE PRESS:
Editor-in-Chief: Jerry Mason
Editor: Adolph Suehsdorf
Art Director: Albert Squillace
Project Art Director: Harry Brocke
Associate Editor: Ruth Birnkrant
Associate Editor: Moira Duggan
Associate Editor: Barbara Hoffbeck
Art Associate: Mark Liebergall
Art Production: Doris Mullane

RESTAURANT ASSOCIATES:
Supervising Chef: Joseph Renggli
Pastry Chef, Four Seasons Restaurant: Bruno Comin
Pastry Chef, Trattoria: Lorenzo Dolcino
Pastry Chef, Publick House-Sturbridge: Richard Stone

Courtesy of B. Altman & Co., New York, in lending objects for
photographic still lifes is gratefully acknowledged.

contents

introduction

Of all the riches lavished on the table, the one least likely to be forsworn willingly is dessert. A first course may be bypassed without regret. Even soup and salad may be refused, if not cheerfully, at least without too much anguish. But the loss of the sweet is sure to be unhappy.

Bread may be the staff of life, but dessert is its cloak of elegance. It represents the fruit of the cook's most ardent labors and comes to table as the consummate achievement of culinary art. It is the happy conclusion to any meal, whether it comes as a many-splendored cake or as an unadorned baked apple.

Dessert has been likened to the epilogue of a play, the resolution of a symphony, and the grand finale of a spectacular ballet. It has been described as the jewel of the kitchen and food for the gods. It has been celebrated in song and story—for example, in an anonymous, seemingly endless poem of the 1880's, entitled "The Dessert," whose opening stanza contains the following lines:

> "Take your two courses, if you have not three
> or say but one, but one and your dessert."

Sweets of a sort have been known to exist since the beginning of history. Originally sacrificial cakes of unbaked crude meal blended with cruder oils and a sweetening that may have been honey, they traveled a long road of refinement until they arrived as dessert at mankind's tables, although even then they were far removed from the irresistible delicacies they were ultimately to become. Desserts probably began their ascent in Egypt. They progressed along the routes of war and conquest to Turkey, thence to ancient Greece, on to Austria and Hungary, and finally to Rome and France. It is the latter which is credited with giving desserts their final polish, but the Italians provided the delectable foundation.

Desserts are now indigenous to almost every country of the world, and each has come to be identified through its native sweet. Strudel is Hungary, although the pastry, originally somewhat less delicate, came from Turkey. The Magyars made it what it is today, a tissue-thin fantasy filled with apples, nuts, poppy seeds, or sometimes with sweetened cheese and even cabbage. When cooked fruit comes to table as filling for puddings and cakes, or when cooked fresh lingonberries provide filling for pancakes you may be fairly certain you are in Denmark, Finland, Norway, or Sweden. If you are in doubt as to which, just ask, but don't be surprised if you find you are in Germany. For that country also favors fruit desserts, as well as schnecken and other nut-filled and spice-flavored torten. Know, however, that schnecken may indicate Austria, and if it and other desserts are well anointed with schlagobers (whipped cream), you may be certain you are in Austria, specifically in Vienna. France is essentially cream country, of the Bavarian and caramel varieties, but the basis for them, which even the French identify as crème à l'anglaise, particularly in trifle, will transport you to England. Italy is ice (granita) and everything frankly and unashamedly rich. Ghurayyibi, if you know how to order it (pronounce it "gribbee") may find you in Lebanon. Baklava will signal your arrival in Greece or Turkey, and kinafe (sometimes "knafee"), an exotic preparation of walnuts combined with a pastry resembling shredded wheat, can only mean you are in Syria. The Orient insists it has no desserts per se, just sweetmeats, but if one of those is pa sze ping kuo (Spun-Silk Apples), you are in China or Hong Kong or, small world that we have become, perhaps in a truly Chinese restaurant in the United States or Britain.

Desserts also have come to represent holidays. You can determine almost certainly which feast day it is by the dessert which comes to table at any particular time of the year. Pancakes served in the spring, the day before Lent, will tell you that it is Shrove Tuesday. A log-shaped cake with a "bark" of butter cream is, in France, a herald of Christmas. Served in February in the United States, the cake salutes the birthday of Abraham Lincoln, the one-time log-splitter. A cake with cherries, served a few days later, greets the birthday of George Washington, the legendary cherry-tree chopper. A heart-shaped cake presented in February is a Valentine's Day remembrance. Pashka is the symbolic cake of Russian Easter, while panettone is for Easter in Italy. Pumpkin pie is for

America's Thanksgiving Day. Fruit cake and plum pudding are Christmas greetings. Eggnog and syllabub greet the New Year. As far as is known there are no desserts to commemorate May Day, Labor Day, Columbus Day, or Groundhog Day, but anybody's birthday any time brings congratulations in a cake. A nuptial day, in June or whenever, has a special cake of its own, varying in size and impressiveness from a two- or three-layer confection to a creation of high-rise proportions.

Dessert can be for all times and every occasion. It adapts itself to matter-of-fact business-breakfast meetings as it does to the casual morning coffee break *à deux* at home. It is as comfortable at a stiffly starched formal banquet as it is at the completely informal family dinner.

Usually the last course of a meal, dessert was once, in colonial times, the first. There are those, particularly among the young, who wish it were still so. Although considerably less ostentatious than they once were, desserts are no less elegant and delicious, and their preparation still requires considerable effort.

The authors of this volume know that the effort is well placed, however, and always appreciated. In collaboration with the fine chefs of Restaurant Associates, they have tested and set down here a wide and handsome variety of both "homey" and company desserts. My own sweet tooth has been happily cosseted by all of them, and I commend them delectably to yours.

—Alvin Kerr

1 | cakes

One dictionary defines cake as a "sweetened mixture of flour and other ingredients, baked in a loaf or mass." That, we think, is too meager a description for one of the great and abiding riches of the table. It might better be called "food for the gods," which in fact it once was. Early fragments of history note that altars were always laden with offerings of cake, and mortal man must frequently have eyed them with envy. For ultimately he decided that the sacrifice was too great, and he reclaimed cake for himself. Since that time cake has become a sweet for all occasions. It celebrates birthdays (as does our own Birthday Cake), serves as a token of affection (as does our Valentine Cake), and it is always a member of the wedding. It is the reward given the winner of a competition, whence came the expression, "It takes the cake." Such is the magic of cake that it transforms even the simplest meal into a distinctive repast.

The cake recipes which follow are all within the compass of even the most timid cook, but you must keep in mind that a cake is only as fine as the quality of the ingredients and the care with which they are prepared. More than for any other dessert, the instructions given for their preparation must be followed strictly. A little more of this or a little less of that can result in a cake's downfall—literally. Too hot an oven or one too cool can be equally disastrous. Observe the rules and you will find cake-making a wonderful adventure.

Genoise | French Sponge Cake

6 eggs　　　　　　　　　　**1 cup sifted cake flour**
1 cup sugar　　　　　　　　**¼ cup Clarified Butter (page 23)**
1 tsp vanilla extract

Preheat oven to 350 degrees. In the top pan of a double boiler over (but not touching) barely simmering water, gently warm together the eggs and sugar, beating constantly with a whisk until the mixture is the consistency of moderately thick syrup. Remove the pan from over the water. Add the vanilla and continue beating, now with a rotary beater, until the mixture is thick enough to flow in ribbons from the withdrawn beater and remain for several seconds on the surface of the mass before blending into it again. Sprinkle the flour over the surface of the mass a little at a time and fold in each addition gently but thoroughly. Similarly fold in the clarified butter, melted and cooled.

Butter a shallow 11 x 15-inch baking pan, cover the bottom with waxed paper, and butter and lightly flour the paper. Or prepare 1 regular 9-inch cake pan or two 9-inch layer-cake pans in the same way. Spread the batter evenly in the prepared pan or pans and bake for 25 minutes or until the top is lightly browned and slightly resistant to gentle pressure. Turn the cake out onto a rack to let it cool and peel off the paper. Serve the cake plain or dusted with confectioners' sugar and cut into squares. Or cut the cake into fancy small shapes and ice as desired as *petits fours.* This recipe provides sufficient genoise for about 20 squares, each 2¾ inches, or the equivalent in other shapes.

Sponge Cake

6 eggs, separated　　　　　**½ tsp vanilla extract**
1 cup sugar　　　　　　　　**1 cup cake flour, sifted 4 times**
1 Tbl strained lemon juice　**¼ tsp salt**

Preheat oven to 350 degrees. In a mixing bowl beat the egg yolks with ½ the sugar and all the lemon juice and vanilla until the mixture can be dripped from the beater in ribbons thick enough to hold their shape for a few seconds before blending into the mass. Thoroughly stir in the flour. In a separate bowl beat the egg whites with the salt to the soft-peak stage. Add the remaining sugar, a little at a time, continuing the beating until the whites are stiff and glossy. Fold them into the yolk mixture. Spread the batter in an ungreased 9-inch tube pan and bake in the preheated oven for 45 minutes or until the top of the cake is lightly resistant to gentle pressure. Set tube over the neck of bottle, cake side down, and cool the cake completely in the pan. Unmold the cake and ice it as desired, or serve plain. This sponge cake provides 8 generous servings.

Applejack Pound Cake

1 cup butter	1 tsp vanilla extract
1½ cups sugar	1½ cups sifted flour
2 eggs, separated	½ cup chopped pecans
3 Tbl applejack	

Preheat oven to 350 degrees. In a mixing bowl cream together to fluffy consistency the butter and 1 cup of the sugar. Beat in the egg yolks. Blend in the applejack and vanilla and gently but thoroughly stir in the flour. In a separate bowl beat the egg whites into soft peaks. Add the remaining sugar, a little at a time, beating constantly until the whites are stiff and glossy. Fold them into the yolk mixture.

Butter and lightly flour a 1½-quart loaf pan. Sprinkle the pecans over the bottom and spread the prepared batter over them. Bake in the preheated oven for 50 minutes or until a cake tester inserted in the center of the cake can be withdrawn clean. Cool the cake in the pan for 10 minutes. Unmold it onto a rack and complete the cooling. Sliced moderately thick, this cake will provide 12 servings.

Pound Cake

2 cups butter, slightly softened	2 Tbl brandy
2¼ cups sugar	4 cups sifted flour
10 large eggs, separated	¼ tsp salt

Preheat oven to 350 degrees. In a mixing bowl whip together the butter and sugar to the consistency of lightly whipped cream. Blend in the egg yolks, beaten until very thick, and the brandy. Add gradually the flour sifted with the salt, stirring just until the mixture is smooth. Excessive stirring will result in a heavy cake. Gently fold in the egg whites, stiffly beaten. Spread the batter evenly in 2 buttered and lightly floured 1½-quart loaf pans and bake in the preheated oven for 40 minutes. Using the blunt side of a buttered table knife, cut a slit about ½-inch deep down the center of each cake and continue the baking for 20 minutes longer or until a cake tester inserted in the center of each loaf can be withdrawn clean. Cool the cakes in the pans for 10 minutes. Unmold them onto a rack and complete the cooling. Serve the cakes, cut in moderately thin slices to provide 16 servings per loaf. Wrapped in foil or plastic wrap and stored in a covered container, the cakes can be kept for several weeks. For neater slices, do not cut the cakes until 24 hours after baking.

Angel Food Cake

1 cup egg whites (7–8), at room temperature	**¼ tsp almond extract**
¼ tsp salt	**1 tsp cream of tartar**
¾ tsp vanilla extract	**1¼ cups fine granulated sugar**
	1 cup sifted cake flour

Preheat oven to 325 degrees. In a mixing bowl combine the egg whites with the salt and beat them to a froth. Stir in the flavorings. Sprinkle the cream of tartar over the whites and continue the beating just until the peaks, formed when the beater is withdrawn, are firm but still moist-looking. Beat no longer. Overbeating will make folding in the dry ingredients very difficult and may result in coarse-textured cake. Gently but thoroughly fold in the sugar, 2 tablespoons at a time. Similarly fold in the flour, sifted over the whites ¼ cup at a time. Transfer the batter to an ungreased 10-inch tube pan and bake in the preheated oven for 1 hour or until the top is lightly browned. Cool the cake completely in the pan, suspended top down with the tube fitted over the neck of a bottle. Run a blunt-edged knife around the edge of the pan and the

tube to release the cake. Serve the cake in wedges, pulled apart with a cake rake or 2 forks. Do not cut it. Angel cake improves in flavor and texture if allowed to season for a day before serving it. This recipe provides 8 to 10 servings.

Buttermilk Cake

1 cup butter, softened
2 cups sugar
2 egg yolks
2 whole eggs
¾ tsp baking soda

1 cup buttermilk
1 tsp vanilla extract
2½ cups sifted flour
Chocolate Icing (page 63)

Preheat oven to 375 degrees. In a mixing bowl beat together the butter and sugar until the mixture is smooth and fluffy. Beat in the egg yolks together and the whole eggs 1 at a time. Stir in the soda dissolved in the buttermilk, and the vanilla. Blend in the flour. Spread the batter equally in 3 buttered and lightly floured 8-inch square cake pans and bake in the preheated oven for 25 minutes or until a cake tester inserted in the center of the cakes can be withdrawn clean. Coat the cakes with the chocolate icing. Each cake provides 6 servings.

Chocolate Buttermilk Cake

1 cup butter	2 cups buttermilk
2 cups sugar	2 tsp baking soda
2 eggs	⅛ tsp salt
3½ cups cake flour	2 Tbl water
½ cup cocoa	1 tsp vanilla extract

Preheat oven to 350 degrees. In a mixing bowl thoroughly cream together the butter and sugar. Beat in the eggs. Sift together the flour and cocoa and blend them into the creamed mixture a little at a time, alternating those additions with small quantities of the buttermilk combined with the soda and salt dissolved in the water. Stir in the vanilla. Spread the batter evenly in a buttered 13 x 9 x 2-inch baking pan and bake it in the preheated oven for 45 minutes or until a cake tester, inserted in the center of the cake, can be withdrawn clean. Ice the cake with vanilla-flavored Butter Cream (page 59) or Chocolate Icing (page 63). Cut the cake lengthwise into thirds and across the width into fourths to provide 12 servings.

Devil's Food Cake

½ cup butter	1 tsp baking soda
2 cups sugar	½ tsp salt
4 eggs, separated	2 cups sour milk (see Note)
1 tsp vanilla extract	6 squares (6 ounces) unsweetened

Preheat oven to 375 degrees. In a mixing bowl thoroughly cream together the butter and sugar and beat in the egg yolks and vanilla. Sift together the flour, baking powder, soda, and salt, and add to the creamed mixture ⅓ at a time, alternating with similar portions of the sour milk. Blend in the chocolate. Spread the batter evenly in a buttered and lightly floured 10-inch tube pan and bake in the preheated oven for 30 minutes or until the top of the cake is lightly resistant to gentle pressure. Remove the cake from the pan and cool it on a rack. Cut the cake into generous-size wedges to provide 12 servings.

NOTE: 2 cups sweet milk can be soured by adding to them 2 tablespoons strained lemon juice or white vinegar and letting the mixture season for 30 minutes.

Gingerbread

½ cup butter	1 tsp salt
½ cup sugar	4 tsp ginger
1 cup light molasses	1 tsp cinnamon
2 eggs	½ tsp ground cloves
2½ cups flour, sifted twice	1 cup hot water
1½ tsp baking soda	

Preheat oven to 325 degrees. In a mixing bowl cream together the butter and sugar. Stir in the molasses and thoroughly beat in the eggs. Blend in the flour, sifted a third time with the soda, salt, and spices, and slowly stir in the hot water. Spread the batter in a 13 x 9 x 2-inch baking pan and bake in the preheated oven 35 minutes or until a cake tester inserted in the center of the cake can be withdrawn clean. Remove the cake from the pan and cool it on a rack. Cut the cake into 3 lengthwise strips of equal size and cut each into 4 to provide a total of 12 servings.

The gingerbread may be served warm or cooled, plain or with whipped cream, or with softened or whipped cream cheese and Lemon Sauce (page 281).

Honey Cake

7 eggs, separated	2 tsp cinnamon
1¾ cups sugar	¼ tsp allspice
1½ cups honey	¼ tsp ginger
1 cup tutti-frutti (see Note)	4½ cups flour
1½ cups shelled pecans	3 tsp baking powder

Preheat oven to 350 degrees. In a mixing bowl beat the egg yolks with ¾ cup of the sugar until they are light in color and very thick. Stir in the honey, tutti-frutti, pecans, and spices. Sift the flour with the baking powder and blend in. In a separate bowl beat the egg whites to soft-peak consistency. Add the remaining sugar a little at a time, continuing the beating until the whites are stiff and glossy. Gently but thoroughly fold them into the yolk mixture. Spread the batter evenly in 2 buttered and lightly floured 8-inch round cake pans and bake in the preheated oven 30 minutes or until a cake tester inserted in the center of the cakes can be withdrawn clean. Serve the cakes unfrosted or with a frosting of your choice. Cut the cakes to provide 6 to 8 servings each.

Honey cakes freeze well. Defrost completely and warm gently before serving.

NOTE: Tutti-frutti is a mixture of preserved fruits, available commercially.

Basler Lebkuchen | Swiss Spice Cake

½ cup sugar	½ tsp ground cloves
1 cup honey	½ tsp baking soda
½ cup unblanched almonds, coarsely chopped	¼ tsp salt
	3 Tbl chopped citron
1 egg	3 Tbl chopped candied orange peel
2½ cups sifted flour	Grated rind of ½ lemon
2 tsp cinnamon	2 Tbl kirsch
½ tsp ground mace	Lemon Icing (page 61)

Preheat oven to 325 degrees. In a saucepan over moderate heat dissolve the sugar in the honey. Bring the syrup to a foaming boil and add the almonds. Immediately remove the pan from the heat and let the syrup cool completely, by which time the almonds should have become well browned. Beat in the egg. Sift the flour with the spices, soda, and salt, and blend in. Stir in the citron, candied peel, grated lemon rind, and kirsch. Spread the dough in a lightly floured, shallow 11 x 15-inch baking pan and bake in the preheated oven for 20 minutes or until the top of the cake is well browned. Remove the pan from the oven and coat the cake with the lemon icing while it is still warm. Cut the cake to provide 12 servings.

Egyptian Cake

½ cup butter	2 Tbl cocoa
1½ cups sugar	1 tsp vanilla extract
3 eggs, separated	1 tsp lemon extract
¾ cup buttermilk	1 cup coarsely chopped nutmeats
2 cups sifted cake flour	12 squares (12 ounces)
¾ tsp baking soda	semisweet chocolate
¾ tsp baking powder	2 cups sour cream
¼ tsp nutmeg	½ tsp orange extract
1 tsp cinnamon	

Preheat oven to 375 degrees. In a mixing bowl cream together the butter and sugar until the mixture is light and fluffy. In another bowl thoroughly combine the egg yolks, well beaten, and the buttermilk. Resift the flour with the baking soda, baking powder, spices, and cocoa, and stir it gently but thoroughly, in small quantities, into the creamed mixture. Alternate those additions with portions of the combined egg yolks and buttermilk. Add the flavorings and nutmeats, and carefully but completely fold in the egg whites, beaten until stiff but not dry. Spread the batter equally in three 8-inch cake pans and bake in the preheated oven for 20 minutes, or until a cake tester inserted in the center of the cakes can be withdrawn clean. Cool the cakes on a rack and arrange them as a 3-layer cake, filled and frosted with the following mixture:

    In the top pan of a double boiler over simmering water melt the chocolate. Remove the pan from over the water and blend in the sour

cream and orange flavoring. Cool the mixture before using it. This cake provides 6 to 8 servings.

Yugoslavian Walnut Cake

6 eggs, separated	**1¼ cups raisins**
1⅓ cups sugar	**1½ cups semolina (see Note)**
1¾ cups ground walnuts	**Syrup (see below)**

Preheat oven to 350 degrees. In a mixing bowl beat together the egg yolks and sugar until the mixture is smooth and creamy. Blend in the nuts, raisins, and semolina. Fold in the egg whites, stiffly beaten. Spread the mixture evenly in 2 buttered and lightly floured 8-inch square cake pans and bake in the preheated oven for 40 minutes or until the tops of the cakes are lightly browned. Cut the cakes into triangles or diamond shapes to provide 6 to 8 servings each and let them cool in the pans. Pour the boiling hot syrup over them and let them absorb it completely.

Syrup:

3 cups sugar

1 cup water

½ tsp vanilla extract

Juice of ½ lemon

In a saucepan combine all of the ingredients and cook them over moderate heat for 10 minutes or until the resulting syrup has thickened somewhat (230 degrees on a candy thermometer).

NOTE: Semolina is fine flour, made from durum or other hard wheat. It is available generally at shops specializing in products used in Middle European cookery.

Madeleines

Thinly peeled rind of ½ lemon

⅔ cup sugar

2 eggs

½ tsp vanilla extract

1 cup sifted cake flour

1 cup warm Clarified Butter
 (see below)

Preheat oven to 375 degrees. In the top pan of a double boiler rub the lemon peel into the sugar, impregnating the granules thoroughly with the zest. Remove and discard the peel. Blend in the eggs. Set the pan over (but not touching) simmering water and beat the mixture with a rotary beater until it is very fluffy and warmed through. Remove the pan from over the water and stir in the vanilla. Gently but thoroughly fold in the flour. Reserve ¼ cup of the warmed clarified butter. Fold the remaining ¾ cup into the batter. Do not stir or beat further. Coat 18 madeleine molds with some of the reserved butter, using as much as may be needed to grease them well. Fill them to about ⅔ their capacity with the prepared batter and bake in the preheated oven for 8 minutes or until the little cakes are lightly browned. Invert them out onto a rack to cool. Rebutter the molds, fill them again with batter and bake as before. This quantity provides about 36 madeleines.

Clarified Butter:

In a saucepan over low heat melt unsalted butter until a froth rises to the top. Skim off the froth and discard it. Drain off the remaining clear golden butter, leaving any sediment at the bottom of the pan.

Clarified butter is rich but slow to burn, which makes it preferred for baking and sautéing. Well contained and under refrigeration, it may be stored for months without deteriorating.

Ladyfingers

4 eggs, separated
¼ tsp salt
1 cup sifted confectioners' sugar
½ tsp vanilla extract
⅔ cup sifted cake flour

Preheat oven to 325 degrees. In a mixing bowl beat the egg whites with the salt to soft-peak consistency. Add ¾ cup of the sugar, a little at a time, continuing the beating until the whites are very stiff and glossy. In a separate bowl beat the egg yolks with the vanilla and remaining sugar until the mixture thickens. Carefully fold it into the egg whites ⅓ at a time, alternating these additions with thirds of the flour. Cover a baking sheet with unglazed paper and, using a pastry bag fitted with a large plain tube, pipe the batter onto it in strips 3½ inches long and ¾-inch wide. Bake in the preheated oven 12 minutes or until the cakes are lightly browned. Run a dull knife under them to free them and cool them on a rack. This provides about 24 ladyfingers.

Baba au Rhum

2 envelopes dry yeast
⅓ cup lukewarm water
8 eggs
⅓ cup sugar
½ tsp salt
3½ cups sifted flour
½ cup butter, softened
Simple Syrup (page 278)
½ cup full-bodied rum
Apricot preserves, melted

In a small bowl soften the yeast in the water. In a larger bowl beat the eggs until the yolks and whites are well combined and stir into them the sugar and salt. Blend in 2½ cups of the flour and the softened butter. Add the prepared yeast with its liquid and gently but thoroughly stir in the remaining flour. Transfer the dough to a buttered bowl, cover it lightly with a cloth, and let it rise in a warm place until it has doubled in bulk, about 1½ hours. Deflate the dough and apportion it equally among 24 buttered baba tins, each about 2 inches in diameter and 2 inches deep. The dough should fill each tin to about ½ its capacity. Set the tins in a warm place and let the dough rise again until it fills them. Preheat oven to 375 degrees.

As soon as the dough has risen sufficiently, transfer the tins to the preheated oven. Bake for 20 minutes or until the cakes are well browned and begin to shrink from the sides of the pans. Cover a rack with a single layer of paper toweling and invert the cakes out onto it. Let them cool somewhat. While they are still warm transfer them to a glass baking dish and pour over them the syrup flavored with the rum. Turn the cakes in the syrup until they absorb all of it uniformly. Brush the babas with the melted preserves. Serve 1 to a serving, plain or with whipped cream.

Babas may be frozen, in which case they should be defrosted and warmed slightly before being moistened with the syrup.

Honey Date Cake

2 eggs, separated
1 cup honey
1 cup sifted dry bread crumbs
¼ cup flour
½ tsp baking powder

¼ tsp salt
1 cup chopped pitted dates
½ cup chopped walnuts
1 tsp vanilla extract
½ cup heavy cream, whipped

Preheat oven to 375 degrees. In a mixing bowl thoroughly combine the egg yolks and honey, and blend into them the bread crumbs, flour, baking powder, and salt, sifted together. Stir in the dates, walnuts, and vanilla. In another bowl beat the egg whites until they are stiff but not dry. Stir ¼ of them into the date-nut mixture and fold in the remainder. Spread the batter evenly in a well-buttered 8-inch square cake pan and bake in the preheated oven for 25 minutes or until the top is lightly resistant to gentle pressure. Remove from the oven. Let the cake remain in the pan for 5 minutes or until it begins to shrink from the sides. Unmold it onto a rack and let it cool a little more. Cut it in half and cut the halves into thirds to provide 6 servings. Serve the cake warm with the whipped cream, well chilled, passed separately.

Layered Fruitcake

1½ cups flaked coconut

1 cup seedless raisins

1 cup walnuts, finely chopped

1 cup butter

2 cups sugar

1 cup blackberry jam

3 eggs

3 cups flour

¼ tsp allspice

1 cup buttermilk

1 tsp baking soda

Fruitcake Filling (page 67)

Preheat oven to 350 degrees. Put the coconut and raisins through the fine blade of a food chopper and combine them with the chopped nuts. In a mixing bowl thoroughly cream together the butter and sugar and stir in the blackberry jam. Beat in the eggs, 1 at a time. Sift the flour with the allspice and fold it into the creamed mixture a little at a time, alternating those additions with small quantities of the buttermilk and soda combined. Stir in the prepared fruit and nuts. Spread the batter evenly in 2 buttered 9-inch layer-cake pans and bake in the preheated oven 45 minutes or until the cakes are very lightly browned. Let the cakes cool in the pans for 5 minutes. Remove them to a rack and complete the cooling. Spread 1 cake thickly with some of the filling and fit the other over it. Frost the layers with the remaining filling. This cake provides 8 servings.

Pecan Fruitcake

¾ cup soft vegetable margarine

½ cup sugar

4 eggs

1 Tbl corn syrup

6 Tbl flour

⅛ tsp salt

1 pound pecan halves

½ pound pitted dates, cut into halves

½ pound candied pineapple slices, cut into small wedges

½ pound candied whole cherries

Preheat oven to 300 degrees. In a mixing bowl combine the margarine and sugar and thoroughly blend in the eggs, 1 at a time. Vigorously beat in the corn syrup. Add the flour, sifted with the salt, and stir in the nuts and fruits. Grease and lightly flour two 1½-quart loaf pans and spread the batter evenly in them. Cover with foil. Bake in the preheated oven for 45 minutes or until the tops of the cakes are lightly browned. Cool the cakes in the pans before unmolding them. Wrap each loaf securely in foil. Refrigerated, the cakes will keep for several weeks. They may also be frozen. Each cake will provide 12 to 16 slices.

White Fruitcake

¾ cup butter	1 pound assorted candied fruit,
1 cup sugar	chopped
5 eggs	1 pound candied whole cherries
2 cups sifted flour	6 ounces dried figs, chopped
2 tsp baking powder	½ cup white rum
⅛ tsp salt	

Preheat oven to 350 degrees. In a mixing bowl thoroughly cream together the butter and sugar. Add the eggs, 1 at a time, beating thoroughly after each addition. Reserve ¼ cup of the flour. Sift the remainder with the baking powder and salt and blend it into the creamed mixture. In another bowl combine the fruits and toss them with the reserved flour, coating the pieces well. Stir them into prepared mixture. Spread this batter in a well-buttered 10-inch tube pan and bake it in the preheated oven for 1½ hours. Remove pan from oven and pour ¼ cup of the rum over the cake. Let the cake cool somewhat and pour over it the remaining rum. Let the cake cool completely before unmolding it.

    Securely wrapped in foil and refrigerated, this cake will keep for about 2 weeks. It should be moistened occasionally with a little more rum. In moderately thin slices the cake will provide about 20 servings. It should be served at room temperature.

Promenade Cheesecake

6 graham crackers	4 eggs
2 pounds cream cheese	Juice & grated rind of 1 lemon
1¾ cups fine granulated sugar	1 tsp vanilla extract

Preheat oven to 325 degrees. Roll the graham crackers into fine crumbs and with them evenly coat the bottom and sides of a buttered cake pan 8 inches in diameter and 3 inches deep. Do not use a spring-form pan. Shake out excess crumbs and reserve them.

In a mixing bowl cream together the cheese and sugar until the mixture is the consistency of whipped cream. Vigorously and thoroughly beat in the eggs, 1 at a time, the lemon juice and rind, and the vanilla. Spread this filling evenly in the prepared pan. Set the pan in the center of a larger pan (9 to 10 inches in diameter but of the same depth) and pour hot water into that pan to a depth of about ½ inch. Bake the cake so in the preheated oven for 2 hours. Turn off heat, but let the cake remain in the slackening oven for 1 hour longer. Remove the cake pan from the larger one and set it on a rack to cool for 2 hours.

Unmold the cake by inverting it out onto a lightly buttered plate. Place a serving platter on the cake (which is now bottom side up) and invert both so that platter is on the bottom and cake is top side up. Sift the reserved cracker crumbs on top. Decorate, if desired, with berries or slices of other fruit. Cut the cake to provide 12 servings.

Ricotta Cheesecake | Torta di Ricotta

2 cups sifted flour	**Grated rind of 2 lemons**
4 tsp sugar	**½ pound ricotta cheese, drained**
1 cup butter, softened	**¼ tsp salt**
⅓ cup plus 2 Tbl sour cream	**1 cup pulverized blanched almonds**
2 egg yolks	

Preheat oven to 350 degrees. Sift together the flour and 1 teaspoon of the sugar into a mixing bowl. Make a well in the center and in it put the butter, 2 tablespoons of the sour cream, 1 egg yolk, and ½ the grated lemon rind. Using your fingers, blend these ingredients into the flour and sugar to produce a soft dough. Chill it in the refrigerator for 15 minutes. Roll out dough into a square about ⅛-inch thick, fit into a buttered and lightly floured 8-inch square cake pan, and trim it around the top of the pan. Line the dough with buttered foil (buttered side down) and fill with dried beans. This is done to prevent the dough from receding during the preliminary baking. Bake in the preheated oven for 12 minutes. Remove the beans and foil and continue the baking for 3 minutes longer or just until the pastry begins to take on a little color. (Don't discard the beans. They are still usable.)

Force the drained ricotta cheese through a fine sieve into a mixing bowl and blend into it all of the remaining ingredients. Spread this filling evenly in the partially baked pastry in the pan and bake it in the oven, still heated to 350 degrees, for 45 minutes or until the top is nicely browned and the filling is set. Turn off the heat and let the cake partially cool in the oven with the door ajar. Complete the cooling at room temperature. Cut the cake in half down the middle, and cut each half into thirds to provide 6 generous servings.

Strawberry Shortcake

1 pint strawberries	**¼ tsp salt**
2 Tbl confectioners' sugar	**⅓ cup butter**
2 cups flour	**½–¾ cup milk**
3 tsp baking powder	**Additional butter, softened**
2 tsp granulated sugar	

Preheat oven to 450 degrees. Hull and wash the strawberries. Place them in a bowl, crush them slightly, and sprinkle them with the confectioners' sugar. Sift the flour with the baking powder, granulated sugar, and salt into a mixing bowl. Blend the butter into it. Add just enough milk to make a dough that is soft but not sticky. Pat evenly in a buttered and lightly floured 9-inch cake pan and bake in the preheated oven for 12 minutes or until the top is lightly browned and a cake tester inserted in the center of the cake can be withdrawn clean. Remove the cake from the pan, split it into 2 layers, and while they are still hot, coat them generously with softened butter. Place 1 layer on a serving platter buttered side up and cover it with ½ the berries. Arrange the second layer, also buttered side up, over them, and spread the remaining berries over it. Let the cake cool and serve it, if desired, with slightly sweetened whipped cream. This shortcake will provide 8 servings.

Applesauce Cake

½ cup butter
¾ cup brown sugar
2 eggs, well beaten
2½ cups flour
2 tsp baking powder
1 tsp baking soda

¼ tsp salt
1 tsp cinnamon
½ tsp ground cloves
2 cups thick applesauce
1 cup chopped raisins
1 cup chopped walnuts

Preheat oven to 325 degrees. In a mixing bowl thoroughly cream together the butter and sugar. Beat in the eggs. Sift together the flour, baking powder, soda, salt, and spices, and blend the mixture into the creamed ingredients, adding it a little at a time, alternately with similar quantities of the applesauce. Thoroughly fold in the raisins and nuts. Spread the batter evenly in a well-buttered 9 x 5 x 2¾-inch loaf pan and bake in the preheated oven for 1 hour or until a cake tester inserted in the center of the loaf can be withdrawn clean. Cool the cake in the pan for a few minutes before removing it to a rack to complete the cooling. Frost the cake as desired and slice it to provide 12 generous servings.

Danish Apple Cake

10 cooking apples
1 cup plus 2 Tbl butter
½ cup Vanilla Sugar (page 70)
½ cup dry white wine
18 Holland rusks
½ cup sugar
¾ cup raspberry jam, melted & cooled

1 cup currant jelly, melted & cooled
¼ cup water
¾ cup sliced blanched almonds
Whipped cream

Preheat oven to 425 degrees. Peel and core the apples and cut each into 8 segments. In a skillet over low heat cook the apples, combined with ½ cup of the butter (1 stick), the vanilla sugar, and wine, until the pieces are soft but not mushy. Stir them occasionally. In a shallow baking pan combine the rusks, coarsely crushed, with another ½ cup of the butter, melted, and the unflavored sugar. Set the pan in the preheated oven and let it remain for 10 minutes or until the crumbs are lightly browned. Stir frequently to coat the crumbs well with the sugar and butter. Remove pan from oven and reduce heat to 350 degrees.

Sift ⅓ of the coated crumbs over the bottom of a buttered 9-inch cake pan and cover them with ½ the cooked apples. Spread them with the raspberry jam combined with ¾ cup of the currant jelly diluted with the water. Sprinkle with ½ cup of the sliced almonds and another ⅓ cup of the crumbs. Spread over them the remaining apples and sprinkle that layer with the remaining crumbs. Dot the top with the remaining butter cut into bits. Bake in the oven at the reduced heat for 45 minutes or until the cake is firm. Let it cool in the pan before unmolding it onto a serving platter. Glaze the top with a thin coating of the remaining currant jelly and decorate it with rosettes of whipped cream, piped from a pastry bag, and the remaining sliced almonds. This pudding-like cake provides 6 to 8 servings.

Pineapple Upside-Down Cake

½ cup butter
¾ cup light brown sugar
8 slices drained canned pineapple
½ cup milk
2 eggs

¼ tsp vanilla extract
1½ cups sifted flour
½ cup granulated sugar
1½ tsp baking powder
¼ tsp salt

Preheat oven to 350 degrees. In a heavy 9-inch skillet over low heat melt ¼ cup of the butter. Stir in the brown sugar and cook the resulting syrup until it thickens somewhat. Arrange the pineapple slices in the syrup in a single layer. Remove the pan from the heat.

In a mixing bowl thoroughly combine the milk, eggs, and vanilla. Sift together the flour, sugar, baking powder, and salt, and blend in. Stir in the remaining butter, melted. Pour the batter over the pineapple slices in the skillet and bake in the preheated oven for 50 minutes or until a cake tester inserted in the center of the cake can be withdrawn clean. Invert the cake onto a serving platter and cut it into wedges to provide 8 servings with, if desired, whipped cream. This cake may also be made with pitted and peeled apricots or peaches, cut in halves.

Sponge-cake layers topped with
whipped cream and whole ripe strawberries
make a delectable spring cake.

Blueberry Cake

½ cup butter	4 tsp baking powder
1 cup sugar	¼ tsp salt
1 egg, beaten	1 cup milk
2 cups flour	1½ cups blueberries

Preheat oven to 350 degrees. In a mixing bowl thoroughly cream the butter with the sugar. Beat in the egg. Reserve 2 tablespoons of the flour and sift the remainder with the baking powder and salt. Stir into the creamed mixture, a little at a time, alternating with small additions of the milk. Dredge the blueberries with the reserved flour and fold them into the batter. Spread in a buttered and lightly floured 8-inch square cake pan and bake in the preheated oven for 35 minutes or until a cake tester inserted in the center of the cake can be withdrawn clean. Remove the cake from the pan and cool it slightly on a rack. Serve it warm, cut to provide 6 servings, with Hard Sauce (page 283) or whipped cream, as preferred.

Chocolate Praline Roll

6 eggs, separated	1 cup Praline Cream (page 71)
1¼ cups confectioners' sugar	½ cup heavy cream, whipped
½ cup dark cocoa, sifted	Shaved semisweet chocolate
⅛ tsp salt	

Preheat oven to 425 degrees. In a mixing bowl beat the egg yolks with ½ the confectioners' sugar until they are thick. Blend cocoa into them. In another bowl beat the egg whites with the salt to the soft-peak stage. Add the remaining confectioners' sugar, a little at a time, continuing to beat until the whites are stiff and glossy. Stir ¼ of them into the yolk mixture. Fold in the remainder.

Butter a shallow 11 x 15-inch baking pan, cover the bottom with waxed paper, and butter the paper. Spread over it the prepared batter and bake it in the preheated oven for 12 minutes or until the top is slightly resistant to gentle pressure. Cool the cake in the pan for 2 to 3 minutes. Invert it onto a lightly buttered rack, peel off the baking paper,

Pennsylvania Dutch Christmas Loaf (page 150)
—and some key ingredients—rest below handsome
Oxford Chocolate Cake (page 46).

and complete the cooling.

Trim the cooled cake of any crisp edges and spread it with the praline cream. Roll the cake down the length and coat it with the whipped cream. Sprinkle with shaved chocolate. Chill the cake before serving it in thick slices to provide 6 servings.

Rum Nut Roll

1¼ cups shelled filberts	Confectioners' sugar
6 eggs, separated	1 cup heavy cream
1 cup sugar	2 Tbl dark rum
2 tsp baking powder	1 Tbl maple syrup

Preheat oven to 350 degrees. Roll the nuts into a fine powder or pulverize them in an electric blender. In a mixing bowl beat the egg yolks with the sugar until they are thick. Stir into them the powdered filberts sifted with the baking powder. Stiffly beat the egg whites and fold them gently but thoroughly into the yolk mixture.

Oil a shallow 11 x 15-inch baking pan, cover the bottom with waxed paper, and oil the paper. Spread the batter evenly in the pan and bake in the preheated oven for 20 minutes or until the top is lightly resistant to gentle pressure. Invert the cake onto a lightly buttered cake rack and let it cool. Peel off the baking paper and slide the cake onto a sheet of waxed paper covered with a 1/16-inch-thick layer of sifted confectioners' sugar. In a chilled mixing bowl partially whip the cream. Stir into it the rum and syrup and continue the whipping until the cream is stiff. Spread it over the cake. Using the waxed paper as a guide, roll the cake down the length enclosing the filling completely. Chill the cake for 1 hour. Sprinkle it with additional sifted confectioners' sugar before serving it. This rum nut roll provides 6 to 8 servings.

Nubian Chocolate Roll, Forum of the Twelve Caesars

4 eggs, separated	½ tsp almond extract
½ cup confectioners' sugar	1½ tsp vanilla extract

6 Tbl cocoa

½ tsp cinnamon

¼ tsp ground anise

1½ cups heavy cream

¼ cup granulated sugar

2 Tbl chopped pistachio nuts

Preheat oven to 325 degrees. In a mixing bowl beat the egg yolks with the confectioners' sugar until the mixture is light in color and thick. Blend in 4 tablespoons of the cocoa and the cinnamon and anise sifted together, and stir in the almond flavoring and 1 teaspoon of the vanilla. Fold in the egg whites, stiffly beaten but not dry. Butter an 8 x 12-inch baking pan, cover the bottom with waxed paper, and butter the paper. Spread the batter evenly in it and bake in the preheated oven for 25 minutes or until the cake shrinks from the sides of the pan. Cool the cake in the pan for a few minutes before inverting it out onto a cake rack. Peel off the baking paper, cover the cake with a lightly dampened cloth, and let it cool completely.

To prepare filling, combine the cream, granulated sugar, and the remaining cocoa and vanilla in a mixing bowl and chill in the refrigerator for at least 1 hour. Beat with a rotary beater until the mixture is moderately thick. Spread the cake with ½ of the mixture and roll it down the length enclosing the filling completely. Coat the roll with the remaining cocoa cream and sprinkle it with the pistachios. Cut the roll into thick slices to provide 6 to 8 servings.

Boston Cream Pie

½ tsp vanilla extract

¼ cup butter, softened

¾ cup sugar

2 eggs, separated

1¼ cups sifted cake flour

1½ tsp baking powder

¼ tsp salt

½ cup milk

Pastry Cream (page 58)

Chocolate Glaze (page 71)

Preheat oven to 375 degrees. In a mixing bowl blend the vanilla into the butter. Beat in the sugar, a little at a time, until the mixture is smooth and light. Stir in the egg yolks. Sift together the flour, baking powder, and salt, and blend into the creamed mixture in thirds, alternating with half portions of the milk. Fold in the egg whites, beaten until stiff but not dry. Pour the batter into a buttered 8-inch pie pan and

bake in the preheated oven for 20 minutes or until the top is lightly resistant to gentle pressure. Cool the cake in the pan for 5 minutes. Remove it to a rack and complete the cooling. Split the cake into 2 layers. Spread filling of pastry cream on bottom layer and reassemble. Coat top thinly with chocolate glaze. This provides 6 servings.
NOTE: Tradition calls this a pie, though it is, of course, a cake.

Lincoln Log

4 eggs	**Coffee Cream Filling (page 66)**
¾ cup sugar	**Mocha Icing (page 63)**
1 tsp vanilla extract	**Sweet Dough (page 135)**
¾ cup sifted cake flour	**½ recipe Butter Cream (page 59)**
1 tsp baking powder	**Candied coffee beans**
¼ tsp salt	**or chocolate bits**

Preheat oven to 400 degrees. In a mixing bowl beat the eggs, adding the sugar gradually until the mixture is pale and moderately thick. Stir in the vanilla. Sift the flour with the baking powder and salt and fold it in a little at a time.

Butter a shallow 11 x 15-inch baking pan, cover the bottom with waxed paper, and butter the paper. Pour in the prepared batter and spread it evenly. Bake in the preheated oven for 12 minutes or until the cake is lightly resistant to gentle touch. Invert it out onto a cloth dampened with cold water and peel off the paper. Trim the cake of any crisp edges and spread it with the coffee cream filling. Using the cloth as a guide, roll the cake down the length, enclosing the filling completely. Coat the cake with the mocha icing and score it with the tines of a fork to resemble a log.

Roll out a small quantity of the sweet dough to a thickness of about ⅛-inch and cut from it 18 crescents, each 2 inches long and somewhat less than ½-inch wide. You will need only 10. The extras (reserve in case of breakage) may be served as cookies if not required. Arrange the crescents on a lightly buttered baking sheet and bake them in a preheated 325-degree oven for 10 minutes or until they are lightly browned. Remove them to a rack and let them cool.

Pipe 10 small ruffles of the butter cream across the top of the log beginning ½-inch from one end and spacing them 1 inch apart. Set a cooled crescent at an angle in each ruffle and pipe a dot of butter cream against the base of each crescent to secure it. Cap each dot of butter cream with a candied coffee bean or chocolate bit. Chill the log briefly before cutting it between the crescents to provide 10 slices. *(See photographs, page 84.)*

Birthday Cake

1 recipe Sponge Cake (page 14)
Confectioners' sugar
Almond-Paste Icing (page 61)
Easy Fondant Icing (page 60)

1½ squares (1½ ounces)
   semisweet chocolate, melted
½ tsp vanilla extract
¼ recipe (1 cup) Praline Pastry
   Cream (page 59)

Bake the cake in 2 buttered and lightly floured 8-inch cake pans, at the temperature indicated in the recipe, for 40 minutes or until a cake tester inserted in the center of the cakes can be withdrawn clean. Cool the cakes on a rack.

Sift confectioners' sugar generously onto a pastry board and over it roll out the almond-paste icing ⅛-inch thick. Cut the sheet into 2 and fit each part on a layer of the cake, covering it completely. Smooth the icing evenly and trim off the excess. Place ½ of the fondant icing in each of 2 bowls. Stir the melted chocolate into one and the vanilla into the other. Over the almond-paste icing coat 1 layer of cake with the chocolate fondant mixture, the other with the vanilla mixture. Spread the chocolate layer with the praline pastry cream and fit the vanilla layer neatly over it. Let the icing set and pipe birthday greetings on the top and decorate with an almond-paste rose, if desired. This cake will provide 6 to 8 servings. *(See photograph, page 83.)*

Valentine Cake

1 recipe Genoise (page 14)
Seedless raspberry jam
Butter Cream, vanilla flavored
  (page 59)

Almond-Paste Icing (page 61)
Pink food coloring
Confectioners' sugar
Almond-Paste Roses (page 85)

Bake the genoise as directed in the recipe, using a 9-inch cake pan. Cool the cake and cut it into a heart shape, following a paper pattern. Split cake into 3 thin layers. Spread 1 of those layers thinly with raspberry jam and cover with butter cream. Arrange the second layer over it and coat it in the same way. Similarly spread and coat the third layer and fit it over the top.

Tint the almond-paste icing with a little of the food coloring. Sift confectioners' sugar onto a pastry board. Using a honeycomb-patterned roller, roll out the almond paste into a sheet somewhat less than ⅛-inch thick. Carefully transfer the sheet to the prepared cake, covering it completely. Smooth the icing evenly and trim off the excess. Pipe an affectionate valentine greeting in butter cream across the top of the cake and decorate with almond-paste roses. This cake provides 6 to 8 servings. *(See photographs, page 84.)*

Polish Chestnut Cake

1 cup almond paste (see Note)
½ cup sugar
⅛ tsp salt
8 egg whites
¼ cup fine dry bread crumbs
2⅓ cups cooked, peeled chestnuts

5 Tbl Vanilla Sugar (page 70)
¼ cup milk
½ cup butter, melted & cooled
2 Tbl dark rum
¾ cup Fondant Icing, lemon
   flavored (page 60)

Preheat oven to 350 degrees. In a mixing bowl combine the almond paste, sugar, salt, and 2 of the egg whites. In another bowl stiffly beat the remaining egg whites and fold them into the almond mixture. Thickly butter two 8-inch layer-cake pans and sprinkle each with ½ the bread crumbs. Spread ½ the batter evenly in each pan and bake in the preheated oven for 20 minutes or until the layers are lightly browned and begin to shrink from the sides of the pans. Remove them from the pans and cool on a rack.

To cook chestnuts, make slits on flat sides and place nuts on a pan in a 450-degree oven for about 6 minutes. While nuts are hot, peel off shells and pare away the inner skin with a sharp knife. Simmer in water 10 to 20 minutes, until nuts are soft. Drain and force nuts through a fine sieve or purée them in an electric blender. In a mixing bowl beat to a smooth mixture the purée, vanilla sugar, milk, and melted butter. Stir in the rum. Use this mixture as filling between the 2 layers. Coat the cake with the icing and cut it to provide 8 to 10 servings. NOTE: Almond paste is available commercially.

Butternut Cake

1 cup butter, softened

2 cups sugar

4 eggs, separated

1½ tsp vanilla extract

3 cups flour

2 tsp baking powder

½ tsp salt

1 cup milk

1 cup coarsely chopped butternuts

Maple Icing (page 62)

Preheat oven to 350 degrees. In a mixing bowl cream the butter with 1 cup of the sugar. In a separate bowl beat the egg yolks with the vanilla and the remaining sugar until the mixture is smooth and thick. Thoroughly combine the yolk and butter mixtures. Sift together the flour, baking powder, and salt, and blend in, a little at a time, alternating with small quantities of the milk. Stir in the butternuts and gently but thoroughly fold in the egg whites beaten until stiff but not dry. Spread the batter evenly in a buttered 10-inch tube pan and bake in the preheated oven for 45 minutes or until the top of the cake is lightly resistant to gentle pressure. Cool the cake in the pan suspended (with the tube fitted over the neck of a bottle) over a rack. Unmold the cake and frost it with maple icing. Cut the cake in wedges to provide 12 generous servings.

Chocolate Bavarian Cake

⅔ cup grated sweet chocolate

¼ cup water

½ cup butter

1 cup sugar

2 eggs, separated

½ tsp vanilla extract

1¼ cups sifted cake flour

½ tsp baking soda

¼ tsp salt

½ cup buttermilk

Pecan Frosting (page 64)

Preheat oven to 350 degrees. In a saucepan over low heat melt the chocolate in the water. Remove pan from heat and let the mixture cool. In a mixing bowl work the butter with a wooden spoon to the consistency of lightly whipped cream. Add the sugar, a little at a time, and the egg yolks, beating them in well. Stir in the vanilla and the cooled chocolate. Sift the flour with the soda and salt and blend it into the creamed mixture, alternating with additions of the buttermilk, each a little at a time. Beat the egg whites until they are firm but not dry and fold them in.

Butter three 9-inch cake pans, line the bottoms with waxed paper, and butter the paper. Spread equal portions of the batter in the prepared pans and bake in the preheated oven for 30 minutes, or until the cakes are slightly resistant to gentle touch. Cool the cakes in the pans for 5 minutes. Remove them to a rack, peel off the baking papers, and complete the cooling. Arrange the cakes in 3 layers. Fill and frost with the pecan frosting. Cake provides 8 to 10 servings.

Torta de Chocolaterias, La Fonda del Sol

½ cup butter	2 tsp baking powder
1 cup sugar	½ tsp baking soda
2 eggs, separated	1 tsp ground cinnamon
1 tsp vanilla extract	½ tsp salt
3 squares (3 ounces) unsweetened chocolate, melted	1¼ cups milk
	Filling and Icing (see below)
2 cups sifted cake flour	Thin Chocolate (see below)

Preheat oven to 350 degrees. In a mixing bowl cream together the butter and sugar until the mixture is smooth and fluffy. Add the egg yolks, lightly beaten, vanilla, and chocolate. Sift the flour with the baking powder, soda, cinnamon, and salt, and blend it in, a little at a time, alternating with additions of the milk. Gently but thoroughly fold in the egg whites, stiffly beaten. Pour ½ the batter into each of 2 buttered and floured 8-inch square cake pans and bake in the preheated oven for 30 minutes or until a cake tester inserted in the center of the cakes can be withdrawn clean. Remove from pans and cool on a rack.

Split the cooled cakes each in 2 and arrange the 4 layers one atop the other, interspersed with part of the filling and icing, using ¼ of the preparation in all. Frost the cake with the remainder. Peel the hardened thin chocolate from the foil and break it into moderately large pieces. Press them into the top and sides of the frosted cake. Chill the cake well before serving it. Cut it vertically into four 2-inch strips and cut the strips in half to provide 8 servings.

Filling and Icing:

12 squares (12 ounces) semisweet
   chocolate, melted

6 eggs, separated

⅔ cup brown sugar, firmly packed

1 tsp cinnamon

½ cup water

1½ tsp vanilla extract

½ tsp orange extract

¼ tsp salt

Pour the melted chocolate into a mixing bowl and beat in the egg yolks 2 at a time. Blend in the brown sugar and cinnamon, and stir in the water gradually. Add the vanilla and orange flavorings. In another bowl beat the egg whites with the salt until they are stiff but not dry and fold them gently but thoroughly into the chocolate mixture. Chill in the refrigerator until firm enough to spread without flowing.

Thin Chocolate:

4 squares (4 ounces) semisweet
   chocolate, melted

Using a pastry brush, thinly spread the chocolate on a sheet of foil and chill it in the refrigerator until it hardens.

Kahlua Chocolate Cake, La Fonda del Sol

1 cup almond paste (see Note)

½ cup butter

10 eggs, separated

4 whole eggs

8 squares (8 ounces) semisweet
   chocolate, melted & cooled

½ cup chocolate bits (3 ounces)

¾ cup sliced almonds

¾ cup chopped walnuts

Grated rind of 3 oranges

1 cup sugar

1 cup flour

2 cups heavy cream

⅓ cup Kahlua liqueur

Preheat oven to 400 degrees. In a mixing bowl thoroughly combine the almond paste and butter. Blend into the mixture the 10 egg yolks and 4 whole eggs, and stir in the melted chocolate, chocolate bits, nuts, and grated orange rind. In a separate bowl beat the 10 egg whites to the soft-peak stage. Add ½ cup of the sugar, a little at a time, continuing the beating until the sugar is incorporated and the whites are stiff and glossy. Fold them into the chocolate mixture, ⅛ at a time, alternating with additions of 2 tablespoons of flour. Butter 2 shallow 11 x 15-inch baking pans, cover the bottom of each with waxed paper, and butter the paper. Spread equal quantities of the batter in the 2 pans and bake in the preheated oven for 15 minutes or until the cakes begin to shrink from the sides of the pans. Invert the cakes onto racks and peel off the baking papers. Let the cakes cool completely.

Stiffly whip the cream with the remaining sugar and blend in the

Kahlua liqueur. Cut the cakes across the width into halves approximately 11 x 7½ inches. Assemble the 4 halves in layers, interspersed and frosted with the prepared Kahlua cream. Cut the cake into equal-size pieces to provide 12 servings.

NOTE: Almond paste is available commercially.

Oxford Chocolate Cake

8 egg yolks
4 whole eggs
1 cup sugar
1 cup flour

½ cup firmly packed cocoa
¼ cup butter, melted & cooled
Chocolate Cream (page 66)

Preheat oven to 350 degrees. In a mixing bowl beat together the egg yolks, whole eggs, and sugar to produce a mixture that is pale yellow in color and very thick. Sift the flour and cocoa together and stir in. Thoroughly fold in the melted butter. Spread the batter evenly in a buttered and lightly floured 9-inch round cake pan and bake in the preheated oven for 30 minutes or until the top of the cake is lightly resistant to gentle pressure. Remove the cake from the pan and cool it completely on a rack. Split it into 3 layers and reassemble them filled and iced with the chocolate cream. Decorate, if desired, with a thick paste of confectioners' sugar and cream. Chill the cake, but remove it from the refrigerator about 30 minutes before serving. The cake provides 10 to 12 servings. *(See photograph, page 34.)*

Three-Layer Chocolate Cake

¾ cup unsalted butter
2¼ cups sugar
4 eggs
6 squares (6 ounces) unsweetened
   chocolate, melted & cooled
1 tsp vanilla extract
2 cups sifted flour

1½ tsp baking powder
¼ tsp salt
1½ cups milk
Chocolate Sour-Cream Icing
   (page 60)
10 shelled walnut halves

Preheat oven to 375 degrees. In a large mixing bowl cream the butter and sugar together until the mixture is light and fluffy. Beat in the eggs, 1 at a time, and stir in the chocolate and vanilla. Sift the flour with the baking powder and salt, and blend it into the chocolate mixture along with the milk, alternating additions of ¼ cup of each at a time.

Butter and lightly flour three 9-inch layer-cake pans and divide the batter equally among them. Bake in the preheated oven for 20 minutes or until the cakes test done. A tester inserted in the center of the cakes should, when withdrawn, be dry and clean. Remove the cakes from the pans and cool them on a rack.

Arrange the cakes one atop the other on a serving platter, interspersing them with the icing spread ¼-inch thick. Coat the top and sides with the remaining icing and decorate the top with the walnut halves. This cake provides 10 servings.

Viennese Nut Cake

10 Tbl butter
1⅓ cups sugar
4 squares (4 ounces) unsweetened
    chocolate, melted & cooled
9 eggs
1⅓ cups finely grated almonds

½ tsp cornstarch
1-inch length vanilla bean
⅓ cup finely chopped walnuts
⅓ cup finely chopped pecans
Chocolate Icing (page 63)

Preheat oven to 300 degrees. In a mixing bowl with a wooden spoon mash and stir 6 tablespoons of the butter until it is soft. Add ½ each of the sugar and chocolate and beat the mixture until it is smooth. Separate 6 of the eggs and blend the yolks into the chocolate mixture. In a separate bowl beat the 6 whites until they are stiff but not dry and fold them into the chocolate mixture, ¼ at a time, alternating each addition with ⅓ cup of the grated almonds. Spread the batter evenly in a buttered and lightly floured 9-inch cake pan and bake in the preheated oven for 45 minutes or until the cake is lightly resistant to gentle pressure. Remove the cake from the pan and cool it on a rack.

In the top pan of a double boiler combine the remaining eggs, the remaining sugar, plus the cornstarch and the vanilla bean. Cook over simmering water, stirring constantly, until thickened. Remove pan from over water and let mixture cool to lukewarm. Remove and discard the vanilla bean. Add the remaining butter and chocolate and beat the mixture until it is velvety smooth. Stir in the walnuts and pecans. Split the cooled cake into 3 layers and reassemble them interspersed with the chocolate nut filling. Coat the cake with the chocolate icing. Cut the cake to provide 10 to 12 servings.

Lemon Mousse Cake

1 recipe Genoise (page 14)
12 egg yolks
3 whole eggs
1½ cups sugar
Juice & rind of 3 lemons
1 cup butter

2 envelopes (2 Tbl) unflavored
  gelatine
½ cup cold water
1½ cups heavy cream, whipped
3 egg whites

Bake the genoise batter in a 9-inch cake pan at the temperature and for the length of time indicated in the recipe. Cool the cake as directed.

In the top pan of a double boiler beat together 5 of the egg yolks, the whole eggs, 1 cup of the sugar, and the lemon juice and rind. Add the butter cut into small pieces. Set the pan over simmering water and cook the mixture, stirring constantly, until it thickens. Remove the pan from over the water and cool the custard completely. Discard the rind.

In a small bowl soften the gelatine in the cold water and dissolve it by setting the bowl in a shallow pan of hot water. Cool the gelatine slightly. In a larger bowl beat the remaining egg yolks with ¼ cup of the sugar until the mixture is thick. Stir in the dissolved gelatine. Combine this yolk mixture with the prepared lemon custard and the whipped cream. In still another bowl beat the egg whites to the soft-peak stage. Add the remaining sugar, a little at a time, and continue the beating until the sugar is completely incorporated and the whites are stiff and glossy. Fold them into the combined mixtures.

Place the cooled genoise in a 9-inch spring-form pan and spread the prepared mousse evenly over it. Chill the cake in the refrigerator for at least 2 hours. Unmold and cut it into wedges to provide 8 servings.

Vanilla and Chocolate Rum Cake

1 recipe Genoise (page 14)
2 cups butter, softened
¾ cup confectioners' sugar
6 egg whites
½ tsp vanilla extract

4 squares (4 ounces) semisweet
   chocolate
¼ cup water
3 Tbl dark rum
1 cup toasted sliced filberts

Bake the genoise in a 9-inch round cake pan at the temperature and for the length of time indicated in the recipe. Cool the cake as directed.

In a mixing bowl thoroughly combine the butter and sugar. Beat in the egg whites gradually until the mixture is light and very fluffy. Transfer ½ of the mixture to another bowl and stir the vanilla into it. In a saucepan over low heat melt the chocolate in the water. Cool, blend in the rum, and stir into the other half of the creamed mixture.

Split the cooled cake into 3 layers. Spread chocolate mixture ½-inch thick on bottom layer. Cover with middle layer and on this spread vanilla mixture ½-inch thick. Top with third layer of cake. Ice the cake with the remaining vanilla mixture and swirl over it the remaining chocolate mixture to achieve a marbled effect. Press filberts into the sides of the cake. When the icing is set, cut the cake into wedges to provide 8 servings.

Hazelnut Cake

5 eggs, separated
¾ cup plus 2 tsp sugar
6 Tbl water
1½ cups flour

1 tsp baking powder
1 cup chopped hazelnuts (filberts)
1 cup heavy cream, whipped
½ cup grated hazelnuts

Preheat oven to 375 degrees. In a mixing bowl combine the egg yolks, ¾ cup of the sugar, and the water, and beat the mixture until it thickens. Stir in the flour, sifted with the baking powder, and the chopped nuts. In a separate bowl beat the egg whites until they are stiff but not dry and fold them gently but thoroughly into the yolk mixture. Spread the batter evenly in a buttered and lightly floured 9-inch cake pan and bake it in the preheated oven for 30 minutes or until the cake is lightly resistant to gentle pressure. Turn the cake out onto a rack and let it cool. Split the cooled cake into 2 layers and fill and frost them with the whipped cream, sweetened with the remaining 2 teaspoons of sugar and combined with the grated nuts. This cake provides 6 to 8 servings.

Variation:

Fill the layers with Pastry Cream (page 58) and coat the top with Chocolate Glaze (page 71).

Pineapple Meringue Cake

½ cup butter
1½ cups sugar
4 eggs, separated
1 cup sifted cake flour
2 tsp baking powder

⅛ tsp salt
5 Tbl milk
2 tsp vanilla extract
¾ cup chopped walnuts
Pineapple Filling (page 67)

Preheat oven to 325 degrees. In a mixing bowl thoroughly cream together the butter and ½ cup of the sugar. Beat in the egg yolks. Sift the flour with the baking powder and salt and stir it into the creamed mixture a little at a time, alternating those additions with small quantities of milk combined with 1 teaspoon of the vanilla. Spread the batter evenly in 2 buttered and lightly floured 8-inch cake pans.

In a separate bowl beat the egg whites to the soft-peak stage. Add the remaining sugar a little at a time, continuing the beating until the whites are very stiff and glossy. Add the remaining teaspoon of vanilla with the final addition of the sugar. Spread the meringue equally over each portion of the batter and sprinkle with equal quantities of the nuts. Bake in the preheated oven for 25 minutes or until the meringue is nicely browned and a cake tester inserted in the center of the cakes can be withdrawn clean. Let the cakes cool in the pans for 2 to 3 minutes. Carefully remove onto lightly buttered racks to complete the cooling. Arrange the cooled cakes one atop the other, with the plain sides together and the pineapple filling between them. This cake provides 10 servings.

Mocha Black-Walnut Cake

½ cup butter
2 cups sugar
3 eggs
3 cups cake flour
3 tsp baking powder

½ cup cold strong brewed coffee
½ cup cold milk
1 cup chopped black walnuts
Coffee Walnut Frosting (page 63)

Preheat oven to 350 degrees. In a mixing bowl beat together the butter and the sugar until the mixture is soft and fluffy. Thoroughly blend in the eggs, 1 at a time. Sift the flour with the baking powder and add it, a little at a time, alternating with small quantities of the coffee and milk combined. Add the nuts and stir the batter until it is smooth. Spread it evenly in 2 buttered and lightly floured 8-inch layer-cake pans and bake in the preheated oven for 25 minutes, or until the tops are lightly resistant to gentle pressure. Remove the cakes from the pans and cool them on a rack. Split the layers each into 2 and arrange them as a 4-layer cake, filled and frosted with the coffee walnut frosting. This cake provides 8 servings.

Greek Yogurt Cake

1 cup butter
2 cups sugar
1 cup yogurt
Grated rind of 1 lemon
5 eggs, separated

3 cups flour
3 tsp baking powder
¼ tsp salt
Confectioners' sugar

Preheat oven to 350 degrees. In a mixing bowl completely cream the butter with the sugar, and blend in the yogurt and lemon rind. Stir in the egg yolks, 1 at a time. Sift the flour with the baking powder and salt and stir it thoroughly into the creamed mixture. Beat the egg whites until they are stiff but not dry and fold them in. Butter and flour a 9-inch tube pan, spread the batter evenly in it and bake in the preheated oven for 1 hour or until the top is lightly resistant to gentle pressure. Remove the cake from the pan and cool it on a rack. Dust it with confectioners' sugar. This cake provides 8 to 10 servings.

Lord and Lady Baltimore Cake

⅞ cup butter, softened
1¾ cups fine granulated sugar
1½ tsp vanilla extract
2 egg whites
3 cups sifted cake flour
3½ tsp baking powder
½ tsp salt
⅞ cup milk (¾ cup plus 2 Tbl)

2 whole eggs
1 recipe Lemon Meringue Icing
  (page 62)
½ cup finely chopped seedless
  raisins
½ cup finely chopped pecans
¼ cup finely chopped maraschino
  cherries

This is actually a union of 2 different cakes, one white, one yellow, but they must be prepared and baked separately. Start with the white.

Preheat oven to 350 degrees. In a mixing bowl cream together 6 tablespoons (¾ stick) of the butter, ½ cup of the sugar, and 1 teaspoon of vanilla until the mixture is smooth (that is, no longer grainy) and very fluffy. In a separate bowl beat the egg whites to the soft-peak stage. Add ¼ cup of the sugar, a little at a time, continuing to beat until the whites are stiff and glossy.

Sift together all of the flour, baking powder, and salt. Set ½ of the mixture aside (to be used for the yellow cake) and blend the remainder a little at a time into the creamed mixture, alternating those additions with ½ cup of the milk, also added in small amounts. Gently but thoroughly fold in the beaten egg whites. Spread the batter evenly in a lightly buttered and floured cake pan measuring 9 inches across and

2 inches deep. Bake in the preheated oven for 25 minutes or until the top of the cake is lightly resistant to gentle pressure. Cool the cake in the pan for 5 minutes before turning it out onto a rack to complete the cooling.

Prepare the yellow cake as follows: Increase the heat of the oven to 375 degrees. In a mixing bowl cream together the remaining butter, sugar, and flavoring as directed for white cake. Vigorously beat in the whole eggs, 1 at a time. Blend in the reserved flour mixture a little at a time, alternating with the remaining milk added in small amounts. Spread this batter in another lightly buttered and floured deep cake pan measuring 9 inches across and 2 inches deep. Bake in the oven at the increased heat for 25 minutes or until a cake tester inserted in the center of the cake can be withdrawn clean. Cool the yellow cake as directed for the white.

Transfer ⅓ of the lemon meringue icing to another bowl and blend into it the chopped raisins, nuts, and cherries. Split the cooled cakes each into 2 layers. Spread the yellow layers and 1 of the white with the mixture. Reassemble the spread layers with the white in the middle. Top with the uncoated white layer. Cover the top and sides of this 4-layer cake with the remaining icing, and cut for 10 to 12 servings.

Italian Trifle | Zuppa Inglese

1 layer Sponge Cake
   (page 14)
6 Tbl Simple Syrup (page 278),
   flavored with 2 Tbl rum
1 cup Pastry Cream (page 58)
½ cup heavy cream, whipped
1 ounce semisweet chocolate,
   grated
1 Tbl finely chopped
   mixed glazed fruit

1 Tbl Sweet Chestnut Purée
   (page 68)
2 slices Panettone (page 149),
   cut horizontally about
   ½-inch thick
2 Tbl coarse macaroon crumbs
5 egg whites
½ cup sugar

Split the single layer of sponge cake in half to make 2 layers. Place 1 slice on a heat-proof dish and douse it with 2 tablespoons of the rum syrup. Combine the pastry cream and whipped cream and spread ½ of that over the layer of cake. Combine the grated chocolate, glazed fruit, and chestnut purée and distribute ½ of that over the cream. Cover with a slice of the panettone. Sprinkle it with 2 tablespoons of the syrup and spread it with the remaining combined creams. Sprinkle the macaroon crumbs over that and cover them with the remaining layer of cake. Dot with the remaining chocolate-fruit-chestnut combination. Place the remaining slice of panettone on top and brush it with the remaining syrup. Chill the filled layers thoroughly in the refrigerator.

Preheat oven to 550 degrees. In a mixing bowl beat the egg whites into soft peaks. Add the sugar gradually, continuing to beat until the whites are whipped to a stiff meringue. Spread it evenly over the chilled cake right down to the serving dish. Set in the preheated oven for 3 minutes or until the meringue is lightly browned. Let trifle cool. Chill it briefly before serving it cut into wedges to provide 6 to 8 servings.

Meringue Layers

2 recipes (double quantity)
  Meringues (page 93)

Preheat oven to 225 degrees. Cover 2 baking sheets with unglazed paper. On one draw 2 circles, each 7½ inches in diameter, spacing them 2 inches from each other and from the edges of the baking sheet. Draw a circle of the same dimension in the center of the paper on the other baking sheet. Prepare meringue batter as directed in the recipe and fill the circles with it, proceeding as follows:

Using a pastry bag fitted with a plain tube, pipe a tight coil of the meringue ¼-inch thick in each circle, beginning at the center and finishing exactly at the edge. Do not go beyond it. Allowance is already made for the coils to spread during the baking to 8 inches in diameter. Bake the meringue layers in the preheated oven for 45 minutes or until they are crisp and just faintly tinged with color. Let the layers cool to warm and remove them. Moisten the underside of the paper if the meringues stick. Use as directed in specific recipes or as desired. The meringues may be stored in a dry place, but not in a covered container.

2 | frostings, fillings, and glazes

Whether you ice a cake or frost it depends on where you do it. In England and in France, a cake is "iced" (*glacé* is the word for it in French). In the United States, a cake may be "iced" or "frosted."

In this volume, we offer recipes for icings, frostings, and glazes, basing our categories on the texture of the preparations. Mixtures that contain unincorporated solids (nuts, for example) we call frostings. Smooth, thick mixtures are designated as icings. Thin icings, used to coat a cake or pastry lightly, or provide a protective coating, are generally classified as glazes (Chocolate Glaze and Apricot Glaze are two given here). Between-layer fillings may be either icings, frostings, or mixtures specially made for the purpose.

We have advised you in the chapter on cakes to follow the recipes closely in order to have success in your baking efforts. The same may be said here. When you have baked an excellent cake, be sure to give it the icing or frosting it deserves—one that pleases by its color, flavor, creaminess, and proper application.

Fondant

3 cups sugar   **¼ tsp cream of tartar**
1 cup water

In a saucepan over low heat dissolve the sugar in the water. Stir in the cream of tartar. Bring syrup to a boil and cook until a drop of the syrup in cool water can be formed into a soft ball (240 degrees on a candy thermometer). Pour syrup onto marble slab or onto a platter dampened with cool water. Let syrup cool to lukewarm and, using a spatula, work it from the edges to the center into a mound. Continue working it so until the mass is creamy white and cool enough to handle. Knead it well on the slab or platter for several minutes. If the fondant is not to be used immediately, it should be stored in a tightly covered jar. So contained, it will keep for several weeks.

Chocolate Fondant:

In a saucepan over simmering water melt together 3 squares (3 ounces) unsweetened chocolate and 1 square (1 ounce) semisweet chocolate. Blend the mixture into the hot syrup on the slab and work the fondant as directed. The recipes provide about 3 cups of plain fondant and 3½ cups of the chocolate.

Pastry Cream

4 cups milk   **¾ cup flour**
8 egg yolks   **2 Tbl butter**
1 cup sugar   **1 tsp vanilla extract**

In a saucepan scald the milk. In a mixing bowl beat the egg yolks with the sugar until the mixture is very thick and flows in a wide ribbon when the beater is withdrawn. Blend in the flour. Gradually pour in the heated milk, stirring constantly. Transfer the mixture to the saucepan and cook it over medium heat, continuing to stir until the lumps (there may be some) are stirred away and the cream is thick and smooth. Blend in the butter and vanilla. This recipe provides about 4 cups of pastry cream. It can be kept in a covered container under normal refrigeration for 1 week or frozen for about 1 month.

Variations:

Chocolate Pastry Cream: Stir 2½ squares (2½ ounces) melted semi-sweet chocolate into the warm pastry cream.

Liqueur- (or Brandy-) Flavored Pastry Cream: Omit the vanilla and stir into the warm cream 1 tablespoon orange-flavored liqueur, kirsch, or cognac.

Praline Pastry Cream: Stir into the warm pastry cream 2 tablespoons Praline Powder (page 71).

Almond Pastry Cream: Omit the vanilla and stir into the lukewarm pastry cream ¼ teaspoon almond extract.

Lemon Pastry Cream: Rub the thin peel of ½ lemon thoroughly into the indicated 1 cup of sugar. Discard the peel. Use the sugar as directed in the recipe. Omit the vanilla.

Butter Cream

1 cup sugar	**5 egg yolks**
⅛ tsp cream of tartar	**1 cup butter, softened**
⅓ cup water	

In a saucepan over low heat dissolve the sugar and cream of tartar in the water. Bring the liquid to a boil and cook it, without stirring, until a small amount dropped into cool water can be formed into a soft ball (240 degrees on a candy thermometer). In a heat-proof mixing bowl beat the egg yolks until they are fluffy. Pour in the syrup in a thin stream, continuing to beat until the mixture is lukewarm, by which time it should be double in bulk and very foamy. Beat the softened butter into it a little at a time. Flavor as desired (see Variations). Chill it until it is firm but spreadable. This makes about 2 cups of the cream.

Variations:

Butter cream of different flavors can be achieved with any of the following additions: 2 teaspoons vanilla; 1 tablespoon cognac, rum, or orange-flavored liqueur; 1 teaspoon instant coffee powder, blended into the warm egg-yolk and syrup mixture before the addition of the butter. For Chocolate Butter Cream, stir in 2 squares (2 ounces) unsweetened chocolate, melted and cooled.

Chocolate Sour-Cream Icing

18 squares (18 ounces) semisweet chocolate

1½ cups sour cream
¼ teaspoon salt

Melt the chocolate in the top pan of a double boiler over simmering water and whisk in the sour cream and salt. Use the frosting while it is still warm. If it becomes too stiff to spread (it stiffens as it cools), warm it briefly over the simmering water. This recipe provides sufficient frosting and filling for a 9-inch cake of 3 layers.

Egg-White Icing

1 egg white

1½ cups (approximate) confectioners' sugar

In a mixing bowl beat the egg white to the soft-peak stage. Add confectioners' sugar in small amounts until the mixture is thick but spreadable. You may need slightly more or less of the sugar. This recipe will ice an 8-inch cake of 2 layers.

Fondant Icing

1 cup Fondant (page 58)

2 Tbl warm water, or more as needed

Melt the fondant in the top pan of a double boiler over simmering water. Stir in as much of the water as needed to produce an icing just liquid enough to flow. It should not be watery. Flavor as desired. This recipe will ice an 8-inch cake of 2 layers.

Easy Fondant Icing

½ cup Simple Syrup (page 278)
2 cups sifted confectioners' sugar

1 egg white
Food coloring (optional)

In a saucepan over low heat warm the syrup. Do not let it boil. Remove

the pan from the heat and thoroughly blend in the sugar. Vigorously beat in the egg white (and food coloring, if used). This quantity of icing is sufficient to coat an 8-inch 4-layer cake.

Lemon Icing

1 recipe Egg-White Icing
  (page 60)
        ⅓ cup strained lemon juice

Prepare icing as directed. Blend in the lemon juice. For a thinner icing, reduce the amount of sugar in the recipe for Egg-White Icing. This recipe will ice an 8-inch cake of 2 layers.

Almond-Paste Icing

1½ cups almond paste (see Note)   **Small quantity egg white**

In a mixing bowl work the almond paste with the egg white, using just enough to produce a smooth but malleable icing. Use as required. This recipe provides sufficient frosting and filling for an 8-inch cake of 3 to 4 layers.

NOTE: Almond paste, generally sweetened, is available commercially in tins. Once opened, the paste should be kept in a tightly covered jar in the refrigerator. So contained and stored, it will keep for a long time.

Maple Icing

6 Tbl butter
1 cup light brown sugar
6 ounces hard maple sugar

¼ cup water
¼ cup light cream
2 cups confectioners' sugar

Melt the butter in a saucepan over low heat. Add the brown sugar and cook until the sugar is slightly caramelized. Add the maple sugar, dissolved in the water, and bring the mixture to a gentle boil. Remove the pan from the heat and stir in the cream. Let the syrup cool, stirring it occasionally. Blend in the confectioners' sugar. This recipe provides sufficient frosting and filling for an 8-inch cake of 3 to 4 layers.

Lemon Meringue Icing

Thin peel of 1 lemon
2¼ cups sugar
3 egg whites

⅓ cup water
¼ tsp cream of tartar
2 Tbl strained lemon juice

Thoroughly rub the lemon peel into the sugar, impregnating the grains completely with the zest. Discard the peel. In the top pan of a large double boiler (about 1½-quart capacity) combine the sugar, egg whites, water, cream of tartar, and lemon juice. Set the pan over boiling water and beat with a rotary beater or electric hand beater for 6 minutes or until the mixture flows from the withdrawn beater in ribbons that hold their shape on the surface of the meringue. Remove the pan from over the water and continue beating until the meringue is firm enough to spread and has cooled completely. Use as required. This recipe provides about 3½ cups of icing.

Mocha Icing

½ square (½ ounce) semisweet
  chocolate, melted
4 Tbl hot brewed coffee
2 Tbl butter

½ tsp vanilla extract
1½ cups sifted confectioners'
  sugar

In a mixing bowl combine the chocolate and coffee. Stir in the butter and vanilla and blend in the sugar to produce a stiff but spreadable mixture. More coffee or sugar may be added to achieve the proper consistency. Use as required. This makes about 1¼ cups of icing.

Coffee Walnut Frosting

½ cup butter, softened
3½ cups confectioners' sugar,
  sifted
4 Tbl hot brewed coffee, or more
  as required

2 Tbl heavy cream
½ tsp vanilla extract
¼ cup finely chopped black
  walnuts

In a mixing bowl thoroughly cream together the butter and sugar. Add the coffee and cream, and beat the mixture until it is smooth and fluffy. It should be just stiff enough to be spreadable. Add more sugar, if needed. Blend in the vanilla and black walnuts. These combined ingredients provide about 3½ cups of frosting.

Chocolate Icing

8 squares (8 ounces) semisweet
  chocolate
¼ cup heavy cream

½ tsp vanilla extract
2⅔ cups confectioners' sugar
  (approximate), sifted

Melt the chocolate in the top pan of a double boiler over simmering water. Thoroughly blend in the cream and vanilla. Beat in just enough of the sugar to produce a mixture that is smooth and spreadable. Use it while it is still warm. If it thickens excessively, stir in a little more cream and reheat the frosting slightly over the simmering water. This recipe provides about 3½ cups of icing.

Pecan Frosting

1 cup evaporated milk	½ cup butter
1 cup fine granulated sugar	½ tsp vanilla extract
3 egg yolks	2 cups finely chopped pecans

In the top pan of a double boiler combine the milk, sugar, egg yolks, and the butter cut into small pieces. Set the pan over simmering water and cook the mixture, stirring constantly, until it thickens. Remove the pan from over the water and stir in the vanilla. Add the pecans and beat the mixture until it is smooth, spreadable, and cool. This recipe provides sufficient frosting and filling for a 9-inch cake of 3 layers.

Frangipane

1 cup butter	Grated rind of 2 lemons
1 cup sugar	¼ tsp salt
2 cups pulverized almonds	5 eggs
(see Note)	⅓ cup cornstarch

In a mixing bowl work the butter with a wooden spoon until it is very soft. Add the sugar by degrees, beating with a rotary beater until the mixture is the consistency of lightly whipped cream. Thoroughly blend in the pulverized almonds, grated lemon rind, and salt. Beat in the eggs, 1 at a time, and blend in the cornstarch. Use as a foundation for fruit or other fillings baked with them in pie or tart shells, or as required. To use as a filling for cakes or crêpes, combine all ingredients except the almonds in the top pan of a double boiler and cook over barely simmering water, stirring constantly until the mixture thickens. Stir in the almonds and let the frangipane cool before using it. This recipe provides about 4 cups of filling. Well contained and stored in the refrigerator, uncooked and cooked frangipane will keep for about a week. The cream may also be frozen for longer storage.
NOTE: Pulverize almonds in an electric blender, or put them through the fine blade of a food chopper, dry them (without browning) in a warm oven, and roll them into a powder between sheets of waxed

paper. Almonds, ground to order or as almond flour, are available in many shops specializing in European-type baking ingredients.

Chocolate Cream

2 cups milk
1 cup sugar
½ cup firmly packed cornstarch
8 egg yolks

1 cup firmly packed cocoa
1 cup grated semisweet chocolate
1 cup butter, softened

In a saucepan combine the milk with ½ cup of the sugar. Blend the remaining sugar and the cornstarch into the egg yolks in a mixing bowl. Bring the milk gently to a boil. Stir just enough of it, a little at a time, into the egg-yolk mixture to heat it through. Combine the yolk mixture with the remaining sweetened milk in the saucepan and continue the cooking over low heat for 2 minutes or just until the mixture thickens. Remove the pan from the heat and immediately blend in the cocoa and grated chocolate. Let the mixture cool somewhat and add the softened butter. Beat the mixture until it is completely cool, creamy, and spreadable. This quantity is sufficient to provide filling and frosting for two 3-layer cakes each 9 inches in diameter and about 4 inches high.

Coffee Cream Filling

½ cup flour
⅓ cup sugar
½ tsp salt
1¼ cups light cream

1 cup strong brewed coffee
2 egg yolks
1 tsp vanilla extract

In the top pan of a double boiler combine the flour, sugar, and salt. Combine cream and coffee and stir in, a little at a time. Set the pan over simmering water and cook, stirring constantly, until the mixture is thick and smooth. Cover the pan, reduce the heat to very low (the water now should barely simmer), and cook for 10 more minutes. In a small bowl stir the yolks and add to them, a bit at a time, just enough of the thickened mixture to heat them through. Combine the yolks with the remaining thickened mixture and continue the cooking for 2 minutes longer. Remove the pan from over the water and stir in the vanilla. Cool the filling before using it as required. This recipe provides about 2½ cups of filling.

Fruitcake Filling

2 cups sugar **1 cup butter**
1½ cups milk

Dissolve the sugar in the milk in a saucepan over low heat. Add the butter, and when it is melted, bring the mixture to a gentle boil. Cook it so for 7 minutes or until it is thick. Use as required, for filling and/or icing, while the mixture is still warm. Yield is 2 cups of filling.

Pineapple Filling

1 cup canned crushed pineapple, **1½ tsp confectioners' sugar**
  well drained **¼ tsp vanilla extract**
1 cup heavy cream

Finely chop the pineapple or force it through a coarse sieve. In a mixing bowl stiffly whip the cream with the sugar. Combine the pineapple and cream and stir in the vanilla. Chill the filling briefly before using it as required. This recipe provides 3 cups of filling.

Semisweet Chocolate Filling

3 squares (3 ounces) semisweet
   chocolate
¼ cup water
3 eggs, separated

1 tsp vanilla extract
¼ tsp salt
⅓ cup brown sugar

In a saucepan over simmering water melt the chocolate in the ¼ cup
of water, stirring until the mixture is smooth. Remove the pan from over
the water and beat in the egg yolks 1 at a time. Stir in the vanilla. In a
mixing bowl beat the egg whites with the salt to the soft-peak stage.
Add the brown sugar, in small quantities, continuing the beating until
the whites are stiff and glossy. Fold them into the chocolate mixture.
Use as directed in specific recipes or to fill one 8-inch pie shell.

Orange Butter

1½ cups butter, softened
¼ cup sugar
Juice & grated rind of 1 orange
Juice & grated rind of 1 lemon

1 Tbl cognac
1 Tbl orange-flavored liqueur
   (Curaçao, Cointreau, or Grand
   Marnier)

In a mixing bowl thoroughly cream together the butter and sugar. Blend
in the juices, rinds, brandy, and liqueur. Chill the butter in the refrigerator. This recipe provides about 2 cups of orange butter, to be used
as required.

Sweet Chestnut Purée

1 2-pound can peeled chestnuts in
   light syrup
½ cup sugar
3 tsp vanilla extract

Peel of ½ orange, in 2-inch strips
Peel of ½ lemon, in 2-inch strips
4 cups water

Drain the chestnuts, reserving the syrup for other uses. Rinse the nuts
under cold running water and combine them in a saucepan with the
sugar, vanilla, and orange and lemon peels. Pour the water over them.

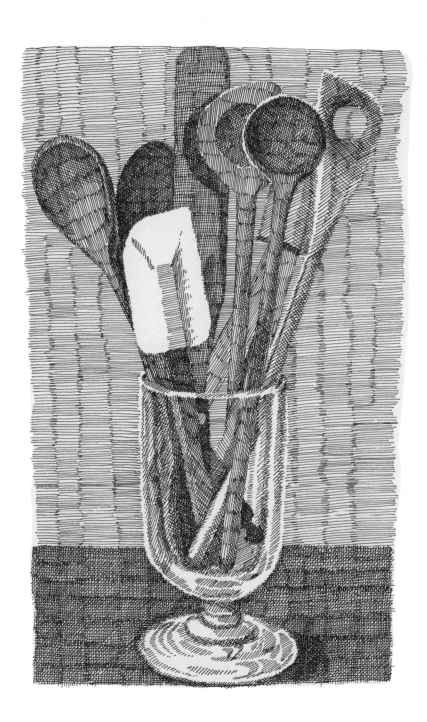

Bring the liquid to a boil and cook the chestnuts, covered, over moderate heat for 30 minutes or until they are very soft. Drain them, reserving the cooking liquid, and force them through a fine sieve or purée them in an electric blender. Thin the purée with a little of the reserved cooking liquid, if necessary, to produce a mixture that is spreadable but thick enough to hold a shape. Use as required. This recipe provides about 1½ cups of purée.

Apricot Glaze

½ cup apricot preserves   **2 Tbl water**

In a saucepan over low heat melt the preserves. Stir in the water and cook for just 1 minute. Strain out the solids and discard them (or reserve them for use as ice cream topping). Use the warm glaze as required. Cooled and contained in a tightly covered jar, it will keep indefinitely. This recipe provides about ½ cup of glaze.

Cinnamon Sugar

1 cup granulated sugar   **⅓ cup cinnamon**

Sift the 2 ingredients together onto a sheet of waxed paper. Pour the cinnamon sugar into a jar or canister for storage and cover it tightly.

Vanilla Sugar

1 vanilla bean   **4 cups sugar, either granulated (2 pounds) or confectioners' (1 pound)**

Split the vanilla bean, cut it into 2-inch lengths, and embed the pieces in the sugar in a jar or canister. Cover the container tightly and let the sugar remain for at least 3 days before using it. Replenish with unflavored sugar.

Chocolate Glaze

13 squares (13 ounces) semisweet   1 cup water
  chocolate

In a saucepan over low heat melt the chocolate in the water, stirring gently to blend. Cool to warm and use as required for a glossy coating. This recipe makes 2½ cups of glaze.

Caramel Glaze

1½ cups sugar

Heat the sugar in a skillet over low heat until it melts and begins to turn amber in color. Pour it immediately over the material to be glazed. This glaze hardens quickly.

Praline Powder

2 cups granulated sugar   ¾ cup shelled almonds
¾ cup shelled filberts

In a skillet over low heat cook the sugar until it begins to melt. Quickly stir in the nuts and continue the cooking, without further stirring, until the sugar caramelizes (that is, until it turns amber in color). Turn the mixture out onto a lightly buttered baking sheet and let it cool and harden completely. Roll this praline, between sheets of waxed paper, into a fine powder, or pulverize it in an electric blender. This recipe provides about 3 cups of praline powder. Stored in an airtight container, it will keep indefinitely.

Praline Cream

⅔ cup Praline Powder (above)   1 cup heavy cream, whipped

Simply fold the praline powder into the whipped cream. Chill the praline cream well.

3 | cake decorating

There was a time, now happily long since gone, when it was considered great culinary artistry to prepare sweet dishes in the likeness of the fish course or the roast. A great cake might be presented at the table as salmon *en Bellevue,* for example. On a smaller scale, such bizarre creations extended even to cake decorating. Those extravagances are now regarded as being in questionable taste, and although home cooks would not even consider attempting them and would be content with simplicity, some may want to try their hands at something a little more complicated than just icing a cake. Wherefore we present on the following pages some of the basic techniques of cake decorating—procedures for icing the cake, using the pastry bag, and making simple piped and applied decorations. Although you may never achieve the virtuosity of a skillful pastry chef (and may not even want to), the fundamentals which follow, plus practice and experimentation, will produce gratifying results.

Equipment

A **pastry bag** is essential to even the simplest kind of decorating. A medium-size plastic-lined bag will serve for most purposes.

Decorating tubes (available in good kitchenware departments and by mail order) come in sizes from small to large, and you should have an assortment. The sizes and styles that follow should cover your needs. Plain tubes:

> #3, for small pastries
>
> #5, for small cookies
>
> #7, for forming small cream puffs and larger cookies
>
> #9, for forming large cream puffs, éclairs, and vacherin rings

Star tubes:

> #2, for decorating small pastries
>
> #4, for making small rosettes
>
> #6, for shaping molded cookies.
>
> #9, for larger confections, such as cream puff pastry swans

Parchment paper, or heavy freezing paper, is frequently used by pastry chefs for making paper cornets for decorating. How this is done will be explained later.

Spatulas, both a rubber one and a metal one, are the utensils you will need to spread icings and fillings.

A **turntable** may be a good investment for a person who does a great deal of decorating. It will not tip over, and since it revolves easily, a smooth job of icing can be done. (A lazy susan also works for this.)

Icing the Cake

Delicacy in coloring is the ideal; artificial and brilliant shades are not appetizing. Food colorings are highly concentrated and should be added drop by drop. For very pastel coloring, dip the point of a knife into a drop of coloring on a piece of waxed paper, then into the icing.

Icing may be applied in several ways, depending upon type. A glaze of melted preserves (such as apricot, page 70) should first be poured over the cake to seal the surface. The cake should be tilted and rotated so that the liquid covers the surface evenly. Generally only the top of the cake requires glazing.

To coat with a spreadable icing, such as Chocolate Icing (page 63), mound a quantity of the icing on the top of the cake and, with a spatula, smooth it over the surface and down the sides. A thick icing, such as the Lemon Meringue (page 62), is used in much the same way but is generally swirled over the top of the cake with a spatula into decorative swirls or spirals.

A rolled almond-paste icing such as that used on the Valentine Cake (page 40), or a rolled fondant icing, is fitted onto the cake, smoothed into place, and the excess trimmed off. Iced in this manner, the cake can then be neatly piped with a greeting or other top ornamentation in keeping with the occasion.

Using the Pastry Bag

To decorate with the pastry bag, proceed as follows: First fold the top of the bag down around the outside to form a cuff about 2 inches wide. Fit the appropriate metal tube into the small opening at the base of the bag, making certain that the tube is properly seated with the tip protruding. Holding the bag over a bowl (to catch any icing that may drip), fill the bag with the icing to about two-thirds of its capacity. Unfold the cuff, close the edges together, and fold down the top into a flap about 1 inch wide. Fold the 2 corners in toward the middle to form a triangle with the point upright. Gently fold the point down and continue folding the top over until it meets the top of the filling. To press out the filling, hold the bag so that the top rests in the palm of your right hand (assuming that you are right-handed) with the fold of the top on the outside; press gently on the top with a sort of rolling motion to force the filling through the tube onto the surface you are decorating, while supporting and guiding the bag with your left hand.

Making a Paper Cornet

It is possible to "write" on a cake by piping the icing through the very small opening of a plain tube, but this is better done with a paper cone, or cornet, which, after a little practice, you can easily make yourself in a few dextrous motions. And when you are finished, the paper is simply discarded.

Start by cutting a large square from a piece of baking parchment or liner paper. Cut the square diagonally into 2 triangles. Hold a triangle with the long side directly in front of and parallel to you. Hold the opposite corner between the thumb and forefinger of your right hand. Take the corner on the left between the thumb and forefinger of your left hand and bring it over against the underside of the corner in your right hand, tugging it so that it points upward. Hold the corners firmly together with your left hand. With your right hand now bring the free corner around the outside of the paper, pulling so that it points upward rather than around the cone. Be sure that the point of the cone is sharp *(see the illustration on page 77).* Fold the 3 corners to secure the cornet. Fill the cone about two-thirds full with the icing to be used and fold the top of the cone over to enclose the filling. With a scissors snip off a small bit from the tip of the cone, the size depending upon whether you wish to write with a fine line or a bold one. Squeeze out into the bowl a test bit of the filling to make certain that it flows evenly. Manipulate the cone in the same way you use the pastry bag, forcing out filling with the right hand and guiding the cone with the left hand.

Piped Decorations

In addition to icings, try using butter cream, softened cream cheese, meringue, and chocolate for making piped decorations.

To Make a Rosette:
The rosette should be pressed out in one continuous motion. Using a pastry bag fitted with a plain tube, start pressing out the icing from the center of a small imaginary circle to form the base of the rosette. Press out a smaller circle directly on top of the bottom circle, continuing in an uninterrupted circle. Spiral the icing in circles of decreasing size until the desired shape is attained.

To Make a Simple Flower:
With the pastry tube or cornet outline 4 hearts with their points together. Then draw a stem coming down from the flower and a leaf

How to make a cornet

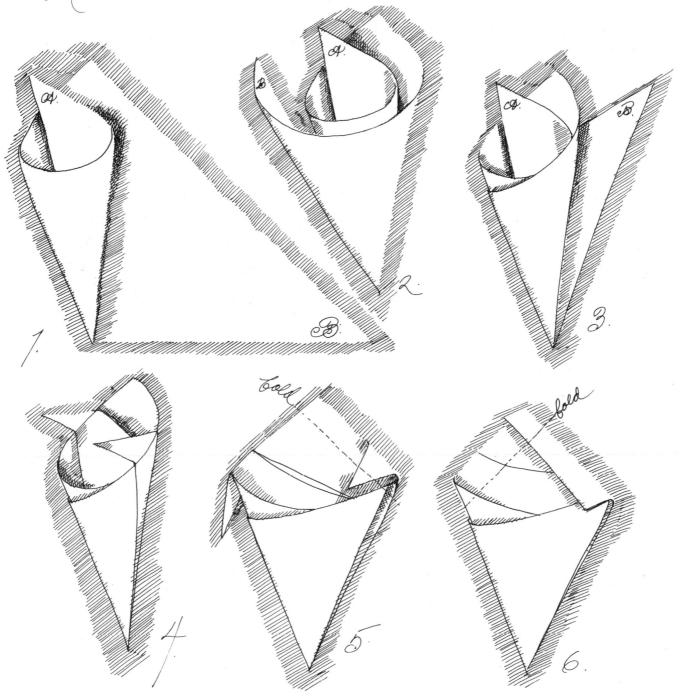

lower down on the stem for balance. After you've made your design with a cornet, go back and thicken it in places where you think it will give the whole more character or, for a more colorful effect, fill in the flower with apricot glaze, tinted with vegetable coloring to any shade you like.

Chocolate for Decorating:

Melt 6 squares of semisweet chocolate. While still warm, put into the refrigerator to chill. Half an hour before you are ready to use it, place in a warm spot until it softens but does not lose its chill; this is called "tempering." Stir occasionally to keep the texture smooth. The best way to test whether it is cold, as it should be for use, is to put a little on your lips (not the inside of your mouth). Put into the pastry bag or cornet and proceed as directed above, or as your imagination dictates.

To Make Meringue Mushrooms:

Prepare Meringue batter (page 93), reserving 2 tablespoons of the sugar as directed in the recipe. Preheat oven to 200 degrees. Line baking sheets as for meringues and, using a pastry bag fitted with a plain tube, pipe onto the paper rounds of meringue about 2 inches in diameter and ½-inch thick, spacing them about 2 inches apart; these are the "caps." Pipe out "stems" about 1 inch long, tapered from ½-inch thickness at the base to a narrow point at the top. Sprinkle caps and stems with the reserved sugar and bake in the preheated oven for 45 minutes or until they are crisp. Remove the pieces while they are still warm. With a skewer or the point of a knife make a hole in the underside of each cap and fit the pointed end of a stem into each. Sprinkle the mushrooms with a light sifting of cocoa.

To Make Swans:

Swans made of cream puff pastry or meringue are a touch of whimsy that children, in particular, enjoy. You can make small swans to use as decoration or larger ones to serve as dessert. For pastry swans to decorate a cake, preheat oven to 400 degrees. Fit a pastry bag with a #9 star tube (about ¾-inch opening) and fill the bag with 1 cup of Pâte à Chou (page 137). Lightly butter 2 baking sheets. On one press out the paste in fluted mounds to form 6 separate "bodies," each about 2 inches long, tapered from 1½ inches wide at one end to a point at the other (the "tail"). Bake in the preheated oven for 15 minutes or until the forms are well puffed and lightly browned. Turn off the heat and let the forms remain in the slackening oven for 5 minutes longer. Cool them on a rack.

Using a small plain tube, such as a #5 (about ¼-inch opening), press out paste onto the other baking sheet to form 6 "necks" and "heads," beginning with a small round for the head and continuing from it to form a question mark in reverse (minus the dot) about 1½ inches long. Pinch a "beak" into the head. Bake the necks and heads in a preheated 400-degree oven for 10 minutes or until they are well puffed and the same degree of brownness as the bodies. Again turn off the heat and let them remain in the slackening oven for 5 minutes. Using a metal spatula, very carefully so as not to break them, remove the neck-head forms to a rack to cool.

How to make a swan

How to make a rose

1.

2.

3.

4.

5.

6.

Split the body forms each into 2 layers, preserving the fluted tops and bases each in 1 piece. Cut each fluted top lengthwise into halves to provide "wings." Mound whipped cream onto the base and fit the wings onto it. Place the base of the "neck" into the whipped cream and sprinkle the swan with sugar. *(See illustration, page 80.)*

Flat swans for decorating or for dessert adornment can be made of meringue. Preheat oven to 225 degrees. Prepare meringue batter as for Meringues (page 93), reserving 2 tablespoons of the sugar. Using a pastry bag fitted with a small plain tube, such as a #5 (about ¼-inch opening), pipe 3 swan shapes of the size desired, all facing in the same direction. Pipe out swans in 1 piece, starting with a small round for the head and proceeding with the neck as directed for the pastry swans. Continue with an outline of the body and fill it with diminishing concentric circles. Press out 3 more swans, facing in the opposite direction from the first 3. Sprinkle the 6 swans with the reserved sugar and bake them in the preheated oven for 45 minutes or until they are crisp and slightly browned. Remove them carefully from the baking paper and use as required. To serve as dessert, fit 2 opposite swans onto a ball of ice cream.

Flat Decorations

Applied decorations are an appealing way to dress a cake for a special occasion. They can be made in several ways.

Chocolate Decorations:

Flat decorations for the top of a cake can be made by spreading a not-too-thin layer of melted chocolate onto a sheet of parchment or liner paper, chilling it until the chocolate hardens (about 30 minutes), and then cutting from it shapes as required. The cutting is more easily accomplished if the chocolate is allowed to soften very slightly after chilling it.

Another way to make such decorations is perhaps even easier. Draw whatever it is you wish to make on waxed paper and then fill it in with Chocolate for Decorating (page 78) or with Butter Cream (page 59), using either a pastry bag or a paper cornet. Refrigerate to harden. Remove from paper and place on the cake.

Individually iced cake layers
and skillful decoration enhance this
festive Birthday Cake (page 40).

1. Cutting cake around heart-shaped pattern.

2. Spreading layers with filling.

3. Rolling paste again for decorative texture.

4. Covering cake with rolled almond paste.

5. Writing message after cake is trimmed.

6. Completed cake, with rose.

1. Spreading cake roll with mocha frosting.

2. Using pastry comb to create bark effect.

3. Adding rows of butter cream.

4. Setting crescents in butter-cream rows.

5. Dotting crescents with butter cream.

6. Presenting log with slice up to show "rings."

To Make a Rose:

An almond-paste rose, like that used on the Valentine Cake, can be made by tinting almond paste with vegetable coloring as desired and shaping the paste into a roll about 1 inch in diameter. Cut the roll into several 1-inch lengths and shape them into balls. Shape each ball into a rose petal, working it as follows: Place the ball on a marble slab or on a sheet of waxed paper on a flat surface and, using a metal spatula, smooth the ball away from you into a petal shape about ⅛-inch thick at the edge nearest you (which will be the base of the petal) and tapering to very thin at the other side. Prepare the remaining balls of almond paste in the same way, reserving 1 to serve as center of the flower. Shape that ball into a cone, in proportion to the size of the flower you are making. Press the base of the petals gently but firmly in layers around the cone, folding the top layers in closely and flaring the petals of the succeeding layers, graduating the flares to simulate the opening flower. Trim the cone even with the bottom layer of petals and place the rose in position on the top of the cake. *(See page 81.)*

Sweet Dough Decorations:

Cookie-like decorations can be made by rolling out Sweet Dough (page 135) very thin. Cut half-moons, stars, circles, or what you will from the dough and place on greased cookie sheets. Bake in a 325-degree oven until golden (12 to 15 minutes).

Practicing

For a beginner, it makes sense not to waste expensive ingredients in practicing decorating. An economical trial-and-error method is to make instant mashed potatoes, to whatever degree of thickness is similar to the job you want to do (thick mashed potatoes for squeezing out cookies, thinner for cake decorations), and use them to practice with. You will also make your job easier if you draw whatever it is you wish to imitate on a piece of cardboard, then with your pastry tube squeeze out the potatoes, following the lines you've set down. Eventually, you will become so skillful that you can do the job freehand, as professional pastry chefs do. And it won't take as long as you think to reach that degree of skill, either.

Basic cake-decorating skills can be
applied in making the Valentine Cake (page 40)
and the Lincoln Log (page 38).

4 | cookies

There is just one problem about cookies: No matter how many are baked, there are never enough. The solution, then, is to bake them often and in quantity. They store well (and all the better if the family cookie jar is kept well hidden).

When you are pressed for time, make cookies by baking one large square and cutting it into smaller squares, as we do with the Ranch Fudge Square. If you are baking primarily for children (and there can be no more eager clientele), concentrate on sturdier, heartier cookies. Most children shy away from the too-fragile (and insufficiently filling) varieties. But you needn't deprive yourself and the rest of your family of the melting delights of such as Tuiles or Brandy Snaps. For parties and special occasions, Sables, with their intricate patterns of brown and white, are impressive. At Christmas, which is the great cookie season of the year, run a joyous gamut and make them all.

Sables

2¾ cups flour   **2 Tbl cocoa**
1 cup butter, cut in small pieces **½ tsp vanilla extract**
½ cup sugar

Sift the flour onto a pastry board, and make a well in the center of the mound. Put into it the butter and sugar, and with your fingers work the flour into them to produce a completely smooth dough. Divide the dough into 2 equal parts. Blend the cocoa into one part, the vanilla into the other. Divide each of these parts into 4, and with them prepare 4 batches of differently designed cookies, proceeding as follows:

On a lightly floured pastry board, roll 1 portion of chocolate dough and 1 portion of vanilla dough each into a square about ½-inch thick. Using a second quarter of each dough, make 2 cylindrical rolls about 1 inch in diameter and the same length as the squares. Place the vanilla cylinder on the chocolate square and the chocolate cylinder on the vanilla square. Roll up each separately, enclosing cylinders completely. Brush the trailing edge of each roll with beaten egg and press to seal the seams. Wrap the rolls in waxed paper and chill them for at least 30 minutes.

Roll out a third quarter of each dough into a square about ⅜-inch thick, and cut each into strips ¾ of an inch wide. On a sheet of waxed paper arrange 2 strips of vanilla dough with a strip of chocolate between them, almost touching. Brush top with beaten egg. Cover that layer evenly with strips in reverse order: 2 strips of chocolate dough with 1 of vanilla between them. Repeat with the remaining strips, alternating vanilla and chocolate in each succeeding layer to produce a checkerboard pattern on the ends. Brush each layer, except the final one, with beaten egg. Wrap the dough in the waxed paper and chill it also.

To the remaining portions of vanilla and chocolate dough add corresponding scraps from the strip-cut dough. Shape the chocolate dough into a cylindrical roll about 1 inch thick. Stretch the remaining vanilla dough into a long rope about ¼-inch thick. Wind the rope around the cylinder in a spiral, covering it completely. Brush the rope with beaten egg and press the ends firmly against the cylinder to secure them. Chill that cylinder along with the other patterns.

Preheat oven to 350 degrees. Lightly grease baking sheets and cover them with waxed paper. Cut each of the chilled dough preparations into slices about ⅜-inch thick and arrange them on the baking sheets. Bake in the preheated oven for 20 minutes or until they are very lightly browned. This recipe provides about 4 dozen sables, about 1 dozen of each design. *(See photograph, page 101.)*

Vanilla Kipferln

1¼ **cups flour**	¼ **cup Vanilla Sugar (page 70)**
¼ **tsp salt**	**Additional Vanilla Sugar,**
½ **cup cold firm butter**	**as required**
½ **cup ground filberts (see Note)**	

Preheat oven to 350 degrees. Sift the flour with the salt into a mixing bowl and cut the butter into it to produce a mixture somewhat like coarse meal. Add the nuts and vanilla sugar and knead quickly to a smooth dough. Wrap the dough in waxed paper and chill it in the refrigerator for at least 30 minutes. Divide the dough into 18 pieces of equal size and form each into a cigar shape about 3 inches long. Bend the "cigars" into crescents. Arrange them on ungreased baking sheets and bake in the preheated oven for 20 minutes or until they are very light golden in color. Sprinkle the 18 kipferln, which this recipe produces, with additional vanilla sugar while the little crescents are still hot. *(See photograph, page 101.)*
NOTE: The filberts can be ground easily in the blender.

Palmiers

Sugar	**1 recipe Puff Pastry (page 135)**

Sprinkle a pastry board generously with sugar and roll the puff pastry out on it into a rectangle about 10 inches wide and ⅛-inch thick. Sprinkle the top with sugar. Mark off the midpoint of the 2 long sides, and then mark off each half into quarters. Fold each long half of the dough over at these points, so that the inside edges of the folds meet in the middle. Fold the 2 halves together to make a long roll with 8 thicknesses of pastry. Sprinkle dough with additional sugar, wrap it in waxed paper, and set it in the refrigerator to chill thoroughly.

Cut the chilled dough across the width into slices about ¼-inch thick, and arrange them, 2 inches apart, on an ungreased baking sheet. Bake in a preheated 400-degree oven for 20 minutes or until the palmiers are well browned and caramelized. Check after they have baked for 10 minutes. If the pastry browns too quickly on the underside, turn the leaves with a spatula and continue the baking for the required length of time. This will provide about 2 dozen palmiers.

Macaroons

1¾ cups confectioners' sugar	1 cup almond paste,
⅔ cup granulated sugar	about ½ pound (see Note)
	4 egg whites

Preheat oven to 275 degrees. In a mixing bowl blend the sugars into the almond paste and thoroughly stir in 3 of the egg whites. Beat the fourth egg white to a froth and add only as much of it as may be needed to produce a mixture that is soft enough to pipe from a pastry bag (fitted with a large plain or a star tube), but firm enough to hold a shape. Pipe the paste in rounds (using the plain tube) or rosettes (with the star tube) about the equivalent of a teaspoonful each and spaced 3 inches apart. Bake them in the preheated oven for 25 minutes or until they are pale-golden in color and slightly crusty. This recipe provides 4½ dozen small macaroons.
NOTE: Almond paste is available in specialty food shops.

Black-Walnut Wafers

½ cup butter, softened	⅓ cup finely chopped black
½ tsp vanilla extract	walnuts
1 cup firmly packed brown sugar	1¼ cups flour

1 egg, beaten **½ tsp baking soda**
½ tsp salt

In a mixing bowl combine the butter and vanilla. Add the sugar, a little at a time, beating until the grains are completely incorporated and the mixture is light and fluffy. Gradually beat in the egg. Stir in the nuts and finally the flour sifted with the soda and salt. On a floured pastry board shape the dough into rolls about 1½ inches in diameter. Wrap them in waxed paper and chill them in the refrigerator for several hours or overnight.

Remove from the refrigerator only as much of the dough as can be worked with at one time and cut it into thin slices. Arrange them about 1½ inches apart on ungreased cookie sheets and bake in a preheated 350-degree oven for 8 minutes or until the cookies are lightly browned. This recipe provides about 6 dozen of these little wafers.

Spiced Walnut Roll-ups

½ pound creamed cottage cheese,
   put through a sieve
1 cup butter, softened
2 cups flour
¼ cup butter, melted

¾ cup light brown sugar
½ tsp cinnamon
¾ cup finely chopped walnuts
1 egg yolk
2 Tbl water

Preheat oven to 400 degrees. Thoroughly combine the cheese and butter in a mixing bowl, and blend in the flour to produce a smooth dough. Divide the dough into 3 equal parts and roll each into a round about ⅛-inch thick. Brush each with some of the melted butter. Combine the sugar, cinnamon, and nuts, and sprinkle ⅓ of the mixture over each round. Cut each into 16 pie-shaped wedges of equal size. Beginning at the wide end, roll up each wedge. Arrange the roll-ups on buttered baking sheets with the seam sides down. Brush the tops with the egg yolk and water beaten together, and bake in the preheated oven for 20 minutes or until the pastry is well browned. As indicated, this recipe provides 48 roll-ups. *(See photograph, page 101.)*

Tuiles

3½ Tbl butter, softened
4½ Tbl sugar
2 egg whites
½ tsp vanilla extract

3–4 drops almond extract
¼ cup sifted cake flour
½ cup thinly sliced blanched
   almonds

Preheat oven to 400 degrees. In a mixing bowl thoroughly cream together the butter and sugar, and stir in the egg whites, lightly beaten, and the flavorings. Gently but thoroughly fold in the flour and almonds combined. Drop teaspoons of the batter about 3 inches apart onto a well-buttered baking sheet and, with the back of a fork, spread them into very thin rounds. Bake them in the preheated oven for 5 minutes or just until the edges of the wafers become tinged with brown. With a metal spatula loosen 1 wafer at a time and place it immediately over a rolling pin; it will shape itself to the curve of the pin, so as to look like a little roof tile (*tuile*). The wafers become crisp very quickly as they cool. Bake only a few wafers at a time and work quickly after you take them from the oven. If they become crisp before you can remove and transfer all of them to the rolling pin, return the baking sheet to the oven for a few seconds until they soften again. This recipe provides about 3 dozen tuiles. *(See photograph, page 102.)*

Currant Cookies

1 cup butter
1 cup sugar
3 cups rolled oats
½ cup currants
¼ cup milk

¾ cup flour
1 tsp baking soda
½ tsp cinnamon
½ tsp ground cloves

Preheat oven to 350 degrees. Soften the butter by mashing it in a mixing bowl with a wooden spoon, and cream it with the sugar. Add the rolled oats and currants, and stir in the milk. Sift the flour with the soda and spices and blend in. Mold the dough into small balls about 1 inch in diameter and arrange them 3 inches apart on buttered baking sheets. The dough will flatten out and spread during the baking. Set the pans, as many at a time as can be accommodated, in the preheated oven and bake for 12 minutes or until the cookies are golden brown. Loosen them with a metal spatula and transfer them to racks to cool. There will be, in all, about 3 dozen.

Meringues

2 egg whites
⅛ tsp salt

⅔ cup sugar

Preheat oven to 225 degrees. In a mixing bowl whisk the egg whites with the salt to the soft-peak stage. Beat ½ cup of the sugar into the whites, 2 tablespoons at a time, to produce a meringue stiff enough to hold a shape and very smooth. It is important that the sugar be completely dissolved.

Cover a baking sheet with unglazed paper and, using a pastry

bag fitted with a plain tube, press out teaspoon-size mounds of meringue batter (or larger, as required), spacing them about 1 inch apart (2 inches for larger meringues). Sprinkle them lightly with the remaining sugar and bake them in the preheated oven for 50 minutes or until they are crisp and just beginning to take on color. Let the meringues cool slightly and remove them. If the meringues stick, moisten the underside of the paper. This recipe provides about 1½ dozen large meringues or twice that number of the small cookies. Store them in a dry place, but not in a covered container.

Spritz Cookies

1 cup butter	2 egg yolks
1 cup confectioners' sugar	2½ cups sifted flour
1 tsp vanilla extract	½ tsp salt

Preheat oven to 400 degrees. In a mixing bowl thoroughly cream together the butter, sugar, and vanilla. Beat in the egg yolks. Sift the flour with the salt and, in small amounts, blend into mixture. Shape dough into a cylinder, wrap it in waxed paper, and chill it well in the refrigerator. Pack into a cookie press equipped with a variety of disks, and press out several different cookie shapes on unbuttered baking sheets. Sprinkle them with coarse sugar, assorted sprinklets, or chopped nuts, and bake them in the preheated oven for 6 minutes or until they are delicately browned. Remove cookies and cool them on a rack; there will be about 5 dozen. *(See photograph, page 101.)*

Langues du Chat | Cat's Tongues

½ **cup butter**
½ **cup sugar**
½ **tsp vanilla extract**

3 **egg whites**
¾ **cup sifted flour**
⅛ **tsp salt**

Preheat oven to 400 degrees. In a mixing bowl cream the butter, sugar, and vanilla together. Add the egg whites, 1 at a time, beating each in thoroughly. Gently but completely fold in the flour sifted with the salt. Pipe the batter through a pastry bag fitted with a plain tube (about ½-inch in diameter) onto buttered and lightly floured baking sheets, pressing them about 2 inches long and spacing the lengths at least 1 inch apart. Bake in the preheated oven 6 minutes or just until the cookies are edged with brown. Transfer them immediately to a rack to cool. This recipe provides about 4 dozen cookies. *(See photograph, page 101.)*

Baci di Dama | Lady's Kisses

1¾ **cups butter**
1 **cup fine granulated sugar**
2 **eggs**

2 **cups flour**
1⅓ **cups yellow cornmeal**
1 **tsp grated lemon rind**

Preheat oven to 350 degrees. In a mixing bowl work the butter until it is soft and creamy. Vigorously stir in the sugar, a little at a time. Beat in the eggs until the mixture is very frothy. Quickly but thoroughly stir in the flour and cornmeal sifted together and the lemon rind. Using a pastry bag fitted with a large star tube, pipe onto buttered baking sheets swirled rosettes 1½ inches wide, spacing them about 4 inches apart (they will spread). Bake them in the preheated oven for 15 minutes or until the cookies are lightly browned around the edges. This recipe provides about 4 dozen cookies.

Dutch Ginger Wedges

1 cup butter
¾ cup sugar
2 cups flour
¼ tsp salt

¼ cup finely chopped, drained,
   preserved ginger
1 tsp syrup from preserved ginger

Preheat oven to 350 degrees. In a mixing bowl thoroughly combine the butter and sugar. Work in the flour, sifted with the salt, and the ginger and syrup. Pat the dough evenly in an 8-inch round layer-cake pan. With the blunt edge of a knife deeply mark dough into 16 wedges. Bake the round in the preheated oven for 45 minutes or until it is nicely browned. Cool it in the pan and cut the marked wedges through.

Joe Froggers

1 cup shortening
2 cups sugar
7 cups flour
1 Tbl salt
1 Tbl ginger
1 tsp ground cloves

1 tsp nutmeg
½ tsp allspice
2 tsp baking soda
2 cups dark molasses
¼ cup rum
¾ cup water

In a mixing bowl thoroughly cream together the shortening and sugar. Make 3 separate combinations from the remaining ingredients: (1) sift together the flour, salt, and spices; (2) stir the soda into the molasses; (3) dilute the rum with the water. Stir into the creamed mixture—in order—½ of each of the 3 combinations. Add the remaining halves in the same order to produce a soft and somewhat sticky dough. Wrap it in waxed paper and chill it in the refrigerator for several hours or overnight. Pat the chilled dough on a lightly floured pastry board into a thickness of about ¼-inch and cut it into 3-inch rounds. Arrange the rounds on buttered baking sheets and bake them in a preheated 375-degree oven for 10 minutes or until they are lightly browned. Check them frequently. If the cookies show signs of browning excessively on the bottom, turn them with a spatula and complete the baking. Let the cookies cool on the sheets briefly before removing them to a rack to complete the cooling. This recipe provides about 2 dozen Froggers. NOTE: These cookies are native to Marblehead, Massachusetts, where they are said to have been created by a man remembered only as Uncle Joe. His neighbors thought the cookies resembled the frogs that inhabited a pond next to his house. Hence the name.

Pfeffernusse | Peppernuts

3 eggs	¼ tsp baking powder
1 cup sugar	½ cup ground blanched almonds
3 cups flour	3 Tbl finely chopped candied
1 tsp cinnamon	orange peel
¼ tsp ground cloves	3 Tbl finely chopped candied
¼ tsp black pepper	lemon peel

In a mixing bowl beat the eggs and sugar together until the sugar dissolves and the mixture is frothy. Sift the flour with the spices and baking powder and blend the mixture into the beaten eggs. Add nuts and candied peel. Knead the dough well on a lightly floured pastry board and roll it out into a sheet about ½-inch thick. Cut from it rounds about 1½ inches in diameter and arrange them on lightly buttered baking sheets (or shape the rounds into nut-size balls). Let the cookies remain so overnight. Bake them in a preheated 325-degree oven for 20 minutes or until they are well browned. Cool them on a rack.

    Pfeffernusse are not generally iced. If desired, however, they may be glazed with a thin mixture of confectioners' sugar and milk. This quantity of batter provides about 4 dozen cookies.

Pariser Stangerl | Parisian Sticks

1 cup ground filberts
½ cup sugar
2 Tbl flour

1 egg white
1 tsp apricot preserves
Egg-White Icing (page 60)

Preheat oven to 300 degrees. In a mixing bowl smoothly combine the nuts, sugar, flour, egg white, and preserves. Pat or roll the dough into a sheet ¼-inch thick and 5 inches wide. Brush it with the icing and let icing dry. Split the sheet lengthwise into 2 strips and cut each across the width into sticks ½-inch wide. Arrange on a lightly buttered baking sheet and bake them in the preheated oven for 15 minutes or just until they are very lightly browned. Loosen them with a spatula and let them cool on the baking sheet. This recipe provides 1½ dozen sticks.

GINGERBREAD MAN

Almond Pretzels

¾ cup butter
¾ cup sugar
Grated rind of 1 lemon
2 eggs

2 cups flour
1½ cups finely ground blanched
   almonds
Thin Lemon Icing (page 61)

Preheat oven to 375 degrees. In a mixing bowl cream the butter and the sugar. Add the lemon rind and thoroughly beat in the eggs, 1 at a time. Combine the flour and ground almonds and blend into the mixture to produce a smooth dough. Turn it out onto a floured pastry board and roll it into a thin sheet. Cut from it strips about ¾-inch wide and 8 inches long, and braid each into a pretzel, proceeding as follows:

With the strip of dough flat on the board, cross 1 end of it over the other, leaving a loop about 1½ inches in diameter with the dangling ends about 1-inch long. Press the joint to secure it, and flip the whole thing over. Bring the under end diagonally to meet the loop and press it into place. Bring the other end diagonally to the opposite section of the loop and secure it also. The pretzel is now complete. Bake the pretzels (there will be about 3 dozen) on greased baking sheets in the preheated oven for 20 minutes or until they are lightly browned. Cool the pretzels on a rack and brush them with lemon icing.

Lucia Pepparkakor | Swedish Christmas Gingersnaps

⅔ cup butter
¾ cup light brown sugar,
   firmly packed
2 Tbl molasses
¼ cup cool water
1 tsp grated lemon rind

2¼ cups sifted flour
1 tsp baking soda
1 Tbl cinnamon
1½ tsp ground cloves
1 tsp ground cardamom

Preheat oven to 350 degrees. In a mixing bowl thoroughly cream together the butter and sugar. Stir in the molasses, diluted with the water, and the lemon rind. Sift the flour with the baking soda and spices and blend it into the creamed mixture. Shape the dough into a ball, dust it with flour, and chill it in the refrigerator. Roll the chilled dough out into a sheet about ⅛-inch thick and, with floured cutters, cut from it Christmas shapes: trees, angels, stars, crescents, etc. Arrange them on buttered baking sheets and bake in the preheated oven for 8 minutes or until the cookies are lightly browned. Cool them on the sheet. Ice, if desired. This recipe provides about 5 dozen cookies.

Sweet-Dough Cookies

¼ **recipe Sweet Dough (page 135)**　　　**1 egg, beaten**

Preheat oven to 350 degrees. Roll the sweet dough out on a lightly floured board to a thickness of about ¼-inch. Cut it as desired and brush the cuts with beaten egg. Decorate as desired with any of the following: halves of maraschino cherries, pine nuts, coarse sugar, chopped pistachio nuts, chopped mixed candied fruit, thin wedges of candied pineapple, chopped or sliced almonds, cashews, or walnuts. Bake in the preheated oven for 15 minutes or until the cookies are brown around the edges. This recipe provides about 3 dozen round cookies or the equivalent in other shapes.

Chocolate Sweet-Dough Cookies:

Blend 1 square (1 ounce) semisweet chocolate, melted and cooled, into each 2 cups of the dough. Proceed as directed.

Oatmeal Florentines

¼ **cup butter**	2 **Tbl flour**
2 **cups rolled oats**	½ **tsp baking powder**
2 **eggs, beaten**	1 **tsp vanilla extract**
⅓ **cup sugar**	

Preheat oven to 350 degrees. In a skillet melt the butter over moderate heat and in it brown the oatmeal flakes well, stirring them constantly. Remove the pan from the heat and let the oatmeal cool. Stir in the eggs. Combine the sugar, flour, and baking powder, and stir in. Stir in the vanilla. Drop the batter by teaspoons onto a buttered and lightly floured baking sheet, spacing them about 1 inch apart. Flatten each

Mélange of cookies includes sugar-sprinkled
Spritz (page 94), slender Langues du Chat (page 95),
black-and-white Sables (page 88),
crescent-shaped Vanilla Kipferln (page 89), and Spiced
Walnut Roll-ups (page 92).

gently with a fork dipped in cool water. Bake in the preheated oven for 10 minutes or until the cookies are nicely browned. This recipe provides about 2½ dozen cookies.

Hermits

¼ **cup butter**	¾ **tsp cream of tartar**
½ **cup sugar**	1 **tsp cinnamon**
½ **tsp salt**	½ **tsp ground cloves**
½ **cup molasses**	½ **tsp nutmeg**
2 **eggs, well beaten**	½ **cup raisins, finely chopped**
2 **cups flour**	3 **Tbl finely chopped citron**
¾ **tsp baking soda**	¼ **cup chopped nut meats**

Preheat oven to 350 degrees. In a mixing bowl thoroughly cream together the butter, sugar, and salt. Stir in the molasses and beat in the eggs. Sift 1¾ cups of the flour with the soda, cream of tartar, and spices, and blend it into the creamed mixture. Coat the fruits and nuts with the remaining flour and stir them into the prepared batter. For 4 dozen hermits, drop batter by tablespoons onto buttered baking sheets and bake in the preheated oven for 10 minutes or until they are nicely browned. For smaller cookies (and twice as many), make them with rounded teaspoons of the batter.

Anise Drop Cookies

3 **eggs**	2 **tsp ground anise seed**
1 **cup sugar**	¼ **tsp baking powder**
1½ **cups sifted flour**	

In a mixing bowl beat together the eggs and sugar until the mixture is very smooth and thick. Sift together the flour, ground anise, and baking powder, and fold in, about ¼ at a time. Drop teaspoons of the batter onto well-buttered baking sheets, spacing them about 2 inches apart. Set the sheets in a cool place (not in the refrigerator) and let them remain, uncovered and undisturbed, for several hours or overnight.

Curved Tuiles (page 92), dark Brandy
Snaps (page 104), and half-tie Almond Pretzels
(page 99) are crisp accompaniments to
strawberries and coffee.

Bake in a preheated 350-degree oven for 5 minutes or until they are very lightly browned. Remove the cookies to a rack and let them cool. This recipe provides about 5 dozen cookies.

Ranch Fudge Squares

1 cup butter, softened	4 eggs, separated
2 cups sugar	1 cup flour
1 tsp vanilla extract	1 cup finely chopped pecans
½ cup cocoa	

Preheat oven to 350 degrees. In a mixing bowl cream together until very fluffy the butter, sugar, and vanilla. Blend in the cocoa and thoroughly beat in the egg yolks. Stir in the flour and pecans combined. In another bowl beat the egg whites until they are stiff but not dry and fold them in gently but well. Butter an 8-inch square baking pan, cover the bottom with waxed paper, and butter the paper. Spread the mixture in the prepared pan and bake in the preheated oven for 40 minutes, or until the square begins to shrink from the sides of the pan. Cool it in the pan for a few minutes. Invert out onto a rack and peel off the baking paper. Cool the square and cut it into 16 smaller squares.

Brandy Snaps

6 Tbl butter	¾ cup sifted flour
6 Tbl sugar	1 tsp ginger
¼ cup molasses	2 tsp brandy
Thin peel of ½ lemon	Whipped cream, brandy flavored

Preheat oven to 325 degrees. In a saucepan gently heat together the

butter, sugar, molasses, and lemon peel, stirring until the sugar dissolves and the ingredients are well blended. Remove the pan from the heat and take out and discard the lemon peel. Sift the flour with the ginger and blend in, ½ at a time. Stir in the brandy. Drop the batter by demi-tasse spoons at 3-inch intervals onto a buttered baking sheet. Bake in the preheated oven for 8 minutes or until the wafers are medium-brown. Let them cool for a moment or two on the baking sheet. Working quickly, remove them, 1 at a time, with a metal spatula and roll them around the handle of a wooden spoon. Slip them off as soon as they are crisp. Bake only a few wafers at a time. If they cool too quickly (they become crisp as they cool), return them to the oven for a few moments to soften. Serve them filled with whipped cream flavored with brandy. This recipe provides about 2 dozen brandy snaps. *(See photograph, page 102.)*

Viennese Jam Pockets

1 cup butter, softened	½ tsp salt
1 cup farmer cheese, put through a sieve (see Note)	1 cup jam
½ tsp finely grated lemon rind	1 egg white
2 cups flour	Confectioners' sugar

Preheat oven to 350 degrees. In a mixing bowl thoroughly cream together the butter, cheese, and lemon rind. Sift the flour with the salt and blend in. Let the dough rest in a cool place for 30 minutes. Roll it out ⅛-inch thick, cut it into 3-inch squares, and place ½ teaspoon of jam in the center of each. Beat the egg white just to a froth and with it brush a ¼-inch border around each square. Fold the dough over the filling to form triangles and seal the edges by pressing them firmly together. Arrange the triangles on lightly buttered baking sheets and bake them in the preheated oven for 20 minutes or until the pastry is golden brown. Cool the "pockets" on a rack and sift a light coating of confectioners' sugar over them. This recipe provides about 2 dozen pockets. NOTE: Farmer cheese, somewhat similar to cottage cheese, is known in some areas as "pressed cheese."

5|pies

Long before apple pie became a measure of Americanism, the English were singing "An apple pie without some cheese/ Is like a kiss without a squeeze." So, there may be a question about how American apple pie *is,* but there can be no question about its popularity; wherever it comes from, it is close to the American heart. No dessert collection would be complete without a good example.

Many other pies, however, are strongly based in American food lore, having been created by early cooks from the fruits and vegetables found in a new and fertile land. From New England came the blueberry pie, from the South the pecan pie, from elsewhere the rhubarb, pumpkin, and berry pies that gave savor to frontier diets of long ago and still are enjoyed today.

Not the least of their attractions are the good smells of pastry, of fruit, of sugar and cream, the good kitchen smell of a pie baking in the oven. These have ever been universal symbols of comfort and pleasure, of warmth and reassurance.

Apple Pie

1 recipe Rich Pastry (page 134)
5–6 medium cooking apples
1 cup sugar
1 tsp cinnamon
¼ tsp nutmeg
1 tsp lemon juice
¼ tsp salt
2 tsp butter
1 egg, beaten

Preheat oven to 375 degrees. Line a 9-inch pie pan with as much of the pastry as needed, rolled ⅛-inch thick. Peel, core, and thinly slice the apples. Combine the sugar, spices, lemon juice, and salt, and coat the apples with the mixture. Spread the slices in the prepared pie shell, heaping them slightly higher in the middle, and dot them with the butter cut into small bits. Roll, also ⅛-inch thick, a top crust of the remaining pastry. Brush the rim of the bottom pastry with beaten egg and fit the top over it, pressing the edges together. Trim off excess and crimp the edges, if desired. Brush the top with beaten egg and prick it in several places with the tines of a fork. Bake in the preheated oven for 1 hour or until the pastry is nicely browned. Serve the pie hot or cooled, cut it to provide 6 servings.

Deep-Dish Apple Pie

½ cup butter, softened
½ cup cream cheese, softened
1¼ cups flour
⅞ cup sugar
   (¾ cup plus 2 Tbl)
½ tsp salt
2 Tbl heavy cream
⅓ cup firmly packed brown sugar
3 Tbl quick-cooking tapioca
1 tsp cinnamon
¼ tsp nutmeg
5 medium cooking apples, cored, peeled & sliced (about 6 cups)
2 tsp butter, melted
1 egg, beaten
Granulated sugar for sprinkling

Prepare pastry in a mixing bowl, beating the butter and cheese together until the mixture is light and fluffy. Sift the flour with 2 tablespoons of the sugar and ½ teaspoon of the salt and quickly work it in. Blend in the cream. Form dough into a ball. Dust it lightly with flour, wrap it in waxed paper or foil, and chill it in the refrigerator for 30 minutes.

Roll out the chilled dough on a lightly floured pastry board into a round about 11 inches in diameter. Preheat oven to 375 degrees.

In another bowl combine the brown sugar, tapioca, cinnamon, nutmeg, the remaining granulated sugar (¾ cup), and the remaining salt. Add the apples and toss them in the mixture, coating the slices well. Sprinkle them with the melted butter. Heap them in a deep 9-inch pie pan, fit the prepared round of pastry over them, and trim off the excess. Crimp the pastry, securing the edges to the pan. Brush the top with beaten egg and sprinkle it with a little additional granulated sugar. Cut 2 small slits in the top of the pastry to allow steam to escape during the baking. Bake in the preheated oven for 45 minutes or until the crust is golden brown. Serve the pie hot, neatly scooped from the pan to provide 6 servings.

Charlie Brown's Apple Lemon Meringue Pie

½ recipe Plain Pastry (page 134)	3 Tbl cornstarch
2 Tbl fine dry bread crumbs	¼ tsp salt
1 cup milk	1½ tsp grated lemon rind
2½ cups sugar	5 cooking apples
8 eggs, separated	6 Tbl butter
1 cup lemon juice	½ tsp cinnamon
1 tsp vanilla extract	1 cup chopped walnuts

Roll pastry ⅛-inch thick and neatly line a 9-inch pie pan. Sprinkle the bread crumbs over the bottom. Preheat oven to 375 degrees.

In a saucepan scald the milk and dissolve in it ½ cup of the sugar. In a mixing bowl thoroughly beat together another ½ cup of the sugar, the egg yolks, lemon juice, vanilla, cornstarch, salt, and 1 teaspoon of the grated lemon rind. Add the hot milk, very little at a time, stirring constantly until the mixture thickens. Set this lemon cream aside to cool.

Peel and core the apples and slice them thinly. In a skillet melt the butter over low heat and in it dissolve ¾ cup of the sugar. Stir in the cinnamon and the remaining lemon rind. Add the apples and cook them just until they are tender, stirring them gently once or twice.

Remove the skillet from the heat and let the apples cool.

In a mixing bowl beat the egg whites until they are stiff and gradually whisk in all but 2 tablespoons of the remaining sugar.

Spread the cooled lemon cream in the prepared pie shell. Cover it with the cooked apples and sprinkle them with the chopped walnuts. Bake in the preheated oven for 30 minutes, or until the pastry is well browned. Remove the pan from the oven and cover the pie evenly with the meringue. Sprinkle it with the reserved 2 tablespoons of sugar and brown the top lightly under a hot broiler. Let the pie cool and cut it into 6 to 8 servings.

Sour-Cream Honey Apple Pie

1 recipe Rich Pastry (page 134)
2 Tbl fine dry bread crumbs
6 medium apples
¾ cup honey
½ cup sour cream

1 tsp cinnamon
½ tsp nutmeg
¼ tsp salt
Beaten egg

Preheat oven to 425 degrees. Line a 9-inch pie pan with ½ the pastry rolled ⅛-inch thick, leaving an overhang of about ¼-inch all around. Sprinkle the bottom with the bread crumbs. Peel, core, and thinly slice the apples. In a mixing bowl stir the honey into the sour cream and blend in the spices and salt. Add the apples, stirring gently to coat the slices evenly. Heap the mixture in the prepared shell, slightly higher in the center. Brush the rim of the shell with the beaten egg. Roll out the remaining dough to the same thickness as the lining. Fit it over the top and press the edges, sealing them together. Trim off the excess. Flute the edges of the pastry and brush the top with beaten egg. Prick it in several places with the tines of a fork and bake in the preheated oven for 45 minutes or until the pastry is well browned. Cut the pie to provide 6 servings.

Peach Pie

1 recipe Rich Pastry (page 134)
Beaten egg
2 Tbl fine dry bread crumbs
5 cups peeled, sliced peaches
½ cup sugar

¼ tsp cinnamon
⅛ tsp nutmeg
⅛ tsp salt
1½ Tbl butter, cut into bits

Preheat oven to 450 degrees. Roll out, ⅛-inch thick, as much of the pastry as is needed for a 9-inch pie pan and line the pan with it. Brush the rim of the pastry lining with beaten egg and sprinkle the bottom with the bread crumbs. Reserve the remaining pastry.

Combine the sugar, spices, and salt, and sift over the peaches in a mixing bowl. Stir peaches gently. Spread the peaches in the prepared pie shell and dot with the bits of butter. Fit the remaining pastry, also rolled ⅛-inch thick, over the top and trim off the excess of both crusts. Press the edges together to seal them. Brush the top with beaten egg. Prick the top in several places with the tines of a fork. Bake in the preheated oven for 10 minutes. Reduce the heat to 350 degrees and continue baking for 35 minutes longer or until the pastry is golden brown. Serve the pie hot or cooled, cut to provide 6 servings.

Peach Tart

½ recipe Rich Pastry (page 134)
2 Tbl fine dry bread crumbs
1 cup Almond Pastry Cream
   (page 59)

4 medium-sized freestone peaches
Simple Syrup (page 278)
1 tsp vanilla extract
Apricot preserves, melted

Preheat oven to 375 degrees. Roll out the pastry ⅛-inch thick and line a 9-inch pie pan with it. Bake the shell as directed for Lemon Meringue Pie (page 116) and let it cool in the pan. Sprinkle the bottom of the baked shell with the bread crumbs and spread the almond pastry cream over them. Peel the peaches by plunging them into boiling hot water and letting them remain for 1 minute. Remove the peaches and when they are cool enough to handle pull off the peel with your fingers. Poach the peaches in the vanilla-flavored syrup for 5 minutes or until they are tender. Do not overcook them. Drain them well, cut them into halves, and remove the stones. Arrange the halves cut sides down in the pastry cream in the pie shell, and brush them with the melted preserves. Serve the pie, cut in wedges to provide 6 to 8 servings.

Pear Tart

Sweet Dough (page 135)
2 Tbl fine dry bread crumbs
2 cups Frangipane (page 64)
1 cup Pastry Cream
   (page 58)

8 halves Poached Pears
   (page 243)
Apricot preserves, melted
4 egg whites
¼ cup sugar

Preheat oven to 400 degrees. On a lightly floured board roll out the sweet dough to fit a 9-inch pie pan and line the pan with it. Sift the bread crumbs over the bottom. In a mixing bowl thoroughly combine the frangipane and pastry cream and spread the mixture in the pie shell. Bake in the preheated oven for 25 minutes or until the filling and pastry are lightly browned. Remove the pan from the oven and let the filling cool. Increase the oven heat to 425 degrees.

Cut the pear halves lengthwise, part-way only, at ½-inch intervals. Arrange the pears on the pie filling, 1 in the center and the others around it, and brush them with the preserves. In a mixing bowl beat the egg whites to the soft-peak stage. Add the sugar, a little at a time, continuing the beating until the meringue is stiff enough to hold a firm shape. Using a pastry bag fitted with a star tube, pipe the meringue decoratively around the pears (see photograph, page 120). Bake in the oven at the increased heat for 10 minutes or until the meringue is set.

Blueberry Pie

4 cups blueberries
1 recipe Plain Pastry (page 134)
1 cup sugar
3 Tbl quick-cooking tapioca
1 tsp cinnamon
¼ tsp salt
1 Tbl lemon juice
2 Tbl butter, cut into bits
Beaten egg

Preheat oven to 450 degrees. Pick over the berries, wash them, and drain them well. Put them in a mixing bowl.

Roll out as much of the pastry as is needed to produce a round 12 inches in diameter and ⅛-inch thick and with it line a 9-inch pie pan. Combine the sugar, tapioca, cinnamon, and salt, and sprinkle 2 tablespoons of the mixture over the bottom of the pie shell. Combine the remainder with the blueberries. Spread that mixture evenly in the pie shell, sprinkle it with the lemon juice, and dot it with the bits of butter. Brush the edges of the pie shell with beaten egg. Roll out the remaining pastry ⅛-inch thick to provide a top crust and fit it over the shell. Trim off excess pastry and seal the edges by pressing them together. Crimp the edges, if desired. Brush the top with beaten egg and cut a few small slits in the top to allow steam to escape during the baking. Bake in the preheated oven for 10 minutes. Reduce the heat sharply, to 350 degrees, and continue the baking for 30 minutes longer or until the pastry is nicely browned. Cool the pie and cut it to provide 6 to 8 servings.

Pecan Pie

½ recipe Rich Pastry (page 134)	1 cup sugar
3 eggs	1 tsp vanilla extract
⅛ tsp salt	⅔ cup pecans, coarsely broken
1 cup dark corn syrup	

Preheat oven to 450 degrees. Roll out the pastry to fit a 9-inch pie pan. Line the pan with it and trim off the excess. In a mixing bowl lightly beat the eggs with the salt. Combine the corn syrup, sugar, and vanilla and thoroughly blend into the eggs. Stir in the pecans. Bake in the preheated oven for 10 minutes. Reduce the heat to 350 degrees and continue the baking 35 minutes longer or until a knife inserted in the center of the filling can be withdrawn clean. Cut the pie to provide 6 to 8 servings topped, if desired, with unsweetened whipped cream.

Cherry Clafoutis | Cherry Pudding Pie

4 cups pitted fresh or drained canned black cherries	2 whole eggs
	1 egg yolk
⅓ cup cognac	¼ tsp almond extract
½ cup sugar	¼ tsp salt
1 cup flour	Confectioners' sugar
1 cup milk	

Preheat oven to 350 degrees. Put the cherries in a glass bowl, pour the cognac over them, and stir in ¼ cup of the sugar. Set the cherries aside to steep.

Prepare a batter by combining in another bowl the remaining sugar, the flour, milk, whole eggs, egg yolk, almond flavoring, and salt,

and beating vigorously until the ingredients are well blended and the mixture is very smooth. Pour ⅔ of the batter over the bottom of a buttered, deep, 9-inch pie pan and bake it in the preheated oven for 2 minutes or until the batter is set. Spread over it the cherries along with any rendered juice and cover them with the remaining batter. Return the pan to the oven and continue the baking for 45 minutes or until the clafoutis is well browned and a knife inserted in the center can be withdrawn clean. Serve warm with a sifting of confectioners' sugar over the top. There will be 6 to 8 servings. *(See photograph, page 120.)*

Lemon Meringue Pie

½ **recipe Plain Pastry (page 134)**	**6 eggs, separated**
2¼ **cups sugar**	¾ **cup lemon juice**
¼ **cup cornstarch**	**Grated rind of 1 lemon**
¼ **cup flour**	**2 Tbl butter**
¼ **tsp salt**	**Additional sugar for sprinkling**
2 cups boiling-hot water	

Preheat oven to 375 degrees. Roll out the pastry to a thickness of ⅛-inch and with it line an 8-inch pie pan. Fit a sheet of buttered foil neatly over the pastry and fill the pan with dried beans (to keep the pastry from shrinking while baking). Bake in the preheated oven for 12 minutes. Remove the beans (save them, since they are reusable) and the foil and continue the baking for 8 minutes longer or until the pastry shell is nicely browned. Set it aside and let it cool in the pan.

Into a saucepan sift together 1½ cups of the sugar, the cornstarch, flour, and salt. Set the pan over very low heat and add gradually the boiling water, stirring constantly until the mixture thickens. In a mixing bowl lightly beat together the egg yolks, lemon juice and rind, and stir in the thickened mixture a little at a time. Pour back into the saucepan and cook, again over very low heat and stirring briskly, for 2 minutes. Remove the pan from the heat and blend in the butter. Let this filling cool to lukewarm and spread it in the baked pie shell. In a mixing bowl beat the egg whites to the soft-peak stage. Add the remaining sugar, ¼ cup at a time, continuing the beating until the meringue is stiff, spreadable, and satiny. Spread it completely over the top of the pie right to and touching the edges of the pan. Sprinkle lightly with additional sugar. Set the pan in a preheated 350-degree oven and let it remain for 10 minutes or until the meringue is delicately browned. Let the pie cool before cutting it to provide 6 servings.

Shaker Pieplant Pie

1 recipe Rich Pastry (page 134)   1½ cups brown sugar
2 cups rhubarb, cut in 1-inch   3 Tbl butter, cut into bits
   lengths (see Note)   Beaten egg
1 Tbl flour

Preheat oven to 450 degrees. Line an 8-inch pie pan with as much of the pastry, rolled to a thickness of ⅛-inch, as required. Similarly, roll out to the same thickness enough of the remaining pastry to provide a top crust.

In a mixing bowl coat the pieces of rhubarb with the flour and sugar combined and spread them in the prepared pie shell. Dot filling with the bits of butter. Brush the edges of the shell with beaten egg and fit on the top pastry. Trim off the excess and press the edges of the 2 crusts to seal them. Brush the top with beaten egg and pierce it in several places to allow steam to escape during the baking. Bake in the preheated oven for 15 minutes. Reduce the heat to 350 degrees and continue baking for 25 minutes longer or until the pastry is golden brown. Cool the pie and cut it to provide 6 servings.
NOTE: Pieplant, of course, is another name for rhubarb.

Apricot Tart

1 recipe Sweet Dough (page 135)   1 8-ounce can apricots, drained
1 8-ounce jar apricot preserves

Preheat oven to 350 degrees. Butter a 9-inch pie pan and line it with as much pastry, rolled ¼-inch thick, as required. Add the preserves to the whole fruit and chop the mixture coarsely. Spread the mixture in the prepared pie shell. Roll out the remaining dough ⅛-inch thick and cut from it enough strips ½-inch wide and 10 inches long to provide a lattice top for the pie. Weave the lattice, securing the strips to the edge of the pastry lining. Fit a border of the dough ½-inch wide around the pie and bake in the preheated oven for 25 minutes or until the pastry is well browned. Cool the tart and cut it to provide 6 to 8 servings.

Tarte aux Épinards Provençale | Provençal Spinach Tart

1 recipe Rich Pastry (page 134)
2 packages frozen chopped
   spinach
½ cup milk
½ cup heavy cream
4 egg yolks

¼ cup sugar
1 tsp vanilla extract
½ tsp grated lemon rind
½ of a pound jar of orange
   marmalade, melted
2 Tbl apricot preserves, melted

Preheat oven to 450 degrees. Line a 10-inch pie pan with as much of the rich pastry as required, rolled to a thickness of ⅛-inch. Cook the spinach according to package directions and drain it thoroughly. In the top pan of a double boiler over simmering water cook the milk, cream, 3 of the egg yolks, and the sugar, well combined, stirring constantly until the mixture coats the spoon. Don't let it thicken too much. Remove the pan from over the water and stir into the custard the vanilla, lemon rind, and drained spinach. Fill the prepared shell with a series of alternating layers of the spinach custard and the melted marmalade, thinly spread. Cover the top with ¼-inch wide strips of the remaining pastry woven into a lattice pattern. Trim the lattice even with the pastry lining and secure the strips to it with the remaining egg yolk beaten with a little water. Brush the tops of the strips also with the yolk. Flute the edges of the crust. Bake the pie in the preheated oven for 25 minutes or until a knife inserted in the center of the filling can be withdrawn clean. Glaze the top with the apricot preserves. Serve the pie warm or cooled, cut to provide 8 servings. *(See photograph, page 119.)*

Tarte aux Épinards Provençal, an
unusual—and unusually attractive—dessert,
surrounded by its ingredients.

Banbury Tarts

1½ recipes Plain Pastry (page 134)

1 cup sugar

1 Tbl fine cracker crumbs

¼ tsp cinnamon

¼ tsp nutmeg

1 cup chopped raisins

1½ tsp grated lemon rind

3 Tbl lemon juice

1 egg, lightly beaten

¼ cup chopped walnuts

Preheat oven to 450 degrees. Roll the pastry into 2 rectangles ⅛-inch thick and cut them into 4-inch squares. In a mixing bowl thoroughly combine the remaining ingredients and place 1 tablespoon of the mixture in the center of each square. Dampen the edges with cold water and fold the squares diagonally to form triangles. Press the edges together with the tines of a fork and prick the tops in several places. Place the tarts on a baking sheet and chill thoroughly. Bake in the preheated oven for 20 minutes or until they are golden brown. Sprinkle the tarts with sugar and serve them warm. This recipe provides about 1½ dozen.

Coconut Cream Pie

½ recipe Rich Pastry (page 134)

7 Tbl cornstarch

1½ cups sugar

8 egg yolks

4 cups milk

1½ cups shredded coconut

2 tsp vanilla extract

4 egg whites

Preheat oven to 375 degrees. Line an 8-inch pie pan with the pastry rolled to a thickness of ⅛-inch. Bake in the preheated oven as directed for Lemon Meringue Pie (page 116). Cool the baked shell in the pan. Maintain oven heat. In the top pan of a double boiler thoroughly blend the cornstarch and ½ cup of the sugar into the egg yolks. In a separate pan scald together the milk and 1 cup of the coconut, and stir the hot mixture, a very little at a time, into the yolks. Set the pan over simmering water and cook, stirring constantly, until the mixture thickens. Remove the pan from over the water and stir in the vanilla. Let the custard cool completely.

In a mixing bowl beat the egg whites to the soft-peak stage. Add

Tempting trio of pies: latticed
Linzertorte (page 128), Cherry Clafoutis (page 114),
and meringue-swirled Pear Tart (page 112).

the remaining sugar, a little at a time, and continue to beat until the sugar is completely incorporated and the egg whites are stiff. Spread the cooled filling in the baked pie shell and spread the meringue over it so that it touches the edges of the shell. Sprinkle the remaining coconut over the top and brown it lightly in the still heated oven. Cool the pie and chill it slightly. It provides 6 servings.

Custard Pie

½ recipe Plain Pastry (page 134)	¼ tsp salt
4 eggs	3 cups milk, scalded
½ cup sugar	½ tsp vanilla extract

Line an 8-inch pie pan with the pastry rolled slightly thicker than ¼-inch. Trim and flute the edges. Preheat oven to 425 degrees. In a mixing bowl beat together the eggs, sugar, and salt until the mixture is smooth and frothy. Gradually stir in the hot milk and blend in the vanilla. Pour the custard mixture into the pie shell and bake in the preheated oven for 10 minutes. Reduce the heat to 350 degrees and continue the baking for 30 minutes longer or until a knife inserted in the center of the filling can be withdrawn clean. Cool the pie before serving it cut into 6 portions.

Black Bottom Pie

½ recipe Rich Pastry (page 134)	3 squares (3 ounces) semisweet
4 egg yolks	chocolate, melted
⅔ cup sugar	2 tsp unflavored gelatine
4 tsp cornstarch	1 Tbl cool water
1½ cups milk	2 Tbl boiling-hot water
1½ cups heavy cream	2 egg whites
2 Tbl dark rum	1 Tbl thinly shaved semisweet
½ tsp vanilla extract	chocolate

Preheat oven to 400 degrees. Line a 9-inch pie pan with the pastry rolled ⅛-inch thick. Bake the shell in the preheated oven blind (that is, without filling), as directed in recipe for Lemon Meringue Pie, page 116. In a saucepan thoroughly combine the egg yolks, ½ cup of the sugar, and cornstarch. In another pan scald the milk and ½ cup of the cream together and stir the liquid gradually into the yolk mixture. Set the pan over low heat and cook, stirring constantly, until the mixture thickens. Remove the pan from the heat and stir in the rum and vanilla. Transfer 1½ cups of the custard to a mixing bowl and blend into it the melted chocolate. Let the chocolate custard cool, stirring it occasionally.

Soften the gelatine in the cool water and dissolve it in the boiling water. Blend it into the plain custard. Beat the egg whites to a froth. Add 1 tablespoon of the remaining sugar, continuing the beating until the whites are stiff, but not dry. Fold them into the cooled plain custard.

Spread the cooled chocolate custard evenly in the baked pie shell and chill until it is set. Cover with the plain custard and return the pie to the refrigerator until that layer is set. Stiffly whip the remaining cream with the remaining sugar and spread it over the chilled pie. Sprinkle with the shaved chocolate. The pie provides 6 to 8 servings.

Eggnog Pie

½ **recipe Rich Pastry (page 134)**	1 **Tbl unflavored gelatine**
4 eggs, separated	¼ **cup cool water**
1 cup sugar	**3 Tbl full-bodied rum**
½ **tsp salt**	½ **cup heavy cream, whipped**
½ **cup hot water**	**Nutmeg**

Preheat oven to 375 degrees. Line a 9-inch pie pan with the pastry rolled ⅛-inch thick and bake it in the preheated oven as directed for Lemon Meringue Pie (page 116). Cool the pie shell in the pan.

In the top pan of a double boiler beat the egg yolks, ½ cup of the sugar, and salt together until the dry ingredients are well incorporated. Stir in the hot water very gradually. Set the pan over simmering water and cook the yolk mixture until it thickens. Soften the gelatine in the cool water and add to the yolk mixture, stirring until it is dissolved. Remove the pan from over the water and add the rum. Let the mixture cool completely.

In a mixing bowl beat the egg whites to the soft-peak stage. Add the remaining sugar, a little at a time, continuing to beat until the whites are stiff. Fold them into the cooled yolk mixture. Pour the filling into the prepared pie shell and chill it in the refrigerator until it is firm. Spread the whipped cream over it and sprinkle lightly with freshly grated nutmeg. Cut the pie to provide 6 to 8 servings.

Chess Pie

½ recipe Rich Pastry (page 134)
4 egg yolks
1 cup sugar
2 tsp cornmeal
1 tsp flour
¼ tsp salt
½ cup butter, melted & cooled
1 cup heavy cream, whipped
Nutmeg

Preheat oven to 300 degrees. Line a 9-inch pie pan with the pastry rolled slightly less than ¼-inch thick. In a mixing bowl lightly beat the eggs. Sift together the sugar, cornmeal, flour, and salt and blend into the eggs. Thoroughly stir in the butter and fold in the whipped cream. Spread this filling in the prepared pie shell and sprinkle the top with a little freshly grated nutmeg. Bake in the preheated oven for 1 hour or until the pastry is lightly browned and the filling is firm. Test by inserting a knife in the center. It should be clean when withdrawn. Cool the pie before cutting it to provide 6 to 8 servings.

Maple Coconut Pie

½ recipe Plain Pastry (page 134)
1 cup shredded coconut, lightly
   toasted
3 eggs, lightly beaten
1 cup maple syrup
¼ cup sugar
¼ tsp salt
6 Tbl butter, melted & cooled

Preheat oven to 400 degrees. Line an 8-inch pie pan with the pastry rolled ⅛-inch thick and sprinkle the bottom with the coconut. In a mixing bowl beat together until well blended the eggs, syrup, sugar, and salt. Stir in the melted butter. Pour the mixture over the coconut

in the pie shell and bake in the preheated oven 45 minutes or until a knife inserted in the center of the filling can be withdrawn clean. Cool and cut to provide 6 servings.

Pumpkin Pie

½ recipe Plain Pastry (page 134)
1½ cups mashed pumpkin,
   cooked fresh or canned
¾ cup sugar
1 tsp cinnamon
½ tsp nutmeg

½ tsp ginger
¼ tsp ground cloves
½ tsp salt
2 eggs, beaten
1¾ cups evaporated milk

Preheat oven to 425 degrees. Line a 9-inch pie pan with the pastry rolled ⅛-inch thick. In a mixing bowl combine the pumpkin, sugar, spices, and salt, and thoroughly beat in the eggs. Stir in the milk, a little at a time. Pour the filling into the prepared pie shell and bake in the preheated oven for 10 minutes. Reduce the heat to 350 degrees and continue baking for 25 minutes longer or until a knife inserted in the center of the filling can be withdrawn clean. Cut to provide 6 to 8 servings, with (if desired) whipped cream flavored with cognac.

Pumpkin Macadamia Chiffon Pie

1 cup brown sugar-cookie crumbs
1¼ cups finely chopped
   macadamia nuts
2 Tbl finely chopped crystalized
   ginger
¾ tsp salt
½ cup butter, melted
4 eggs, separated

1 cup sugar
2 cups cooked fresh or
   canned pumpkin
½ cup milk
½ tsp cinnamon
½ tsp nutmeg
1 envelope unflavored gelatine
¼ cup cool water

Preheat oven to 375 degrees. In a mixing bowl combine the crumbs, ¾ cup of the nuts, 1 tablespoon of the ginger, and ¼ teaspoon of the salt, and stir in the melted butter until the mixture is smooth. Press it evenly in a 9-inch pie pan and bake it in the preheated oven for 15 minutes or until the filling is heated through. The filling must not bubble. Remove the pan from the oven and let the pie shell cool.

In the top pan of a double boiler beat the egg yolks with ½ cup of the sugar and the remaining salt until they are very thick. Blend in the pumpkin, milk, spices, and remaining ginger. Set the pan over simmering water and cook the mixture until it begins to clear the sides of the pan. Soften the gelatine in the water and add, stirring until it is dissolved. Let the mixture cool completely and stir in the remaining nuts.

Beat the egg whites to the soft-peak stage. Add the remaining sugar, a little at a time, continuing to beat until the whites are stiff. Fold them into the cooled pumpkin mixture. Spread the filling in the pie shell and chill it in the refrigerator until it is set. Serve the pie cut into 6 to 8 portions with, if desired, whipped cream.

Rice-Pudding Pie

½ recipe Rich Pastry (page 134)	4 egg yolks
1 cup sugar	Juice & grated rind of 2 lemons
¼ tsp salt	3 egg whites
3 cups milk	¼ cup sliced blanched almonds
¾ cup rice	

Preheat oven to 375 degrees. Line a 9-inch pie pan with the pastry rolled slightly thicker than ⅛-inch and bake it without filling in the preheated oven (see directions for Lemon Meringue Pie, page 116). Let the baked shell cool in the pan. Maintain the oven temperature.

In a saucepan combine ½ cup of the sugar, the salt, and the milk. Cook the rice in this mixture over low heat for 30 minutes or until the rice is tender. Vigorously beat in the egg yolks, lemon juice, and rind. Let the filling cool somewhat and spread it in the baked pie shell. Beat the egg whites to the soft-peak stage. Add the remaining sugar gradually, continuing to beat until the egg whites are stiff and glossy. Spread the egg whites evenly over the filling and sprinkle the top with the almonds. Bake the pie in the still heated oven for 5 minutes or until the topping is lightly browned. Serve warm or cool. Pie provides 6 to 8 servings.

Whiskey Cream Pie

½ recipe Rich Pastry (page 134)
¾ cup sugar
7 egg yolks
3 Tbl lemon juice
1 Tbl finely grated lemon rind
4 tsp unflavored gelatine
   (1 envelope plus 1 tsp)

2 Tbl cool water
3 Tbl boiling-hot water
½ cup whiskey (bourbon or Irish)
2 cups heavy cream, whipped
4 egg whites

Preheat oven to 375 degrees. Line a deep 9-inch pie pan with the pastry rolled ⅛-inch thick and neatly trim the edges. Bake the shell in the preheated oven as directed for Lemon Meringue Pie (page 116). Cool the shell completely in the pan.

Reserve 3 tablespoons of the sugar, and beat the remainder gradually and thoroughly into the egg yolks in a mixing bowl. Add the lemon juice and rind. Soften the gelatine in the cool water, dissolve it in the hot water, and add it to the yolks. Pour in the whiskey and stir to blend. Reserve ¼ of the whipped cream and fold in the remainder.

In a separate bowl beat the egg whites to the soft-peak stage. Add the reserved sugar and continue beating until the whites are stiff. Fold them into the yolk mixture. Spread the filling in the baked pie shell and chill in the refrigerator until firm. Decorate the top with the remaining whipped cream. Cut the pie to provide 8 servings.

Linzertorte

¾ cup butter, softened
¾ cup sugar
1½ tsp cinnamon
1 tsp grated lemon rind
¼ tsp vanilla extract
3 eggs

1½ cups ground filberts
2 cups flour
¼ tsp baking powder
1 cup preserves (cherry, currant,
   raspberry, or other)

Preheat oven to 375 degrees. In a mixing bowl thoroughly cream together the butter, sugar, cinnamon, lemon rind, and vanilla. Beat in 2 of the eggs, 1 at a time. Blend in the ground nuts and the flour sifted with the baking powder. Wrap the dough in waxed paper and chill it in the refrigerator for at least 1 hour.

On a lightly floured pastry board roll out ½ of the chilled dough to a thickness of about ¼-inch and line a 9-inch pie pan with it. Spread the jam over it. Roll the remaining dough between the palms of your hands into a rope about ¼-inch in diameter. With part of the rope weave a lattice over the top of the filled pie. Trim the edges neatly and brush them with the remaining egg, beaten. Secure the remaining rope over the edge of the lattice to form a rim for the pie. Brush the rim also with beaten egg. Bake the pie in the preheated oven for 35 minutes or until the pastry is golden brown. While the pie is still hot fill it with more jam, using a funnel to add it between the spaces of the lattice. Cool the pie and cut it as required for 8 to 10 servings. *(See photograph, page 120.)*

Shaker Sugar Pie

½ recipe Rich Pastry (page 134)
½ cup butter, softened
1 cup maple or light brown sugar
¼ cup flour, sifted

2 cups heavy cream
½ tsp vanilla extract or rosewater
¼ tsp nutmeg

Preheat oven to 450 degrees. Line an 8-inch pie pan with the pastry rolled to a thickness of ⅛-inch. In a bowl beat the butter with a wooden spoon until it is the consistency of whipped cream. Spread 2 tablespoons of it over the bottom of the pie shell and sprinkle it with ¼ cup of the sugar. Repeat, alternating butter and sugar for 3 more double layers. Sift the flour evenly over the top. Flavor the cream with the vanilla or rosewater and pour it into the pie shell. Sprinkle it with the nutmeg. Bake in the preheated oven for 10 minutes. Reduce the heat to 350 degrees and bake 45 minutes longer or until the filling has begun to solidify and the top is well browned. Cool the pie and chill it in the refrigerator for 2 hours. Let the pie return to room temperature before cutting it to provide 6 servings.

Shoo Fly Pie

½ recipe Rich Pastry (page 134)
1 cup sifted flour
½ tsp salt
½ tsp cinnamon
⅛ tsp nutmeg

⅛ tsp ground cloves
2 Tbl butter
½ tsp baking soda
¾ cup boiling-hot water
½ cup light molasses

Preheat oven to 375 degrees. Roll out the pastry to a thickness slightly less than ¼-inch and line a 9-inch pie pan with it. Trim the edge neatly and crimp with the tines of a fork. Into a mixing bowl sift together the flour, salt, and spices. Using your fingers, work the butter into the dry ingredients until the mixture is crumbly. In another, smaller bowl dissolve the soda in the hot water and stir in the molasses. Pour the molasses mixture into the prepared pie shell and cover evenly with crumbed mixture. Bake in preheated oven for 30 minutes or until the filling is firm. Serve warm, cut for 6 to 8 servings.

Frozen Lime Pie

1 cup graham cracker crumbs
3 Tbl sugar
¼ cup butter, softened
1 15-ounce can sweetened
   condensed milk
4 eggs

½ cup fresh lime juice
2 Tbl grated lime rind
4–5 drops green food coloring
½ pint vanilla ice cream, slightly
   softened

In a mixing bowl blend the crumbs and sugar thoroughly into the butter and pat the mixture firmly over the bottom and around the sides of an 8-inch pie pan. Chill for 1 hour. In another bowl beat together with a rotary beater the condensed milk, eggs, lime juice, 1 tablespoon of the grated lime rind, and the food coloring. The ingredients must be completely combined. This can be done much more simply and thoroughly in an electric blender. Pour the mixture into the chilled pie shell and freeze it until it is set, 3 hours or longer. Spread the top with the ice cream and continue the freezing overnight. Serve the pie sprinkled with the remaining grated lime rind and cut to provide 4 to 6 servings.

Frozen Pumpkin Pie

½ recipe Plain Pastry (page 134)
1 pint Vanilla Ice Cream (page 160)
1 cup puréed fresh cooked or
   canned pumpkin
1 cup granulated sugar
1 tsp cinnamon

½ tsp nutmeg
¼ tsp ground ginger
¼ tsp allspice
½ tsp salt
1 cup heavy cream, whipped

Preheat oven to 375 degrees. Line a 9-inch pie pan with the pastry rolled about ¼-inch thick and bake it in the preheated oven as directed for Lemon Meringue Pie (page 116). Cool the pie shell completely in the pan, and spread it evenly with the ice cream. Freeze until the ice cream is firm. In a mixing bowl thoroughly combine the pumpkin, sugar, spices, and salt, and fold in the whipped cream. Spread the mixture over the frozen ice cream. Return the pie to the freezer until the filling is completely frozen. Cut the pie to provide 6 to 8 servings.

6 | pastries

The art of making pastry is said to be a gift rather than an accomplishment. Either you are born with it, the experts insist, or you will never have it. That, of course, is so much nonsense. Whether you are making plain, rich, or sweet-dough pastry, you need only to observe a few basic rules to get good results. These rules include having all the ingredients cold, preferably chilled, blending them thoroughly but quickly, and not overdoing it. As one accomplished pastry maker advises, "Don't fiddle around with it." Practice will make you, too, a born pastry maker.

Many cooks learn to make perfect pastry for pies and tarts, yet are timid about attempting puff pastry (which the French call leafed or layered pastry). They would be more adventurous, perhaps, if they knew that the making of puff pastry is not so much difficult as it is time-consuming. Even if the enclosed butter is accidentally forced through the surface of the paste in the rolling process, the damage is not irreparable. A little patching will put it all to rights again.

Pâte à chou, the classic paste of cream puffs, is probably the simplest of all pastries to make, especially with the ingredients assembled in the order in which they are to be used. An important requisite, however, is a strong arm capable of vigorous stirring.

Plain Pastry

2½ cups flour
½ tsp salt
¾ cup chilled firm shortening

¼ cup ice-cold water, more or less, as required

Sift the flour and salt together into a mixing bowl. Using your fingers (or, if you prefer, two knives or a pastry blender), work in the shortening to produce a mixture that resembles coarsely ground meal. Work quickly so that the shortening stays cold and retains as much of its firmness as possible. Sprinkle over the flour mixture only as much of the cold water as is needed to blend it to a dough that just holds together and is not at all sticky. The total amount required depends upon the absorbency of the flour used. Start with 1 tablespoon of the water, sprinkling it over evenly. Toss the flour mixture with your fingers to moisten as much of it as possible. With the tines of a table fork "spear" up, a little at a time, *all* of the flour mixture so moistened. Remove each forkful to a sheet of waxed paper. Continue to prepare the remaining flour mixture in the same way, reducing the amount of water each time as the flour mixture is reduced, until finally only a drop or two may be needed. Mass the accumulated dough gently into a ball, wrap it in the waxed paper, and chill it in the refrigerator for at least 2 hours before using it as required. The pastry will keep under normal refrigeration for several days or in a freezer for several weeks. NOTE: Using butter only makes for fine flavor, but not always the most tender pastry; a mixture of ⅔ butter and ⅓ vegetable shortening or lard is ideal for pastry of well-balanced flavor and tenderness; using vegetable shortening only or lard only makes for magnificent tenderness but not always—particularly with lard—desirable flavor. This recipe provides sufficient pastry for one 9-inch 2-crust pie.

Rich Pastry

2 cups flour
½ tsp salt

¼ cup ice-cold water, more or less, as required

1 cup chilled firm shortening (see Note, above)

Proceed exactly as for Plain Pastry (above). This recipe provides sufficient pastry for one 9-inch 2-crust pie.

Sweet Dough

4 cups butter	**¼ tsp salt**
2 cups sugar	**8 egg yolks, stirred to blend**
1 tsp vanilla extract	**9 cups flour**
1 tsp grated orange rind	**¼ tsp baking powder**

In a mixing bowl thoroughly cream together the butter, sugar, vanilla, orange rind, and salt. Stir in the egg yolks, a little at a time, and gradually blend in the flour sifted with the baking powder. Chill the dough in the refrigerator for at least 30 minutes before using it as required. Sweet dough will keep under normal refrigeration for 4 or 5 days. Frozen and stored in the freezer, it can be kept for about 2 months. This recipe provides sufficient dough for five 8-inch 2-crust pies or the equivalent.

Puff Pastry

1½ cups sifted flour	**¼ cup ice-cold water**
½ tsp salt	**1 cup (2 sticks) very cold butter**

Sift the flour and salt together into a mixing bowl and stir in the cold water. Turn the dough out onto a lightly floured pastry board and knead it until it is satiny smooth and elastic. Divide the dough into 2 equal parts and roll out each into a rectangle about 12 inches long and 6 inches wide. Cut each stick of butter lengthwise into 3 slices and arrange each 3 parallel to each other, centered on one half of each rectangle. Fold the other half of each rectangle over the butter, enclosing the 3 slices completely. Maintaining the 6-inch width, roll out each piece of dough to a length of 18 inches. Fold each of the lengths into thirds, bringing one end over and folding the other end over that (as you would fold a sheet of long letter paper). Wrap the folded strips each in foil and chill them in the refrigerator for 30 minutes.

Work on 1 piece of the dough at a time and work quickly so that the enclosed butter remains as firm as possible. Place the piece of chilled dough on the pastry board with a narrow end parallel to you, and roll it out away from you again into a rectangle 18 inches long and 6 inches wide. Fold it as before and chill it again. Repeat the rolling, folding, and chilling 4 more times. Store the puff pastry, wrapped in foil, in the refrigerator until needed. It will keep under normal refrigeration for several weeks. Frozen and kept so, it will be usable for a year or more. Use as required.

Strudel Dough

4 cups sifted flour	**½ tsp salt**
2 eggs	**⅔ cup warm water, more or less,**
2 Tbl bland cooking oil	**as required**

Sift the flour in a mound onto a pastry board. Make a well in the center and in it put the eggs, oil, and salt. Work them into the flour along with as much of the warm water as needed to produce a moderately soft paste. Beat the paste until it becomes firm and elastic. A good way to do that is to pick up the dough and slap it down on a lightly floured pastry board. You may have to do this 100 times before the dough acquires the proper elasticity. Form the dough into a ball, brush it lightly with oil, and cover it with a bowl to keep it warm. Let it rest so for 1 hour.

Spread a cloth over a large table and sprinkle the cloth lightly with flour. Set the dough in the center and roll it out into the largest and thinnest circle possible without tearing it. It is still not as thin as it must be. Flour your hands, slip them under the dough, and start stretching it. Use the backs of your hands and stretch the dough all around, working from the center to the outer edges. When it is tissue-paper thin, it is ready. Trim off the thick edge of the dough and set it aside. It may be used, if desired, to prepare noodles. Let the strudel dough

dry for a few minutes—but only a very few, 10 minutes at the most. It must not become brittle. Use it immediately as required.

Pâte à Chou | Cream Puff Pastry

½ **cup butter**	**1 cup sifted flour**
1 cup water	**4 eggs**
¼ **tsp salt**	

In a saucepan over low heat melt the butter in the water. Stir in the salt and bring the mixture to a boil. Add the flour all at once and stir vigorously until the mixture clears the sides of the pan and is formed into a ball. Remove the pan from the heat and thoroughly beat in 3 of the eggs, 1 at a time. In a small bowl lightly beat the remaining egg and add just enough of it to produce a batter just thick enough to drop from a spoon. Use the batter warm as required.

Pâte à Brioche

5 packages dry yeast
1 cup lukewarm milk
7 eggs
¾ cup sugar

1 Tbl salt
7 cups sifted cake flour
1½ cups butter

Soften the yeast according to package directions and stir it into the warm milk. In a mixing bowl stir the eggs just enough to blend the yolks and whites and combine with them the sugar and salt. Add the combined yeast and milk, and blend in the flour. Turn the dough out onto a lightly floured pastry board and knead it vigorously until it is very elastic. Thoroughly knead in the butter, a little at a time. Put dough in a bowl and dust with flour. Cover it lightly with a cloth and let it rise in a warm draft-free place for about 1½ hours or until it has doubled in bulk. Deflate the dough, re-cover it, and let it rise until it has again doubled in bulk. Deflate it once more and use it as required.

Ice Cream Shells

⅔ cup (7 ounces) almond paste
 (see Note)
¼ cup sugar

2½ Tbl flour
4 egg whites

Preheat oven to 300 degrees. In a mixing bowl thoroughly combine the almond paste with the sugar and flour and gradually but vigorously beat in the egg whites to produce a smooth dough. Butter a large piece of cooking parchment and place it on a baking sheet. Spread the prepared dough thinly on the paper in rounds about 5 inches in diameter. Bake them in the preheated oven for 15 minutes or until they are golden brown. Quickly remove the rounds from the parchment with a metal spatula and place them immediately in fluted molds of about 3¼-inch diameter. Press them down gently with another fluted mold of the same size to produce fluted shells. Let them cool in the molds before removing them. This recipe provides about 18 ice cream shells.

NOTE: Almond paste in tins is available commercially.

Paris-Brest

1 recipe Pâte à Chou (page 137)
1 egg yolk
2 Tbl milk
⅓ cup toasted sliced almonds

½ recipe Praline Pastry Cream
 (page 59)
Confectioners' sugar

Preheat oven to 400 degrees. On a buttered and lightly floured baking sheet trace a circle about 8 inches in diameter. With a pastry bag fitted with a large plain tube, pipe inside the circle a ring of the paste about 2 inches wide. Brush the top of the ring with some of the egg yolk and milk, beaten together, and sprinkle it with the almonds. Bake in the preheated oven for 20 minutes or until the ring is well puffed and nicely browned. With the tines of a cooking fork pierce the ring in several places around the sides (to dry out the inside of the pastry) and leave the ring in the oven, with the heat turned off and the oven door ajar, for 10 minutes longer. Carefully remove the ring to a rack and let it cool completely.

Split the cooled ring into 2 layers and remove any remaining soft parts. Fill the layers with the pastry cream and fit them together again. Dust the top with confectioners' sugar. Cut the Paris-Brest to provide 6 servings.

Cream Puffs and Éclairs

1 recipe Pâte à Chou (page 137)
½ tsp sugar

1 egg, beaten

Preheat oven to 400 degrees. Augment the ingredients for the Pâte à Chou with the sugar, to be added to the boiling water and butter, and continue as directed in the recipe. For large puffs, to provide 10 to 12 servings, drop tablespoons of the paste onto lightly floured but un-buttered baking sheets, making mounds about 2 inches in diameter and 1 inch thick at the center, and spaced 2 to 3 inches apart. Brush the tops lightly with some of the beaten egg and bake in the preheated oven for 20 minutes or until the mounds are well puffed and golden brown. Pierce the sides of the puffs in several places with the tines of a cooking fork (to dry out the insides) and let them remain in the oven, with the heat off and the oven door ajar for 10 minutes longer. Transfer the puffs to a rack, in a place free from drafts, and let them cool completely. Fill as desired with your choice of sweetened whipped cream, or plain or flavored Pastry Cream (page 58). Pipe in the filling with a pastry bag fitted with a plain tube through a small slit cut in the side of each puff. Dust the tops with confectioners' sugar or glaze them.

For small puffs, about 3 dozen, drop teaspoons of the paste onto the prepared baking sheet, making mounds about 1 inch in diameter and ½-inch thick, and spaced about 2 inches apart. Bake and fill as for larger puffs and glaze as desired.

For standard-size éclairs, to provide about 1 dozen, pipe the paste into strips about 1½ inches wide, ¾-inch thick, and 3 inches long, spacing them about 2 inches apart. Bake and fill as for puffs.

For small éclairs, usually called *carolines,* pipe the paste finger width and thickness and just 1½ inches long. Bake in the preheated oven for 15 minutes and dry out in the slack oven for 10 minutes longer. Fill and glaze as for puffs to provide about 2 dozen carolines.

Nut Strudel

½ recipe Strudel Dough (page 136, or see Note below)
¼ cup butter, melted
Fine dry bread crumbs
1 cup ground filberts

¼ cup seedless raisins
¼ cup sugar
¼ tsp cinnamon
1 Tbl grated lemon rind
2 Tbl sour cream

Preheat oven to 400 degrees. Cut the dough into 4 sheets of equal size. Place 1 on a lightly dampened cloth, brush it with some of the melted butter, and sprinkle it lightly with bread crumbs. Fit the remaining sheets of dough over it, brushing and sprinkling each in the same way. In a mixing bowl combine the nuts, raisins, sugar, cinnamon, and lemon rind, and blend in the sour cream. Spread the mixture along one end of the prepared dough and, using the cloth as a guide, roll the 4 dough sheets together, jelly-roll fashion, enclosing the filling completely. Transfer the roll to a buttered baking sheet, seam side down. Brush

the top with melted butter and sprinkle it lightly with bread crumbs.
With a sharp knife mark the roll to indicate 6 to 8 servings. Bake in
the preheated oven for 30 minutes or until the pastry is golden brown.
NOTE: Commercially prepared strudel dough, 4 sheets to a package,
is available in most shops specializing in Middle European food
products.

Apple Strudel

½ recipe Strudel Dough (page 136,   ¼ cup sugar
    or see Nut Strudel Note)   ¼ cup raisins
¼ cup butter, melted   2 Tbl chopped nuts
Fine dry bread crumbs   ½ tsp cinnamon
2–3 cooking apples   Grated rind of 1 lemon

Preheat oven to 400 degrees. Cut the strudel dough into 4 sheets of equal size and prepare them for filling, brushing each with melted butter and sprinkling it with bread crumbs, as directed for Nut Strudel (page 140).

Peel and core the apples and cut them into small thin slices. Combine them in a mixing bowl with the remaining ingredients. Spread this filling along one end of the prepared dough and roll it, jelly-roll fashion, enclosing the filling completely. Place the roll on a buttered baking sheet, seam side down. Brush the top with melted butter and sprinkle it with bread crumbs. With a sharp knife mark the roll to indicate 6 to 8 servings. Bake in the preheated oven for 30 minutes or until the pastry is golden brown.

Cheese Strudel

½ recipe Strudel Dough (page 136, or see Nut Strudel Note)
¼ cup butter, melted
Fine dry bread crumbs
1 Tbl butter, softened
4 Tbl sugar
4 eggs
1 pound cottage cheese, put through a sieve
3 Tbl sour cream
½ tsp vanilla extract
⅓ cup seedless raisins

Preheat oven to 400 degrees. Cut the strudel dough into 4 sheets of equal size and prepare them for filling, brushing each with melted butter and sprinkling it with bread crumbs, as directed for Nut Strudel (page 140).

In a mixing bowl cream together the softened butter and the sugar, and thoroughly beat in 1 of the eggs. Blend in the cottage cheese and sour cream, and beat in the remaining eggs, 1 at a time. Stir in the vanilla and raisins. Spread the mixture along one end of the prepared dough and roll it, jelly-roll fashion, enclosing the filling completely. Place the roll on a buttered baking sheet, seam side down. Brush the top with melted butter and sprinkle it with bread crumbs. With a sharp knife mark the roll to indicate 6 to 8 servings. Bake in the preheated oven for 30 minutes or until the pastry is golden brown.

Shaker Apple Dumplings

6 cooking apples   1½ Tbl rosewater
¾ cup sugar   1 recipe Rich Pastry (page 134)
3 Tbl cream   ¾ cup maple syrup, heated

Preheat oven to 450 degrees. Peel and core the apples and fill the centers with the sugar, cream, and rosewater combined. On a lightly floured board roll out the pastry ⅛-inch thick and cut it into 6 squares each large enough to enclose an apple. Set the apples each in the center of a square. Bring the dough up around them, enclosing them completely. Moisten the seams with cool water and press them together to seal them. Prick the pastry in several places with a fork. Place the dumplings in a baking pan and bake them in the preheated oven for 15 minutes. Baste with some of the hot maple syrup. Reduce the oven heat to 350 degrees. Continue the baking for another 15 minutes and baste the dumplings again. Bake for a final 15 minutes. Remove the pan from the oven and baste the dumplings once more. Serve the 6 dumplings hot with, if desired, Hard Sauce (page 283).

New Orleans French Market Doughnuts

1 cup milk   1 egg
2 Tbl sugar   2 Tbl vegetable oil
¾ tsp salt   3½ cups sifted flour
½ tsp nutmeg   Fat for deep frying
1 envelope dry yeast   Sifted confectioners' sugar
2 Tbl lukewarm water

Scald the milk, dissolve in it the sugar and salt, and add the nutmeg. Let the milk cool to lukewarm and combine with it the yeast softened in the lukewarm water. Stir in the egg and the oil and thoroughly blend in the flour, a little at a time. Cover the bowl lightly with a cloth and let the dough rise in a warm place until it has doubled in bulk, about 1½ hours. Turn the dough out onto a well-floured pastry board, deflate it, and knead it gently. Roll it out into a rectangle 18 inches long and 12 inches wide and cut it into 36 pieces, each 3 inches by 2 inches.

Cover them lightly with a towel and let them rise on the pastry board for 30 minutes.

In a fryer or large saucepan heat fat for deep frying to 375 degrees and in it cook the little rectangles, a few at a time, until they are golden brown. Drain them quickly, dust them immediately with confectioners' sugar, and serve them at once piping hot.

Peach Dumplings

1 recipe Plain Pastry (page 134)
3 fresh peaches, peeled, halved & stoned
6 Tbl raspberry jam
Beaten egg
½ cup heavy cream, whipped

Preheat oven to 400 degrees. Roll out the pastry ⅛-inch thick and cut from it six 5-inch squares. Fill each peach half with 1 tablespoon of the jam. Invert each half onto a piece of the dough, centering it in the square. Brush the edges of each square with beaten egg and bring the 4 corners up over the peach half, overlapping the edges of the dough slightly. Seal the seams by pressing them together. Arrange the dumplings on a buttered baking sheet and bake them in the preheated oven for 45 minutes or until they are golden brown. Serve the 6 dumplings with the whipped cream or with Vanilla Sauce (page 287).

Berliner Balls | German-Style Filled Doughnuts

2 envelopes dry yeast
⅓ cup lukewarm water
1 cup milk
4 cups flour
5 Tbl butter
¼ cup sugar
⅛ tsp salt
Grated rind of ½ lemon
2 whole eggs
2 egg yolks
Fruit preserves or jelly
Fat for deep frying
Additional granulated sugar

In a mixing bowl soften the yeast in the lukewarm water and stir into it the milk heated just to lukewarm. Blend in 1 cup of the flour. Cover

the bowl lightly with a cloth, set it in a warm place, and let the dough remain until it doubles in bulk, about 1 hour. In a separate bowl cream together the butter, sugar, and salt, and stir in the lemon rind. Add the whole eggs, 1 at a time, and the egg yolks, beating well after each addition and continuing the beating until the mixture is light and frothy. Deflate the risen dough and work the creamed mixture into it along with the remaining flour. Turn the dough out onto a lightly floured board and knead it thoroughly. Return it to the bowl, cover it with the cloth, and let it rise again until it doubles in bulk. Deflate it, roll it out on the board to a thickness of about ¼-inch, and cut from it rounds 2 to 3 inches in diameter. You should have about 24 rounds. On each of 12 of the rounds place a small teaspoon of fruit preserves or jelly. Moisten the edges of those rounds with water and fit the remaining 12 over them. Seal the edges by pressing them together. Let the prepared rounds remain on the pastry board for 20 minutes.

In a fryer or deep saucepan heat fat for deep frying to 375 degrees and in it cook the rounds, 2 or 3 at a time, for about 2 minutes on each side or until they are golden brown. Drain the 12 doughnuts on paper toweling and roll them in sugar.

Danish Pastry Dough

6⅓ **cups flour**
1 tsp salt
5 eggs
¼ cup sugar
1 tsp vanilla extract

2 envelopes dry yeast
⅓ cup lukewarm water
1½ cups butter
1 cup lukewarm milk, more or less,
    as required

Sift 6 cups of the flour with the salt into a mound on a pastry board. Make a well in the center and in it put the eggs, sugar, vanilla, the yeast softened in the warm water, and ½ cup of the butter, cut in small pieces. With your fingers work the ingredients contained in the well into the flour, adding, a little at a time, just enough of the milk (or more as required) to produce a dough that is moderately soft but not sticky. Knead the dough gently for a few minutes until it is smooth. Dust the dough lightly with a little of the flour and let it rest for a few minutes on the pastry board.

Thoroughly combine the remaining butter and flour and shape the mixture into a square block about ½-inch thick. Roll out the dough into a rectangle ½-inch thick and mark off the dough to indicate 3 sections of equal size. Place the prepared butter in the center section and fold a side section over it. Cover with the opposite section. Place the dough with the open ends parallel to you and roll it out away from you into a rectangle the size of the original, taking care not to dislodge the butter. Fold it, as before, and let it rest, lightly covered, on the board for 15 minutes. Roll the dough again toward the open ends into a rectangle of the original size, and fold it as before. Wrap it in waxed paper and let it rest in the refrigerator for 2 hours before using it as required. This quantity of dough is sufficient for about 3 dozen small pastries or the equivalent in larger shapes. The filled shapes will keep in the refrigerator for several days, to be baked as needed.

Cheese Danish Pastries

1 cup cream cheese	2 egg yolks
2 Tbl sugar	⅓ recipe Danish Pastry Dough
1 Tbl cornstarch	(page 146)
½ tsp grated lemon rind	1 whole egg, beaten

Preheat oven to 400 degrees. In a mixing bowl thoroughly combine the cheese, sugar, cornstarch, and lemon rind, and beat in the egg yolks. On a lightly floured pastry board roll out the dough to a thickness of ⅛-inch and cut it into 12 squares of equal size. Place about 1 tablespoon of the cheese mixture in the center of each square. Brush the corners of the dough with some of the beaten egg and fold them in to the center, overlapping them slightly. Press them together to secure them. Brush the tops with beaten egg and arrange the pastries on a lightly buttered baking sheet. Let them rise in a warm place for 30 minutes and bake in the preheated oven for 20 minutes or until they are golden brown. Brush them, if desired, while they are still warm, with confectioners' sugar reduced to a thin paste with a little milk and flavored with a drop or two of vanilla. Cool the 12 pastries on a rack.

Prune Danish Pastry

⅓ **prepared Danish Pastry Dough**
  (page 146)
1 cup thickly puréed prunes

1 tsp grated orange rind
1 egg, beaten

Preheat oven to 400 degrees. Roll the dough ⅛-inch thick and cut it into 12 rectangles of equal size. Combine the puréed prunes and orange rind and spread about 1 tablespoon of the mixture lengthwise along the center of each rectangle. Brush the edges of the rectangles with some of the beaten egg and fold them over the fillings, securing the seams by pressing them together. Cut 4 or 5 gashes about ¼-inch deep along the seam edge of each pastry and arrange these "cockscombs" on a lightly buttered baking sheet. Let the pastries rise in a warm place for 15 minutes or just until they begin to puff. Brush them with beaten egg and bake them in the preheated oven for 20 minutes or until they are golden brown. Cool them on a rack.

Cinnamon Danish Pastry Roll

⅓ **recipe Danish Pastry Dough**
  (page 146)
1⅓ cups Frangipane (about
  ⅓ recipe on page 64)

4 tsp Cinnamon Sugar (page 70)
1 egg, beaten

Preheat oven to 400 degrees. Roll out the dough ⅛-inch thick, spread it evenly with the frangipane, and sprinkle it with the cinnamon sugar. Roll up the dough firmly, jelly-roll fashion. Brush the seam with some of the beaten egg and press it to the roll to secure it. Chill the dough in the freezer for 15 minutes or until it is firm enough to cut. Do not let it freeze. Brush the roll with beaten egg and cut it into 12 slices of equal size.

Arrange the rolls on a lightly buttered baking sheet and bake them in the preheated oven for 20 minutes or until the edges are nicely browned. Cool the slices on a rack.

2 envelopes dry yeast
⅓ cup lukewarm water
5 cups flour
1 cup butter, melted &
   cooled to lukewarm
9 egg yolks
⅔ cup orange-flower water,
   heated to lukewarm

⅔ cup sugar
½ tsp salt
1 tsp vanilla extract
1 Tbl honey
¾ cup seedless raisins
¾ cup chopped mixed glazed fruit
1 Tbl butter
1 egg, beaten

Soften the yeast in the lukewarm water. Blend it, with the water, into 1¼ cups of the flour. Shape the dough into a ball and set it in a lightly buttered bowl. Cover bowl lightly and let dough rise in a warm place, free of drafts, for 30 minutes. Deflate the dough and work into it the remaining flour, the melted butter, egg yolks, warmed orange-flower water, sugar, salt, vanilla, and honey. Knead dough until it is very smooth, about 15 minutes, steadily. Spread dough into a square and sprinkle over it the raisins and glazed fruit. Fold dough in half over them and in half again. Knead it for 5 minutes to distribute the fruit evenly throughout. Shape dough into a ball, return it to the buttered bowl, and let it rise again, lightly covered, for 30 minutes. Deflate the dough. Divide it into 3 equal-size pieces and form each into a ball. Place each in a lightly buttered round baking pan, 8 inches in diameter and 3 inches deep.

Cover pans lightly with cloths and let the pieces of dough rise until they double in bulk, about 1½ hours.

Preheat oven to 375 degrees. Cut a cross in the top of each piece of risen dough and place 1 teaspoon of the butter in each. Brush the tops with the beaten egg. Set pans, staggered (on 2 shelves, if necessary, but not directly over each other), in the preheated oven and bake for 45 minutes or until a cake tester inserted into center of loaves can be withdrawn clean. Remove loaves from pans and set them on racks to cool. Each loaf will provide about 6 to 8 servings.

Cape Cod Coffee Cake

1 cup cranberries	**2 cups flour**
½ cup water	**3 tsp baking powder**
1 cup plus 2 Tbl sugar	**¼ tsp salt**
½ cup butter	**⅛ tsp ground cloves**
3 eggs	**⅛ tsp cinnamon**

Preheat oven to 350 degrees. In a saucepan over moderate heat cook the cranberries in the water with 2 tablespoons of the sugar for 5 minutes or just until the berries are soft but not mushy. Drain them and set them aside to cool.

In a mixing bowl thoroughly cream together the butter and remaining sugar. Add the eggs, 1 at a time, beating well after each addition. Sift together the remaining ingredients and blend into the mixture. Spread ⅓ of the batter evenly in a buttered 8-inch square cake pan and cover it with ½ the prepared berries. Spread over them another ⅓ of the batter and the remaining berries. Cover with the remaining batter. Bake in the preheated oven 45 minutes or until a cake tester inserted in the center of the cake can be withdrawn clean. Remove the cake from the pan and cool it on a rack. This cake provides 6 servings.

Pennsylvania Dutch Christmas Loaf

1½ cups milk	**¾ cup seedless white raisins**
1 package dry yeast	**⅔ cup chopped**

¼ **cup lukewarm water**
3–3½ **cups sifted flour**
¼ **tsp salt**
½ **cup unsalted butter**

assorted candied fruit
½ **cup currants**
¼ **cup sliced walnuts**

Scald 1 cup of the milk, pour it into a mixing bowl, and let it cool to lukewarm. Soften the yeast in the lukewarm water. Sift 1½ cups of the flour with the salt and stir it into the lukewarm milk. Blend in the softened yeast. Cover the bowl lightly with a cloth, set it in a warm place and let it remain overnight. Next day scald the remaining milk in a saucepan and melt the butter in it. Let it cool to lukewarm and stir it into the risen yeast mixture. Beat in 1½ cups of the remaining flour and all of the raisins, candied fruit, currants, and nuts. Turn the dough out onto a floured board and knead it until it is no longer sticky. Add more flour, if necessary. Brush the bowl with melted butter, replace the dough in it, and lightly butter the top. Cover the bowl again, return it to a warm place, and let it remain for 1½ hours or until it has doubled in bulk.

Butter and lightly flour a 9 x 5 x 2¾-inch loaf pan. Deflate the risen dough and turn it out onto a lightly floured board. Pat it into a square about 1 inch thick and shape it into a sort of double scroll by rolling 2 ends in to the middle. Set the shaped dough in the prepared pan and let it rise until it again doubles in bulk. Preheat the oven to 375 degrees and bake the loaf in it for 45 minutes or until the top is lightly browned and the loaf begins to shrink slightly from the sides of the pan. Cool the loaf on a rack and cut it into ½-inch slices to provide 18 servings. The slices may be toasted and served topped with ice cream. *(See photograph, page 34.)*

Schnecken | Viennese Pastry Snails

1½ cups flour

¼ cup sugar

½ tsp salt

6 Tbl butter, cut in small pieces

½ cup sour cream

2 eggs

1 envelope yeast

¼ cup lukewarm water

⅓ cup currants or raisins

⅓ cup ground pecans

¼ tsp cinnamon

¼ cup butter, softened

¾ cup dark brown sugar

2 tsp light corn syrup

24 pecan halves

Onto a pastry board sift together the flour, sugar, and salt into a mound. Make a well in the center and put into it the pieces of butter, sour cream, 1 of the eggs, and the yeast softened in the warm water. Using your fingers work the wet ingredients into the dry to produce a dough that is moderately soft but not sticky. Blend in a little more flour, if necessary. Transfer the dough to a buttered bowl, cover it lightly with a cloth, and chill it in the refrigerator for several hours or overnight.

Deflate the dough (it will have risen somewhat in the refrigerator) and turn it out onto a lightly floured pastry board. Divide the dough into 2 parts. Roll out each part into a rectangle ¼-inch thick and spread it evenly with the fruit, ground pecans, and cinnamon combined. Roll up the rectangles, jelly-roll fashion, across the width, and seal the seams with a little of the remaining egg, beaten.

In a mixing bowl thoroughly combine the softened butter, brown sugar, and corn syrup. Place about 2 teaspoons of the mixture in the bottom of each of 24 small muffin tins (2 sets) and place a pecan half topside down in each tin. Cut the prepared pastry rolls each into 12 slices and place 1 slice in each tin. Set the tins in a warm place and let them remain for 20 minutes or until the slices have risen somewhat. Preheat oven to 350 degrees.

Bake in the preheated oven for 30 minutes or until the slices are puffed and nicely browned. Remove the pan from the oven and immediately invert the schnecken along with the glaze and pecans out onto sheets of lightly buttered foil. Let the pastries cool or serve them slightly warm.

Kugelhopf, Brasserie

2 envelopes dry yeast	¾ cup sugar
½ cup lukewarm water	12 egg yolks
5¾ cups flour	1 tsp vanilla extract
¼ tsp salt	1 cup Frangipane (page 64)
½ cup milk, scalded & cooled	2 tsp cinnamon
to lukewarm	1 cup seedless raisins
½ cup butter	Confectioners' sugar

Soften the yeast in the lukewarm water. Sift together into a mixing bowl 2¼ cups of the flour and the salt. Combine the softened yeast and the lukewarm milk, and blend in. Work the dough until it is smooth. Cover it lightly with a cloth and let it rise in a warm place until it doubles in bulk.

In another bowl cream together the butter and all but 2 tablespoons of the sugar; reserve those 2 tablespoons. Into the creamed mixture thoroughly beat the egg yolks, 2 at a time, and stir in the vanilla. Deflate the risen dough and stir the creamed mixture into it. Work in the remaining flour, a little at a time, to produce a stiff but smooth dough. Roll the dough into a rectangle about 20 inches long and 10 inches wide. Spread it evenly with the frangipane, leaving bare a 1-inch border all around. Combine the cinnamon and reserved sugar and sift the mixture over the frangipane. Sprinkle with the raisins. Roll up the rectangle across the width. Moisten with a little cold water the edge toward which the rectangle is rolled and press it to the roll to secure the seam. Bring the ends of the roll together to form a ring and fit one end into the other. Butter a fluted 10-inch kugelhopf pan and arrange the prepared ring in it. Cover it lightly with a cloth and let it rise in a warm place until it fills the pan, which it should do in about 45 minutes. Preheat the oven to 375 degrees and bake the risen ring in it for 45 minutes or until a cake tester inserted in the center can be withdrawn clean. Remove the cake to a rack and let it cool. Serve the kugelhopf dusted with confectioners' sugar and cut to provide 10 to 12 servings.

Ghurayyibi

1 cup butter	1 Tbl orange-flower water
1 cup sugar	1½ cups semolina (see Note)
1 Tbl rosewater	

Preheat oven to 475 degrees. In a mixing bowl soften the butter by mashing it with a wooden spoon and beat it until it is light and fluffy. Beat in the sugar, a little at a time, along with the rosewater and orange-flower water. Reserve 3 tablespoons of the semolina and beat the remainder gradually into the creamed mixture. Sprinkle the reserved semolina evenly over the bottom of a 9 x 13-inch baking pan and spread the prepared mixture over it. Bake in the preheated oven for 15 minutes or until the pastry is firm. Let it cool and cut it into 18 triangular-shaped serving pieces.

NOTE: Semolina, a fine flour ground from durum wheat, is available in most shops specializing in Middle European food products. Farina or cream of wheat may be substituted.

Baklava

1 cup unsalted butter, melted	3 cups sugar
1 pound filo pastry (see Note)	2½ cups water
2 cups ground walnuts	1 Tbl lemon juice

Preheat oven to 200 degrees. Brush an 11 x 15-inch baking pan with a little of the melted butter and line it with ½ the filo, buttering each sheet with melted butter. Brush the top sheet generously and spread it with the ground nuts. Cover them with the remaining pastry, brushing each of those sheets also with melted butter. Coat the top with the remaining melted butter. With a sharp knife mark the pastry into diamond-shaped serving pieces, but do not cut them through. Bake in the preheated oven for 2½ hours, by which time the pastry will be crisp but still quite pale in color.

Well before the pastry is taken from the oven, prepare a syrup with the sugar, water, and lemon juice combined in a saucepan. Cook the mixture over medium heat for 20 minutes or until the syrup is quite thick. The pastry removed from the oven, pour the syrup over it a little at a time, while both are still hot, until syrup is completely absorbed. Cool the baklava and serve it with, if desired, whipped cream. This recipe provides about 2½ dozen pieces.

NOTE: Filo (also spelled *phyllo)* is a Greek pastry similar to strudel dough, which may be substituted, although the ingredients are not quite the same. Filo pastry contains no eggs. It is available commercially in shops specializing in Greek food products.

Kinafe

12 Shredded Wheat biscuits	**¼ cup butter, cut into bits**
2 cups warm milk	**1¼ cups water**
1 cup finely chopped walnuts	**1 Tbl lemon juice**
2 cups sugar	

Preheat oven to 400 degrees. Arrange the biscuits in a deep platter and pour the warm milk over them. Turn them rapidly in the milk 2 or 3 times until they are softened but not soggy. Immediately drain off the excess milk. Carefully split the biscuits and coat the cut sides equally with the nuts and ½ cup of the sugar combined. Reassemble the halves and carefully fold the filled biscuits down the length into neat miniature rolls. Transfer the rolls to a baking pan, seam sides down, and dot them equally with the bits of butter. Bake them in the preheated oven for 20 minutes or until they are golden brown.

In a saucepan combine the remaining sugar with the water and lemon juice and cook the mixture over medium heat until it is reduced to a thick syrup, which should be ready when the biscuits are taken from the oven. Pour the syrup over them at once and let the rolls absorb it completely. Cool the kinafe and apportion them 2 to a serving.

7 | frozen desserts

Thomas Jefferson may not have introduced ice cream to the tables of America, as he is frequently credited with having done, but his recipe, the first American one for that dessert and still the only one in the handwriting of a president of the United States, certainly was instrumental in making Americans the greatest ice-cream-eating people in the world.

The ingredients for ice cream have changed very little, if at all, since Mr. Jefferson penned his famous recipe. Ice cream is still basically a custard, made of cream, sugar, and egg yolks, blended and then frozen. Until the mid-eighteen hundreds, when the hand-operated churn was invented, the freezing was quite similar to our modern refrigerator method: The custard was placed in a container set in a bucket of ice and salt, and stirred or shaken at intervals until it became firm.

Ice cream was served in England almost two hundred years before it arrived here, having made its first appearance in 1667 at a banquet in Windsor Castle. China is reputed to have tasted it, in its original form as an ice, some thirteen centuries earlier. Presumably Marco Polo discovered it in China, took it back to Italy, and transformed it into Bisquit Tortoni, of which we present a counterpart on page 168.

Basic Ice Cream

3 cups light cream	**¼ tsp salt**
¾ cup sugar	**1 cup heavy cream**
8 egg yolks	

In the top pan of a double boiler scald the light cream and dissolve ⅓ cup of the sugar in it. In a mixing bowl beat the egg yolks with the salt and remaining sugar until the yolks are light in color and thick. Pour the sweetened hot cream into the yolk mixture very gradually in a thin stream, stirring constantly. Pour the mixture into the double-boiler pan and cook it over simmering water, continuing to stir, until it coats the spoon. Strain the custard into a heat-proof bowl and add the required flavoring (see specific recipes which follow on pages 159 through 161). Let the custard cool and stir in the heavy cream, liquid or whipped, depending on method of freezing (see below). Freeze as desired. This quantity of mixture with the required flavoring will provide about 1 quart (6 to 8 servings) of ice cream.

Refrigerator or Deep-Freezer Ice Cream:

Prepare the ice-cream mixture as directed in the recipe, adding the flavoring to the strained custard, but whip the heavy cream and fold it in. Pour the mixture into a stainless-steel bowl and set it in the freezing compartment of the refrigerator with the temperature control at its coldest point, or in a deep freezer. Cover the bowl with waxed paper or plastic wrap and freeze the mixture for 2 hours, stirring it every 20 minutes. Continue thereafter to freeze without further stirring until the cream is firm.

If cream is to be frozen in a deep freezer, it should be stirred or beaten at 10-minute intervals during the first 2 hours and allowed to freeze thereafter without further stirring.

Check the consistency of the ice cream well ahead of serving time. If it is frozen hard, remove the bowl from the freezer about 1½ hours before the ice cream is to be served. Let ice cream stand at room temperature until it softens. Beat it well with a rotary beater and return it to the freezer for 30 minutes, or just until it is again firm.

Churn-Frozen Ice Cream:

Prepare the ice-cream mixture as directed in the recipe, with liquid heavy cream and the required flavoring. Pour the mixture into a 2-quart drum of a churn freezer with the dasher in place. Cover the drum, set it in place in the freezer, and pack around it alternating layers of 6 cups crushed ice and 1 cup coarse rock salt until the packing is level with the top of the drum. Churn at moderate, constant speed until the drum begins to turn with difficulty. Remove the cover of the drum, carefully so that no ice or salt falls into it, remove the dasher, and pack down the ice cream. Cover the cream with waxed paper or plastic wrap (to prevent cream from crystalizing) and replace the lid of the drum. Repack the freezer with ice and salt as before, wrap it in burlap or several thicknesses of newspaper, and let the ice cream remain so to mellow for several hours before serving it.

Caramel Ice Cream

Proceed as directed for Basic Ice Cream (page 158), stirring 2 tablespoons caramel syrup and ½ teaspoon vanilla into the strained custard.

Chocolate Ice Cream

Proceed as directed for Basic Ice Cream (page 158), stirring 2 squares melted unsweetened chocolate into the strained custard.

Coffee Ice Cream

Proceed as directed for Basic Ice Cream (page 158), dissolving 2 tablespoons powdered instant coffee in the strained custard.

Lemon Ice Cream

Proceed as directed for Basic Ice Cream (page 158), stirring the grated rind and juice of 1 large lemon into the strained custard.

Mocha Ice Cream

Proceed as directed for Basic Ice Cream (page 158), stirring 1 square melted unsweetened chocolate and 1 tablespoon powdered instant coffee into the strained custard.

Peach Ice Cream

Proceed as directed for Basic Ice Cream (page 158), stirring into the strained custard 3 very ripe peaches, peeled, the pits removed, and the fruit puréed in an electric blender or forced through a sieve.

Pistachio Ice Cream

Proceed as directed for Basic Ice Cream (page 158), stirring into the strained custard ½ cup finely ground pistachio nuts and 1 or 2 drops of green food coloring.

Rum Ice Cream

Proceed as directed for Basic Ice Cream (page 158), stirring ¼ cup full-bodied rum into the strained custard.

Strawberry Ice Cream

Proceed as directed for Basic Ice Cream (page 158), stirring into the strained custard 1 pint fresh strawberries, hulled, washed, and crushed.

Vanilla Ice Cream

Proceed as directed for Basic Ice Cream (page 158), stirring 2 tablespoons vanilla extract into the strained custard.

How to Make Ices and Sherbets

Ices simply are mixtures of juice or purée (or both), flavoring, and sugar syrup. A mixture for ice becomes one for sherbet when the ingredients are augmented by a stabilizer such as egg white or gelatine.

Any of the following ice mixtures may be converted to provide sherbet by adding 2 stiffly beaten egg whites or 2 tablespoons unflavored gelatine softened in ½ cup cool water and dissolved in a little heated simple syrup.

Drained canned fruit, puréed, may be used instead of fresh fruit in the ice and sherbet recipes. The syrup of the canned fruit may be used also; if it is, add only enough of the Simple Syrup required in the recipe to provide the total liquid sweetening required.

The freezing process for ices and sherbets is the same as for ice cream: Follow directions for Churn-Frozen Ice Cream, or for Refrigerator or Deep-Freezer Ice Cream under recipe for Basic Ice Cream (page 158).

If the ice or sherbet is to be refrigerator- or deep-frozen, it should fill the container to no more than ¾ of its capacity. Ices and egg-white sherbets should be stirred (or, better still, beaten with a rotary beater) at 10-minute intervals after they start to freeze, and only during the first hour. Thereafter, freezing should continue without further stirring or beating. However, if a sherbet is made with gelatine and frozen in the refrigerator or deep freezer, it generally needs stirring only once, after the initial freeze.

Apricot Ice

2 cups unsweetened puréed   **1½ cups Simple Syrup (page 278)**
  cooked apricots   **1 cup milk**

In a mixing bowl thoroughly combine all ingredients. Freeze as desired to provide 1½ pints of ice.

Black-Coffee Ice

4 cups strong brewed coffee, cooled

2 cups Simple Syrup (page 278)
½ tsp vanilla extract (see Note)

In a mixing bowl thoroughly combine all of the ingredients. Freeze as desired to produce about 3 pints of ice.

NOTE: Vary the flavor by substituting for the vanilla 2 tablespoons cognac, full-bodied rum, or orange-flavored liqueur.

Lemon Ice

2 cups strained lemon juice
3 cups Simple Syrup (page 278)

Grated rind of 2 lemons
¼ tsp salt

In a mixing bowl combine the lemon juice and 2 cups of the syrup. In a saucepan combine the remaining syrup with the lemon rind and heat, without boiling, for 2 minutes. Strain it into the mixture in the bowl. Add the salt and stir to blend. Cool the mixture thoroughly before freezing it as desired to produce 1 quart of ice.

Minted Lime Ice

2 cups strained lime juice
3 cups Simple Syrup (page 278)
Grated rind of 2 limes

2 Tbl green crème de menthe
¼ tsp salt

In a mixing bowl combine the lime juice and 2 cups of the syrup. Heat the remaining syrup and lime rind for 2 minutes without boiling. Let the syrup cool and strain it into the mixture in the bowl. Stir in the liqueur and salt. Freeze as desired. This recipe provides about 1 quart of ice.

Orange Ice

3 cups orange juice

¼ tsp salt

¼ **cup strained lemon juice**
3 cups Simple Syrup (page 278)
Grated rind of 1 orange
Grated rind of ½ lemon

1 Tbl orange-flavored liqueur
   (Cointreau, Curaçao, Grand
   Marnier, or such)

Strain the orange juice through a coarse sieve into a bowl, letting some of the pulp seep through. Combine that juice with the lemon juice and 2 cups of the simple syrup. In a saucepan heat together the remaining syrup and the 2 fruit rinds for 2 minutes, but do not let the syrup boil. Remove the pan from the heat and let the mixture cool. Strain it into the bowl with the combined juices. Discard the grated rinds. Stir in the salt and the liqueur. Freeze as desired, preferably in a stainless-steel bowl. This recipe provides about 1 quart of ice.

Pear Ice

3 cups puréed cooked pears,   **¼ cup lemon juice**
    unsweetened   **¼ tsp salt**
3 cups Simple Syrup (page 278)   **2 Tbl pear brandy**

In a mixing bowl thoroughly combine the purée, syrup, and lemon juice. Add the salt and stir to dissolve. Stir in the pear brandy. Freeze as desired to provide about 3 pints of ice.

Plum Ice

2½ cups puréed unsweetened   **Juice & rind of 1 lemon**
    cooked plums   **⅛ tsp salt**
3 cups Simple Syrup (page 278)

Thoroughly combine all of the ingredients in a bowl, preferably made of stainless steel. Freeze in the refrigerator or deep freezer, or transfer the mixture to the drum of a churn freezer and freeze until firm. This quantity of mixture provides about 3 pints of ice.

Raspberry Ice

3 pints fresh raspberries (see Note)   **½ cup cool water**
1 cup fine granulated sugar   **1 Tbl strained lemon juice**
⅛ tsp salt

Wash the raspberries very gently in a pan of cool water. Drain them partially and put them in a bowl. Sprinkle them with the sugar and let them stand in the refrigerator for at least 2 hours. Force the berries, along with any rendered juice, through a sieve into a bowl in which the ice will be frozen (preferably a stainless-steel bowl). Use a sieve fine enough to retain the seeds. Or purée the berries in an electric blender and strain out the seeds. Dissolve the salt in the water and lemon juice combined and add the liquid to the purée. Freeze as desired to provide about 1 quart.

NOTE: Two 10-ounce packages of frozen raspberries may be substituted for the indicated quantity of fresh berries. Purée the berries along with the syrup in which they are contained. Decrease the sugar to ⅓ cup and increase the amount of water to 1 cup.

Strawberry Ice

3 pints firm ripe strawberries	Juice of 1 lemon, or more to taste
3 cups Simple Syrup (page 278)	¼ tsp salt

Hull and wash the berries and force them through a fine sieve into a mixing bowl or purée them in an electric blender. There should be 2 cups of the purée or slightly more. Combine with it the syrup, lemon juice, and salt, and freeze as desired. The mixture provides about 1 quart of ice.

Watermelon Ice

2½ cups seeded ripe watermelon pulp (see Note)	2 Tbl lemon juice
	¼ tsp salt
1½ cups Simple Syrup (page 278)	1 cup pale ginger ale

Force the watermelon pulp through a fine sieve into a mixing bowl or purée it in an electric blender. Combine with it the simple syrup, lemon juice, and salt, and gently stir in the ginger ale. Freeze as desired. This recipe provides about 1 quart of ice.
NOTE: For different melon ices, substitute 2½ cups seeded honeydew melon pulp, or 2 cups seeded ripe cantaloupe pulp. Purée pulp and combine with the 1½ cups of Simple Syrup, 3 tablespoons each of lemon and orange juice, ½ cup dry Madeira, and the salt. Omit the ginger ale.

Coupes

The coupe is the most elegant member of a trio which includes also the fruit cup and the fruit cocktail. It is presented in a champagne or sherbet glass (the custom from which the dessert takes its name). To make a coupe, begin by placing the basic fruit mixture in a glass. Over this place an ice cream, ice, or sherbet. The whole is embellished generally with whipped cream, and occasionally with liqueur, cognac, nuts, or candied flowers, as well.

Following are some of the more familiar coupes with the ingredients arranged in order of preparation.

Coupe Andalouse

Peeled orange sections, steeped in maraschino liqueur, and Lemon Ice Cream (page 159).

Coupe Clo-Clo

Coarsely chopped marrons glacés, Vanilla Ice Cream (page 160), half-and-half combination of puréed strawberries and whipped cream, and a whole marron glacé. *(See photograph, page 170.)*

Coupe Elizabeth

Cooked (or canned, drained) cherries steeped in kirsch, soft-frozen whipped cream, and a sprinkling of cinnamon.

Coupe Gressac

Vanilla Ice Cream (page 160), small macaroons moistened with kirsch, ½ peeled fresh peach filled with Bar-le-Duc, and whipped cream.

Coupe Jamaique

Diced cooked fresh pineapple steeped in rum, Coffee Ice Cream (page 159), and candied coffee beans.

Coupe Montmorency

Brandied cherries and Vanilla Ice Cream (page 160).

Frozen Lemon Cream

3 egg yolks	⅛ tsp salt
½ cup sugar	3 egg whites, stiffly beaten
¼ cup lemon juice	1 cup heavy cream, whipped
½ tsp grated lemon rind	¾ cup vanilla-wafer crumbs

In the top pan of a double boiler beat together the egg yolks and sugar and blend in the lemon juice, rind, and salt. Set the pan over simmering water and cook the mixture, stirring constantly until it thickly coats the spoon. Cool the custard and chill it thoroughly. Fold into it the beaten egg whites and the whipped cream. Sprinkle ½ the wafer

crumbs over the bottom of an 8-inch square baking pan and spread the lemon cream evenly over them. Sprinkle with the remaining crumbs. Freeze until firm and cut to provide 8 to 10 servings.

Baked Alaska

1 quart ice cream, flavored as
    desired (see Note)
1 pint sherbet, of compatible flavor
    (see Note)

1 8-inch layer Genoise (page 14)
5 egg whites
¾ cup sugar

Line a 6-cup dome-shaped mold with waxed paper or foil with an overhang of about 2 inches all around. Spread the mold with a thick shell of the ice cream and pack the center with the sherbet. Cover the filling with waxed paper and freeze until hard. Place the cake layer on a heatproof serving platter and invert the mold over it. Wipe the top of the container rapidly with a cloth dampened with hot water. Pull the lining overhang in several places to loosen the filling and unmold it. Have ready a stiff meringue of the egg whites beaten with the sugar added gradually, and quickly cover the ice cream and cake with it right down to the platter. Bake immediately in a preheated 450-degree oven for 5 minutes, or until the meringue is delicately browned. Present the Baked Alaska at table immediately and cut for 10 to 12 servings.
NOTE: Compatible combinations may be vanilla ice cream and raspberry sherbet; melba ice cream and strawberry sherbet; praline ice cream and plum sherbet; peach ice cream and lemon sherbet; chocolate ice cream and orange sherbet; rum ice cream and black-coffee sherbet; or ginger ice cream and café au lait sherbet.

Bisquit Tortoni

1 cup heavy cream
5 Tbl fine granulated sugar
½ cup finely chopped toasted
    blanched almonds

1 Tbl Marsala wine
1 egg white, stiffly beaten

The special tang of home-made ice creams and sherbets makes them a favorite dessert (see pages 158-165).

In a mixing bowl whip the cream until it begins to thicken. Add the sugar gradually, continuing to beat until the cream is stiff. Reserve 1 tablespoon of the almonds and stir the remainder into the cream along with the wine. Fold in the egg white. Fill eight 2-inch paper cups with the mixture and sprinkle the tops with the reserved almonds. Freeze in the refrigerator until the cream is firm. Each bisquit is a serving.

Boule de Neige | Ice Cream Snowball

¾ **cup diced mixed glazed fruit**　　**Sweetened whipped cream**
¼ **cup seedless white raisins**　　　**Candied violets**
¼ **cup kirsch**
1 quart Vanilla Ice Cream
　(page 160)

In a bowl steep the fruit, including the raisins, in the kirsch for 1 hour, stirring frequently. Put the ice cream into the bowl and blend into it the steeped fruit along with any remaining kirsch. Pack the ice cream into a 6-cup dome-shaped mold and freeze until solid. Unmold the cream onto a chilled metal tray or removable bottom of a flan pan and cover the dome completely with small rosettes of whipped cream, piped from a pastry bag fitted with a star tube. Decorate with candied violets (available commercially). Return the Boule de Neige to the freezer until serving time. Cut it into wedges to provide 8 to 10 servings.

Mint Strawberry Ring

3 pints Lemon Ice (page 162)　　**2 pints strawberries**
⅓ **cup crème de menthe**

Line an 8-cup ring mold with 6 equally spaced strips of waxed paper, each 1 inch wide and 12 inches long, allowing the ends to overhang the edges of the mold. In a mixing bowl soften the ice slightly and blend the crème de menthe into it. Spread it evenly in the prepared mold, cover it with foil, and freeze it until it is firm.

　　About 3 hours before the ice is to be served unmold the ring onto

Patrician Parfait sprinkled with pistachios
(page 172), Coupe Clo-Clo with a whole marron
glacé (page 166), Peach Melba (page 173),
and Coffee Ice Cream (page 159) topped with walnuts
and served in a demitasse.

a chilled metal tray or baking sheet: Remove the foil, dip the mold very briefly in warm water and invert it onto the tray; pull the ends of the waxed paper strips gently until the ring is worked loose and unmolded. Remove the strips of paper and return the ring to the freezer to remain until serving time. Carefully transfer the ring to a chilled shallow bowl and fill the center with the strawberries, hulled, washed, and sweetened to taste. This recipe provides 6 to 8 servings.

Soufflé Glacé à l'Orange

6 navel oranges
6 egg yolks
1 cup confectioners' sugar
1½ cups heavy cream, whipped

2 Tbl Grand Marnier liqueur
1 egg white
12 fresh mint leaves

Cut a slice from the top of each orange about 1 inch thick. Carefully scoop out the pulp of the lower parts and press out the juice through a sieve into a bowl. Set aside ½ cup of the juice and reserve the remainder for morning drinking. In the top pan of a double boiler beat the egg yolks with the sugar until the mixture is very thick and stir in the ½ cup of orange juice. Set the pan over simmering water and cook the mixture, stirring it constantly until it thickly coats the spoon. Remove the pan from over the water and let the custard cool. Stir into it the whipped cream and the liqueur. Fill the orange shells with the mixture and freeze them overnight. Brush the orange tops with a little of the egg white and place 2 of the mint leaves on top of each. Freeze the tops separately. At serving time, replace the tops on the 6 filled and frozen oranges and serve them at once.

Patrician Parfait

¾ cup Chocolate Sauce
(page 281)
1 quart Vanilla Ice Cream
(page 160)

18 brandied cherries with a little
of their juice
⅓ cup cognac
Chopped pistachio nuts

In each of 6 parfait glasses pour 2 tablespoons of the chocolate sauce and cover with ¼ cup of the ice cream. Add 3 of the cherries along with a little of their juice and about 1 tablespoon of the cognac. Fill each glass equally with the remaining ice cream and smooth each filling into a cone shape. Sprinkle each equally with chopped pistachios. Six parfaits equal 6 servings. *(See photograph, page 170.)*

Peach Melba

3 firm ripe peaches, peeled, halved
   & pitted
1 cup Simple Syrup (page 278)

6 scoops Vanilla Ice Cream,
   about 1 pint (page 160)
¾ cup Melba Sauce (page 284)

In a saucepan over medium heat poach the peach halves in the syrup for 10 minutes. Allow to cool in syrup. Drain peaches well and place 1 half in each of 6 sherbet glasses. Fill centers each with a scoop of ice cream. Pour 2 tablespoons of sauce over each and serve.

Sicilian Coffee Cream

2 eggs
½ cup light cream
½ cup milk
½ cup sugar

1 Tbl instant coffee powder
⅛ tsp salt
2 tsp grated orange rind
1½ cups heavy cream

In the top pan of a double boiler beat the eggs with a rotary beater until they are frothy. Add the light cream, milk, sugar, coffee powder, salt, and orange rind, and continue beating until the ingredients are well blended. Set the pan over simmering water and cook the mixture, stirring it constantly until it coats the spoon. Remove the pan from over the water and strain the custard into a mixing bowl. Discard the grated rind. Let the custard cool and fold into it the heavy cream, stiffly whipped. Fill a 1-quart mold with the mixture and cover it with a sheet of buttered waxed paper. Fit the mold cover in place or seal the top with foil. Freeze until firm, about 6 hours or overnight. Unmold onto a chilled serving platter to provide 6 to 8 servings.

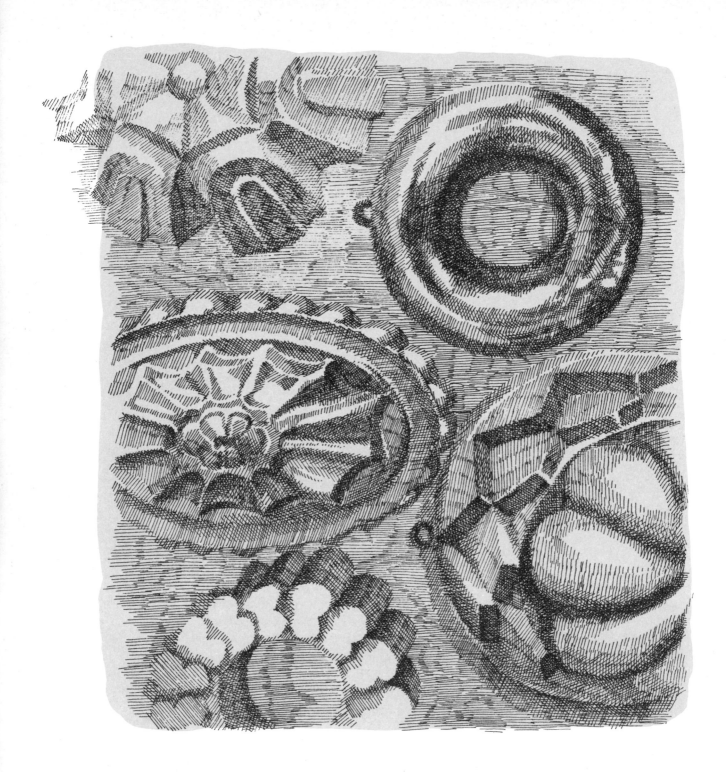

8 | gelatines and creams

In the rarefied realm of dessert cookery, the Bavarian cream is considered to be without peer. The chilled soufflé may seem to have more stature, but that is only the result of tying a paper collar around its container to give it greater height. Otherwise the difference between a chilled soufflé and an ordinary cream is frequently imperceptible.

Molded jellies are considered to be more demanding. A well-made jelly should be clear, bright, and properly firm, which is to say firm enough to hold a shape, but still soft enough to quiver. In unmolding a jelly which has become too firmly set, the inexperienced cook is cautioned to remain calm. Never use force in trying to separate the jelly from its mold. To do so is to court disaster and possibly to ruin the contents of the mold. Instead, very calmly half immerse the mold in warm water for a few seconds, then invert it onto a chilled platter; the recalcitrant jelly will very meekly unmold.

Basic Custard Cream

4 egg yolks
⅔ cup sugar
½ tsp cornstarch

⅛ tsp salt
1½ cups milk, scalded

In the top pan of a double boiler beat together the egg yolks, sugar, cornstarch, and salt. Gradually add the hot milk, pouring it in a thin stream while beating constantly. Set the pan over simmering water and cook the mixture, still stirring, until it coats the spoon. Flavor and use, hot or cooled, as required. If cooled, stir the cream occasionally to prevent skin from forming. This recipe provides 2 cups of custard cream for use in making gelatine desserts.

Amor Frío | Spanish Cold Love

2 cups diced pulp of honeydew or
  Spanish melon
2 cups peeled seedless orange
  segments
2 halves Poached Pear (page 243),
  diced
2 Tbl confectioners' sugar

1 cup white rum
1½ envelopes (1½ Tbl) unflavored
  gelatine
1 recipe Basic Custard Cream
  (above)
¾ cup heavy cream, whipped

In a glass or china bowl combine the fruits and sprinkle them with the sugar. Pour the white rum over them and let steep for 2 to 3 hours. Drain off the remaining rum and soften the gelatine in it. Dissolve the gelatine in the hot custard cream. Let the mixture cool. Stir the steeped fruit into it and fold in the whipped cream. Spread the mixture evenly in a 2-quart mold and chill it in the refrigerator for 2 hours, or until it is completely set. Unmold it onto a chilled serving platter to be apportioned for 8 to 10 servings.

Apricot Ring

1 cup apricot purée (see Note)

⅓ cup cool water

2 Tbl apricot liqueur
1½ envelopes (1½ Tbl) unflavored
   gelatine

2 cups heavy cream, whipped
5 egg whites
½ cup fine granulated sugar

In a mixing bowl combine the purée and liqueur. In the top pan of a double boiler soften the gelatine in the water and dissolve it by setting the pan over hot water. Blend the dissolved gelatine into the apricot purée. Let the mixture cool and fold in the whipped cream. In a mixing bowl beat the egg whites to the soft-peak stage. Add the sugar a little at a time, continuing the beating until the whites are stiff. Fold them into the purée mixture. Spread that mixture evenly in a 6-cup ring mold rinsed in ice-cold water and drained. Chill the apricot mixture in the refrigerator for 3 hours, or until it is very firm. Unmold it onto a chilled serving platter to be apportioned for 6 to 8 servings. Fill the center of the ring, if desired, with whole apricots, peeled, pitted, and cooked (or with drained canned apricots).

NOTE: This quantity of purée is derived from ½ pound apricots, peeled, pitted and cooked, or from the apricots of a #2 can, without syrup.

Couronne Mexicaine | Mexican Crown of Cream

½ recipe Pâte à Brioche (page 138)
Frangipane (page 64)
1 envelope (1 Tbl) unflavored
   gelatine
¼ cup cool water
1 recipe Basic Custard Cream
   (page 176)

½ cup mixed candied fruit
2 Tbl rum
¾ cup heavy cream, whipped
Small slices pineapple
Maraschino cherries
Apricot Glaze (page 70)

Preheat oven to 425 degrees. Prepare brioche dough as directed in the recipe and with it fill an 8-cup ring mold to ½ its capacity. Let the dough rise until it fills the pan and bake in the preheated oven for 20 minutes, or until the ring is well puffed and nicely browned and a cake tester inserted in the center can be withdrawn clean. Remove the brioche to a rack and let it cool. Cut the cooled brioche into enough slices ½-inch thick to surround a 4-cup dome-shaped mold. Spread the slices, on 1 side only, with frangipane and return them to the pre-heated oven for 5 minutes, or until they are golden brown. Remove and cool them.

Soften the gelatine in the water and dissolve it in the hot custard cream. Stir in the candied fruit and the rum and let the mixture cool. Fold in the whipped cream. Rinse the 4-cup dome-shaped mold in ice-cold water and drain. Pour in the mixture. Chill it in the refrigerator for 2 hours or until it is firm. Unmold the cream onto a large, round, chilled serving platter and arrange the browned slices of brioche around the mold, overlapping them slightly. Decorate every other slice with a tiny slice of pineapple and the intervening slices of brioche each with a maraschino cherry. Brush the prepared slices with apricot glaze. Cut the crown at the table to provide 6 servings.

Blackberry Charlotte

1 recipe Ladyfingers (page 24)
1 recipe Basic Custard Cream
   (page 176)

¼ cup cool water
3 cups fresh blackberries
½ cup Simple Syrup (page 278)

1 envelope (1 Tbl) unflavored gelatine	**1 cup heavy cream, whipped**

Split 8 to 10 of the ladyfingers into halves and trim 1 end of each half to a point. Fit a round of waxed or baking liner paper in the bottom of a 6-cup-capacity soufflé dish and place the trimmed ladyfingers on it, arranging the halves around the dish, with the split sides up and the points meeting at the center. Line the sides of the dish with the remaining whole ladyfingers.

Prepare the custard cream as directed in the recipe, reducing the milk to 1 cup. Soften the gelatine in the water and dissolve it in the hot custard. Purée the blackberries by forcing them through a sieve or reducing them in an electric blender and straining out the seeds. Combine the purée with the custard cream and blend in the syrup. Let the mixture cool and fold in the whipped cream. Pour the mixture into the cake-lined soufflé dish, taking care not to dislodge the ladyfingers. Cover the dish with waxed paper or foil, and chill the mixture for 2 hours, or until it is very firm. Peel off the top paper. Loosen the rim of ladyfingers by running a sharp knife between it and the edge of the bowl, and invert the charlotte out onto a chilled serving platter. Peel off the lining paper, and cut the charlotte at the table to provide 6 servings.

Charlotte Russe

24 Ladyfingers (page 24)	**½ cup Melba Sauce (page 284)**
¼ cup cognac	**½ tsp vanilla extract**
2 envelopes (2 Tbl) unflavored gelatine	**2 squares (2 ounces) semisweet chocolate, melted & cooled**
⅓ cup cool water	**1½ cups heavy cream**
2 recipes (double quantity) Basic Custard Cream (page 176)	

Split the ladyfingers into halves and sprinkle them lightly with the cognac. Lightly butter a 2-quart dome-shaped ice-cream mold and line it with as many of the ladyfinger halves as needed. Reserve the remainder. Soften the gelatine in the water and dissolve it in the hot custard cream. Divide the cream into 3 equal parts, each in a separate bowl. Stir the Melba sauce into one, flavor another with the vanilla, and stir the melted and cooled chocolate into the third. Let the creams cool completely but do not allow them to set.

Stiffly whip the cream; it will double in bulk to provide 3 cups. Fold 1 cup into the Melba cream and pour that mixture into the cake-lined mold. Chill it in the refrigerator until it is set. (As you work, stir the other 2 creams frequently to keep them from setting.) Fold another cup of the whipped cream into the vanilla cream and pour that over the set cream in the mold. Chill again until that layer is set. Fold the final cup of whipped cream into the chocolate cream, pour that over the set layers and gently cover it with the remaining ladyfinger halves. Chill the Charlotte Russe for 2 hours, or until it is completely firm. Unmold onto a chilled serving platter and decorate, if desired, with rosettes of whipped cream piped from a pastry bag fitted with a star tube. Return the charlotte to the refrigerator until serving time. Cut it in wedges to provide 8 to 10 servings.

Almond Bavarian Cream

1 recipe Basic Custard Cream
  (page 176)
1 envelope (1 Tbl) unflavored
  gelatine

¼ cup maraschino liqueur
1 cup finely ground almonds
1 cup heavy cream, whipped
2 egg whites

While the custard cream is still hot, dissolve in it the gelatine softened in the liqueur. Stir in the almonds and let the custard cool completely. Transfer it to a metal bowl and chill it in the refrigerator just until it begins to gel; do not let it become set. Immediately fold into it the whipped cream and the egg whites, beaten until they are stiff but not dry. Pour the mixture into a 6-cup mold rinsed in ice-cold water and drained. Chill in the refrigerator for 2 hours, or until the cream is completely set. Unmold it onto a chilled serving platter and decorate, if desired, with rosettes of whipped cream, lightly sweetened and flavored with pure almond extract. Apportion for 6 servings.

Avocado Bavarian Cream

2½ envelopes (2 Tbl plus 1½ tsp)
  unflavored gelatine
⅔ cup fresh orange juice
Thin peel of ½ lemon
½ recipe (about 1 cup) Basic
  Custard Cream (page 176)

2 large avocados
Juice of 1 lime
¼ cup honey
2 Tbl light rum
½ cup heavy cream, whipped
2 egg whites, stiffly beaten

Soften the gelatine in the orange juice and add the mixture, along with the lemon peel, to the prepared hot custard cream. Stir to dissolve the gelatine. Let the cream cool completely, and remove and discard the peel. Peel the avocados, remove the pits, and force the pulp through a sieve or ricer into a mixing bowl. Add the lime juice, honey, and rum, and beat to a smooth paste. Blend the cooled custard cream into the avocado paste, and fold in the whipped cream and beaten egg whites. Spread the mixture in a 6-cup mold, rinsed in ice-cold water and drained. Chill in the refrigerator until the Bavarian cream is set. Unmold it onto a chilled serving platter to be apportioned for 6 to 8 servings. Sprinkle the molded cream, if desired, with finely chopped pistachio nuts.

Chocolate Bavarian Cream Pie

½ recipe Plain Pastry (page 134)
½ recipe Basic Custard Cream
   (page 176)
¾ cup grated semisweet chocolate
   (about 3 ounces)

1 envelope (1 Tbl) unflavored
   gelatine
¼ cup cool, strong-brewed coffee
1 cup heavy cream, whipped
2 egg whites

Roll out the pastry to a thickness of about ⅛-inch and with it line a 9-inch pie pan. Crimp the edges. Bake the shell as directed for Lemon Meringue Pie (page 116) and let it cool in the pan.

    Prepare the custard cream as directed in the recipe, and during the last 2 or 3 minutes of cooking add the chocolate, stirring until it melts. Remove the pan from the heat. Soften the gelatine in the coffee and dissolve in the custard. Let the custard cool completely and chill it in the refrigerator until it just begins to gel. Do not let it become set. Immediately fold into it the whipped cream and the egg whites, beaten until stiff but not dry. Spread the Bavarian cream in the cooled pie shell. Chill again in the refrigerator for 2 hours, or until the filling is completely set. Spread the top, if desired, with whipped cream and decorate it with chocolate curls. This pie provides 6 to 8 servings.

Coconut Bavarian Cream

2 cups milk
½ cup shredded coconut
½ recipe Basic Custard Cream
   (page 176)
1 envelope (1 Tbl) unflavored
   gelatine

¼ cup cool water
2 cups heavy cream, whipped
2 egg whites
⅓ cup toasted shredded coconut

Scald the milk in a saucepan. Add the ½ cup coconut and let it steep until the milk cools. Strain the milk through several thicknesses of cheesecloth into a bowl, squeezing the coconut to press out as much of the milk as possible. Discard the coconut. Use the coconut milk to prepare the custard cream. While the cream is still hot dissolve in it the gelatine softened in the water. Let the cream cool and chill it in the refrigerator just until it begins to gel. Fold in ½ the whipped cream and all of the egg whites, beaten until stiff but not dry. Spread the Bavarian cream evenly in two 8-inch cake pans that have been rinsed in ice-cold water and drained. Set the pans in the refrigerator and let them remain until the cream is thoroughly set.

Unmold one of the cream layers onto a chilled serving platter. Coat the layer with ½ the remaining whipped cream and unmold the other layer over it. Coat the top and sides with the remaining whipped cream and sprinkle them with the toasted coconut. Chill until serving time. Cut the layered Bavarian cream to provide 6 servings.

Molded Ginger Cream

½ recipe Basic Custard Cream
  (page 176)
2 envelopes (2 Tbl) unflavored
  gelatine
½ cup cool water

3 Tbl finely chopped preserved
  ginger
¼ cup syrup from preserved ginger
1 tsp vanilla extract
2 cups heavy cream, whipped

Use the custard cream hot and dissolve in it the gelatine softened in the water. Stir in the ginger, syrup, and vanilla, and let the custard cool completely. Set the pan in a bowl of cracked ice and stir the custard until it begins to gel. Do not let it set. Immediately fold in the whipped cream. Rinse a 6-cup mold with ice-cold water and drain it well. Pour in the ginger cream and chill it in the refrigerator for 2 hours or until it is set. Unmold onto a chilled serving platter to provide 6 servings.

Coffee Spanish Cream

1 recipe Basic Custard Cream
  (page 176)
1 envelope (1 Tbl) unflavored
  gelatine
¼ cup cool water
½ cup milk

2 Tbl instant coffee powder
¼ tsp pure almond extract
2 egg whites
2 Tbl sugar
Whipped cream

Prepare the custard cream as directed in the recipe, reducing the egg yolks to 2. Soften the gelatine in the water and dissolve it in the hot custard. Stir in the milk, coffee powder, and flavoring. Let custard cool completely. In a mixing bowl beat the egg whites to the soft-peak stage. Add the sugar and continue beating until the egg whites are stiff. Fold them into the cooled custard. Pour the mixture into a 1-quart mold rinsed in ice-cold water and drained. Chill the cream in the refrigerator for 2 hours, or until it is completely set. Unmold it onto a chilled serving platter. Apportion for 4 to 6 servings, with a topping of whipped cream.

Coffee Jelly

3 envelopes (3 Tbl) unflavored
   gelatine
5½ cups strong-brewed coffee

3 Tbl sugar
½ tsp vanilla extract, or 1 tsp anise
   liqueur

Soften the gelatine in ½ cup of the cool coffee. Heat the remaining coffee in a saucepan and dissolve the sugar and softened gelatine in it. Let the coffee cool and stir into it the vanilla or liqueur. Pour the liquid into a 6-cup mold, rinsed in ice-cold water and drained. Chill in the refrigerator for 3 hours or until the jelly is completely set. Apportion for 6 to 8 servings, and serve with whipped cream, if desired. *(See photograph, page 187.)*

Mocha Jelly

¼ cup instant coffee powder
3 cups boiling-hot water
⅓ cup sugar
⅛ tsp salt
1 envelope (1 Tbl) unflavored
   gelatine

¼ cup cool water
¼ cup crème de cacao liqueur
Whipped cream, slightly sweetened

In a mixing bowl dissolve the coffee powder in the hot water. Stir in the sugar and the salt. Soften the gelatine in the cool water and dissolve it in the hot coffee. Add the liqueur. Cool the mixture and chill it in the refrigerator until it gels. Apportion the jelly among 6 stemmed glasses and serve with slightly sweetened, very cold whipped cream.

Rote Grütze | Molded Red Fruit Jelly

1 pint fresh raspberries
1 pint fresh red currants
3 cups light, dry red wine
¾ cup cool water
1 cup sugar, or to taste
2-inch length thin lemon peel

2-inch length thin orange peel
1 envelope (1 Tbl) unflavored
 gelatine
1 egg white
Vanilla Sauce (page 287)

Pick over the berries, wash and drain them, and combine them in a saucepan with the wine, ½ cup of the water, the sugar, and the citrus peels. Set the pan over medium heat and cook the mixture at a slow boil for 10 minutes, or until the berries are cooked apart. Remove and discard the peels, and strain the berry mixture through a fine sieve. You should have about 5 cups of juice. If it is less than that, replenish with red port wine. Return the juice to the saucepan and cook it over low heat for 5 minutes or until the juice is clear. Soften the gelatine in the remaining cool water and dissolve it in the hot juice. Cool the juice and chill it in the refrigerator until it gels. Do not let it become firm. Fold into it the egg white, stiffly beaten, and transfer the mixture to a 6-cup mold rinsed in ice-cold water and thoroughly drained. Continue chilling until the jelly is firm. Unmold it onto a chilled serving platter to be apportioned for 6 to 8 servings with vanilla sauce.

Molded Honey Walnut Meringue

1 cup honey
¾ cup cool water
⅓ cup sugar
2 squares (2 ounces) unsweetened
   chocolate, shaved
1 envelope (1 Tbl) unflavored
   gelatine

3 egg whites
½ tsp vanilla extract
1 cup finely chopped walnuts
1¼ cups heavy cream, whipped

In a saucepan combine the honey, ½ cup of the water, the sugar, and the chocolate, and cook the mixture over medium heat until a small bit of it dripped from the spoon into a cup of cool water forms a soft ball (238 degrees on a candy thermometer). Remove the pan from the heat. Soften the gelatine in the remaining ¼ cup cool water and dissolve in the syrup. Pour the syrup in a thin stream into the egg whites, stiffly beaten in a mixing bowl, beating constantly until the syrup is completely incorporated. Stir in the vanilla and the chopped nuts, and let the meringue cool. Fold in the whipped cream. Spread the mixture in an 8-cup mold rinsed in ice-cold water and drained, and chill it in the refrigerator until it is completely set. Unmold the meringue cream onto a chilled serving platter and, if desired, decorate with rosettes of whipped cream piped from a pastry bag. This provides 8 servings.

Wine Jelly

1 envelope (1 Tbl) unflavored
   gelatine
1 bottle Sauternes (slightly more
   than 3 cups)

1 cup Simple Syrup (page 278)
2 Tbl yellow Chartreuse

In the top pan of a double boiler soften the gelatine in ½ cup of the wine. Set the pan over hot water and let it remain until the gelatine dissolves. Remove the pan from over the water and let the dissolved gelatine cool somewhat. In a glass bowl combine the remaining wine, the syrup, and Chartreuse, and stir in the gelatine. Chill the mixture until it gels. Apportion the jelly among 6 chilled sherbet glasses for serving.

Coffee Jelly (page 184) served
as a mold and in parfait glasses, embellished
with whipped cream and coffee beans.

Champagne Jelly:

Substitute dry champagne for the Sauternes. (Note that champagne designated as "dry" is actually quite sweet.) Omit the Chartreuse and add 2 tablespoons cognac.

Gelée à la Russe:

Chill the wine-gelatine mixture (of either Sauternes or champagne) until it just begins to gel. Do not let it become firm. Beat it lightly with a fork and pour it into a 1-quart mold rinsed with ice-cold water and drained. Chill until firm. Unmold onto a chilled serving platter.

If you like, the Gelée à la Russe can be embellished with a ring of Green Grape Mousse, prepared as follows: Finely chop 1 cup seedless green grapes and force them through a sieve. Discard the skins. Or, reduce the grapes whole in an electric blender and strain out any remaining skins. In a mixing bowl blend into the purée 1 tablespoon Simple Syrup (page 278) and 1 teaspoon dissolved gelatine. Chill the mixture until it just begins to gel and is not firm. Fold in ½ cup whipped cream. Pipe the mousse around the unmolded Gelée à la Russe from a pastry bag fitted with a plain tube. Chill until firm.

Mousses

It is said that too many cooks spoil the mousse . . . by adding egg white. Agreed. Mousse should contain little more than egg yolk, whipped cream, sugar, and flavoring. If you encounter a little egg white in some of the recipes which follow, or even all egg white and no egg yolk at all, make light of it—as it is intended to do for the mousse.

Almond Pear Mousse

1½ envelopes (1½ Tbl) unflavored gelatine	2 Tbl pear brandy
⅓ cup cool water	1 tsp vanilla extract
2 egg yolks	2 Tbl sliced almonds, toasted
⅓ cup sugar	2 cups heavy cream, whipped
	3 Poached Pears (page 243)

Soften the gelatine in the water in the top pan of a double boiler. Set

Riz Malta (page 197), enhanced by orange
segments, strawberry, and orange apricot sauce,
with Blanc Mange (page 201) in background.

the pan over simmering water and let it remain until the gelatine dissolves. Remove the pan from over the water and let the gelatine cool somewhat. In a mixing bowl beat together the egg yolks and sugar until the mixture is very thick. Stir into it the dissolved gelatine, the pear brandy, and vanilla. Blend in the almonds and fold in the whipped cream. Cut the pears lengthwise each into 4 slices and arrange them decoratively in the flat bottom of a 6-cup chilled and lightly oiled mold. Pour the mousse over them and chill it in the refrigerator for 2 hours or until it is set. Unmold it onto a chilled serving dish, carefully so as not to dislodge the pears, to be apportioned for 6 servings.

Cheese Mousse

½ cup finely chopped or grated Munster cheese

⅓ cup cream cheese

3 eggs, separated

Grated rind of 1 lemon

Juice of 1 lemon

2 Tbl full-bodied rum

1½ envelopes (1½ Tbl) unflavored gelatine

⅓ cup cool water

2 cups heavy cream, whipped

1 cup confectioners' sugar

Force both cheeses together through a sieve into a mixing bowl and work to a smooth paste with the egg yolks, lemon rind and juice, and the rum. Soften the gelatine in the water in the top pan of a double boiler and dissolve it over hot water. Stir the dissolved gelatine into the cheese mixture. Let the paste cool and stir into it 1 cup of the whipped cream. Fold in the remainder. Partially whip the egg whites. Add the sugar, a little at a time, and continue beating until the whites are stiff. Fold them into the cheese mixture. Spread in a 6-cup mold rinsed in ice-cold water and drained. Chill the mixture in the refrigerator for 2 hours, or until it is completely set. Unmold it onto a chilled serving platter to be apportioned for 6 to 8 servings.

Lemon Mousse

8 large lumps sugar

⅔ cup cool water

4 lemons
2 Tbl dry white wine
1½ envelopes (1½ Tbl) unflavored
   gelatine

1 cup sugar
8 egg yolks
¼ tsp salt
2 cups heavy cream, whipped

Rub the lumps of sugar into the lemon rind until they are well moistened with the lemon oil. Squeeze the juice of the lemons into a saucepan and combine with it the wine and lemon sugar. Heat the mixture gently to dissolve the sugar. Soften the gelatine in ⅓ cup of the water and dissolve it in the hot lemon liquid. In another saucepan combine the sugar and the remaining water, and cook the resulting syrup over medium heat until a couple of drops of it form a soft ball in a bowl of cold water (238 degrees on a candy thermometer). In a mixing bowl stir the egg yolks with the salt and, beating constantly, gradually add the prepared hot syrup, pouring it in a thin stream. Combine the still-warm lemon syrup and the egg yolks. Cool the mixture completely. Fold in the whipped cream. Pour the mousse into a 2-quart mold rinsed in ice-cold water and drained, and chill it in the refrigerator for 2 hours, or until it is completely set. Unmold the mousse onto a chilled serving platter to be apportioned for 6 to 8 servings.

Lime Mousse with Orange Ice-Cream Sauce

1 envelope (1 Tbl) unflavored
   gelatine
1 cup Simple Syrup (page 278)
3 egg yolks
¾ cup lime juice

Green food coloring
2 cups heavy cream, whipped
Orange Ice-Cream Sauce
   (see below)

Soften the gelatine in the syrup in the top pan of a double boiler. Set the pan over simmering water and heat the syrup just until the gelatine dissolves. In a mixing bowl beat the egg yolks until they are light. Add the syrup with the dissolved gelatine, pouring in gradually while beating constantly. Let the mixture cool, and stir into it the lime juice and 1 or 2 drops of the coloring. Fold in the whipped cream. Spread the mixture in a 6-cup mold rinsed in ice-cold water and drained. Chill the mousse in the refrigerator for 2 hours, or until it is completely set.

Unmold it onto a chilled serving platter to be apportioned for 6 servings with Orange Ice-Cream Sauce.

Orange Ice-Cream Sauce:

1 cup Vanilla Ice Cream (page 160)   **2 Tbl Grand Marnier liqueur**
Grated rind of 1 orange

In a mixing bowl soften the ice cream to the consistency of lightly whipped heavy cream and stir into it the orange rind and liqueur. Transfer the sauce to a proper dish for serving.

Maple Mousse

1 recipe Basic Custard Cream   **⅓ cup cool water**
  (page 176)   **½ cup ground filberts**
¾ cup maple sugar   **1½ cups heavy cream, whipped**
1½ envelopes (1½ Tbl) unflavored   **2 egg whites**
  gelatine

Prepare custard cream as directed in the recipe, substituting the maple sugar for the granulated. Soften the gelatine in the water and dissolve it in the hot custard. Stir in the nuts and let the mixture cool completely. Fold in the whipped cream and the egg whites, stiffly beaten. Spread mixture in a 6-cup mold rinsed in ice-cold water and drained. Chill the mousse in the refrigerator for 2 hours, or until it is completely set. Unmold it onto a chilled serving platter to be apportioned for 6 to 8 servings with, if desired, Mocha Sauce (page 286).

Marron Mousse

Contents of 1 9-ounce bottle mar-   **¼ cup cool water**
  rons in vanilla syrup   **⅛ teaspoon salt**
1 envelope (1 Tbl) unflavored   **¼ cup cognac**
  gelatine   **1 cup heavy cream, whipped**

Into a saucepan strain the syrup from the marrons to remove any bits of vanilla bean. Heat the syrup but do not let it boil. Soften the gelatine in the water, seasoned with the salt, and dissolve it in the heated syrup. Force the marrons through a fine sieve into the syrup along with the cognac, or reduce the marrons to a purée in an electric blender, adding the cognac to facilitate the blending. Blend the purée thoroughly into the syrup. Let the mixture cool and fold into it the whipped cream. Pour the mixture into a 1-quart mold rinsed in ice-cold water and drained. Chill it in the refrigerator for 2 hours, or until it is set. Unmold the mousse onto a chilled serving platter to be apportioned for 4 to 6 servings.

Strawberry Mousse

3 pints strawberries
1 cup Simple Syrup (page 278)
1½ envelopes (1½ Tbl) unflavored
   gelatine

⅓ cup cool water
1 cup heavy cream, whipped
2 egg whites
¼ cup sugar

Hull and wash the berries and force them through a sieve or purée them in an electric blender. In a mixing bowl stir the syrup into the purée. In the top pan of a double boiler soften the gelatine in the water. Set the pan over hot water and let it remain until the gelatine dissolves. Stir the dissolved gelatine into the purée. Let the mixture cool and fold into it the whipped cream. In a mixing bowl beat the egg whites to the soft-peak stage. Add the sugar a little at a time, continuing to beat until the whites are stiff. Fold them into the purée. Pour the mixture into a 6-cup mold rinsed in ice-cold water and drained. Chill the mousse in the refrigerator for 2 hours, or until it is set. Unmold it onto a chilled serving platter to be apportioned for 6 to 8 servings.

Mincemeat Mousse

3 egg yolks
½ cup sugar
1 envelope (1 Tbl) gelatine
¼ cup cool water
1 cup mincemeat

2 cups heavy cream, sweetened to
   taste & whipped
1 9-inch layer Sponge Cake (page
   14), about ½-inch thick

In a mixing bowl beat the egg yolks with the sugar until they are very thick. In the top pan of a double boiler soften the gelatine in the water. Set the pan over hot water to dissolve the gelatine. Stir the dissolved gelatine into the egg yolks. Let the mixture cool and stir the mincemeat into it. Fold in the whipped cream. Spread the mixture in a 6-cup mold rinsed in ice-cold water and drained. Trim the cake to fit the mold and place it over the mousse mixture. Reserve the trimmings and reduce them to crumbs. Cover the mold with foil or plastic wrap and chill the mixture in the refrigerator for 2 hours, or until it is completely set. Unmold it onto a chilled serving platter, carefully so as not to dislodge the base of cake. Sprinkle the mousse with the cake crumbs and cut it, as for a cake, to provide 6 to 8 servings. Serve, if desired, with Vanilla Sauce (page 287), additionally flavored with 2 tablespoons cognac.

Tangerine Mousse

8 tangerines, peeled
1½ envelopes (1½ Tbl) unflavored
   gelatine
½ cup sugar

1 Tbl cognac
5 egg whites
2 cups heavy cream, whipped

Separate the tangerines into segments and force them through a food mill to extract the juice. Discard the pulp. In a saucepan soften the gelatine in the tangerine juice and heat it gently until the gelatine dissolves. Stir in the sugar and let the juice cool. Add the cognac. In a mixing bowl beat the egg whites until they are stiff but not dry. Fold into the cooled juice a part at a time, alternating with portions of the whipped cream. Spread the mixture in a 2-quart mold rinsed in ice-cold water and drained. Chill the mousse in the refrigerator for 2 hours or until it is set. Unmold the mousse onto a chilled serving platter to be apportioned for 8 servings with, if desired, an accompaniment of Sauce Laura (page 284).

Wine Raspberry Mousse

1 pint fresh raspberries
1½ cups dry white wine
¾ cup sugar
1½ envelopes (1½ Tbl) unflavored
   gelatine

⅓ cup cool water
1 cup heavy cream, whipped

Wash and drain the berries. In a saucepan heat together the wine and sugar. Add the berries and cook them over medium heat for 1 minute. Drain the berries and set them aside. Return the hot syrup to the pan and in it dissolve the gelatine softened in the water. Let the mixture cool completely and fold the whipped cream into it. Gently fold in the berries. Spread the mixture in a 1-quart mold rinsed in ice-cold water and drained. Chill for 2 hours, or until the mixture is set. Unmold the mousse onto a chilled serving platter to be apportioned for 4 to 6 servings.

Chilled Chocolate-Cinnamon Soufflé

1 recipe Basic Custard Cream
  (page 176)

4 squares (4 ounces) semisweet
  chocolate, shaved

2 squares (2 ounces) unsweetened
  chocolate, shaved

½ tsp cinnamon

1 envelope (1 Tbl) unflavored
  gelatine

¼ cup cool water

½ tsp vanilla extract

1½ cups heavy cream, whipped

4 egg whites

Prepare custard cream as directed in the recipe and, during the last 2 or 3 minutes of cooking, add the chocolate and cinnamon, stirring until the chocolate melts and is blended into the cream. Soften the gelatine in the water and dissolve it in the hot custard. Add the vanilla. Let the mixture cool completely and chill it in the refrigerator just until it begins to gel. Do not let it become set. Immediately fold into it the whipped cream and the egg whites, stiffly beaten.

Increase the height of a 6-cup (1½ quart) soufflé dish by tying a 4-inch-wide, heavy waxed-paper collar around the rim. Pour in the soufflé mixture and chill it in the refrigerator for 2 hours, or until it is completely firm. Remove the paper collar before serving the soufflé to provide 8 servings. Decorate the soufflé, if desired, with pipings of whipped cream sprinkled with grated chocolate.

Burnt-Almond Sponge

1½ cups sugar

1¼ cups milk

¼ tsp salt

1 envelope (1Tbl) unflavored
  gelatine

¼ cup cool water

1 tsp vanilla extract

¾ cup slivered blanched almonds,
  darkly toasted

1½ cups heavy cream, whipped

Reserve ⅓ cup of the sugar. Melt the remainder in a skillet over low heat until the resulting syrup turns dark amber, stirring only until the sugar melts. In a saucepan scald the milk and stir into it the remaining sugar and the salt. Add the sugar syrup, pouring it in very gradually and stirring constantly until it is completely incorporated. The syrup may harden as it is added, but will ultimately dissolve as the mixture is stirred. Soften the gelatine in the water and dissolve it in the still-hot milk. Cool the mixture, add to it the vanilla, and chill it in the refrigerator until it gels but is not firm. Remove the pan from the refrigerator and beat the mixture with a rotary beater until it becomes spongy. Whisk in the almonds and fold in the whipped cream. Chill briefly before apportioning the sponge among 6 sherbet glasses for serving.

Riz Malta

⅔ cup long-grain rice
2 cups milk
1½ envelopes (1½ Tbl) unflavored
   gelatine
⅓ cup cool water
Juice of 1 orange
Shredded thin peel of 1 orange

½ cup coarsely chopped candied
   orange peel
1 Tbl orange-flavored liqueur
2 cups heavy cream, whipped
Peeled orange segments
Orange Apricot Sauce
   (see below)

In a covered saucepan over low heat cook the rice in the milk for 30 minutes, or until the milk is absorbed and the grains are tender. Soften the gelatine in the water in the top pan of a double boiler. Set the pan over hot water and let it remain until the gelatine dissolves. Stir it into the rice with the orange juice, fresh and candied orange peel, and liqueur. Let the mixture cool completely and fold in the whipped cream. Transfer to a 6-cup mold rinsed with ice-cold water and drained. Chill the mixture in the refrigerator for 2 hours, or until it is completely firm. Unmold it onto a chilled serving platter and decorate with the orange segments. Serve the Riz Malta apportioned for 8 servings with the Orange Apricot Sauce. *(See photograph, page 188.)*

Orange Apricot Sauce:

¾ cup Apricot Glaze (page 70)
1½ cups orange juice

3 Tbl shredded orange peel
3 Tbl orange-flavored liqueur

Dilute the glaze with the orange juice and stir in the orange peel and liqueur.

9 | puddings and custards

In colonial Virginia, which may well have been the birthplace of American *haute cuisine,* dessert was served as the first course, and the most favored dessert was pudding. By this time, of course, pudding had been considerably refined from its original form: a casing laden with seasoned, chopped meat and dough—or some such filling—and boiled to a sodden mass. Even so, for some reason pudding suddenly fell from popularity and ultimately was banished from the table altogether. "Too heavy," people said, with new-found concern for their figures. "Puddings," in fact, came to be the not-too-complimentary term for over-plump children.

This about-face was most unfair, since puddings *can* be light. If not as light as gossamer spun sugar or thistle-down meringue, certainly pudding can be as delicate as the silken custard which is its frequent companion. It is time that pudding was restored, not perhaps to its former order of service, but surely to a place of honor at table. Wherefore we present these recipes.

Quick Apple Pudding

3 tart cooking apples	¾ cup flour
1 cup sugar	1 tsp baking powder
1 egg	¼ tsp salt
½ cup milk	1 Tbl butter, melted

Preheat oven to 375 degrees. Peel, core, and chop the apples, and sprinkle them with the sugar. In a mixing bowl beat together the egg and milk, and blend in the flour sifted with the baking powder and salt. Add the melted butter and thoroughly fold in the apples. Pour the batter in a buttered 8-inch square baking pan and bake in the preheated oven for 20 minutes, or until the pudding is firm and nicely browned. Apportion the pudding to provide 4 to 6 servings with liquid heavy cream or, if desired, Hard Sauce (page 283).

Apple Brown Betty

6 medium cooking apples	1 tsp cinnamon, or ¼ tsp nutmeg
2 cups soft bread crumbs, preferably of raisin bread	¼ tsp salt
	⅓ cup water
½ cup light brown sugar	1 Tbl orange-flower water
¼ cup granulated sugar	3 Tbl firm butter, cut in small pieces
½ tsp grated orange rind	Vanilla Sauce (page 287)

Preheat oven to 375 degrees. Peel and core the apples, and cut them into thin slices. In a mixing bowl combine the bread crumbs (including raisins, if such bread is used), brown and granulated sugar, orange rind, cinnamon (or nutmeg), and salt. Butter a deep, 6-cup baking dish and spread ⅓ of the bread-crumb mixture over the bottom. Cover with ½ the apple slices. Combine the water and orange-flower water and pour ½ the liquid over the apples. Sift over them another ⅓ of the bread crumbs and sprinkle with ½ the pieces of butter. Continue with a layer of the remaining apples, moistened with the remaining liquid, the remaining bread crumbs, and the remaining bits of butter. Bake, covered, in the preheated oven for 30 minutes. Remove the cover and continue the baking for 15 minutes longer or until the apples are soft but not mushy and the bread crumbs are browned and crisp. Serve warm or cooled, apportioned for 6 servings, with the vanilla sauce passed separately.

Allemande Pudding

20 slices white bread, trimmed	¼ tsp cinnamon
1¼ cups dry white wine	6 eggs
½ cup dark brown sugar	Orange Apricot Sauce (page 197)

Preheat oven to 350 degrees. Tear the bread into small pieces, place them in a mixing bowl, and pour the wine over them. Turn the pieces frequently, so that they absorb the wine uniformly. Reduce the softened bread to a paste by forcing it through a sieve or a ricer into the bowl again. Blend into it the sugar and cinnamon, and thoroughly beat in 2 whole eggs and 4 egg yolks. In a separate bowl beat the 4 egg whites until they are stiff but not dry, and fold them into the bread mixture also. Spread the mixture in a buttered 6-inch-diameter soufflé dish and bake in the preheated oven for 1 hour, or until the pudding is well puffed and browned. Let it cool completely before unmolding it onto a serving platter to provide 6 servings. Serve with the sauce.

Blanc Mange

¼ cup cornstarch	2⅓ cups milk
⅓ cup Vanilla Sugar (page 70)	2 egg whites, stiffly beaten
⅛ tsp salt	

In the top pan of a double boiler combine the cornstarch, vanilla sugar, and salt. Add ⅓ cup of the milk and stir to dissolve the dry ingredients. Scald the remaining milk and stir it in gradually. Set the pan over simmering water and cook, stirring constantly until the mixture thickens. Cover the pan and continue cooking for 15 minutes or until the mixture no longer tastes starchy. Stir occasionally. Remove the pan from over the water and let the mixture cool partially. Fold in the beaten egg

whites and transfer the pudding to a mold rinsed in ice-cold water and drained. Chill in the refrigerator until the pudding is firm. Unmold it onto a chilled serving platter and apportion it to provide 6 servings with, as desired, fresh berries, stewed fruit, or a sauce of choice. *(See photograph, 188.)*

Bread Pudding

6 slices slightly dry white bread	**¼ tsp salt**
½ cup butter	**2 eggs, separated**
2 cups milk	**½ tsp vanilla extract**
½ cup sugar	**¼ cup confectioners' sugar**

Preheat oven to 350 degrees. In a skillet, lightly brown the slices of bread on both sides in as much butter as needed. Arrange the slices in a 1-quart baking dish. Scald the milk and dissolve in it the sugar and salt. Let it cool, and beat in the egg yolks. Stir in the vanilla. Pour the mixture over the bread in the baking dish and bake in the preheated oven for 45 minutes. Remove the dish from the oven and spread the pudding with the egg whites stiffly beaten with the confectioners' sugar. Increase the oven heat to 400 degrees, and when that temperature has been reached return the dish to the oven and let the meringue brown. Serve warm or cooled with, if desired, light cream. This pudding provides 4 to 6 servings.

Chocolate Bread Pudding: Blend into the scalded milk 1½ squares (1½ ounces) unsweetened chocolate, and proceed as recipe directs.

Cherry Macaroon Pudding

18 small macaroons

3 eggs, separated

1 cup semisweet light white wine,
     such as Rhine wine

¼ cup sugar

1 layer Sponge Cake (page 14)

1 cup pitted red cherries

2 Tbl currant jelly

Preheat oven to 325 degrees. Break the macaroons into small pieces and distribute ½ of them over the bottom of a buttered 6-cup baking dish. In a saucepan over low heat beat together the egg yolks, wine, and sugar to produce a thick frothy custard. Do not let it boil. Spread ¼ of this custard over the macaroon bits in the baking dish. Split the cake into 2 layers and trim them to fit the baking dish. Place 1 layer over the layer of custard and sprinkle it with the cherries. Complete the filling with, in order, a second quarter of the custard, the second layer of cake, a third quarter of the custard, and the remaining bits of macaroon and the final part of custard. Bake in the preheated oven for 30 minutes. Remove the pan from the oven and increase the heat to 400 degrees. Beat the egg whites until they are stiff and blend into them the currant jelly. Spread this meringue over the contents of the baking dish and continue the baking at the increased temperature for 10 minutes, or until the meringue is golden brown. Cool the pudding before apportioning it to provide 6 servings.

Sa-Nwin-Ma-Kin | Burmese Coconut Pudding

4 cups milk

1¼ cups water

⅛ tsp salt

⅔ cup shredded coconut

1⅓ cups semolina

⅔ cup sugar

¼ cup butter

2 egg whites

⅓ cup raisins

Almonds (or sesame seeds or
     poppyseeds)

Preheat oven to 300 degrees. In a saucepan cook together at simmer for 10 minutes the milk, water, salt, and coconut. Strain the liquid into a mixing bowl through several thicknesses of cheesecloth, pressing the coconut to extract as much of the liquid as possible. Discard the coconut. Blend into the liquid the semolina and sugar and let the mixture cool for 30 minutes. Return the pan to the heat and bring the mixture to a boil. Add the butter and fold in the egg whites, beaten until frothy but not stiff. Stir the mixture constantly, always in the same direction, until it is quite thick. Do not let it stiffen. Stir in the raisins and transfer the mixture to a buttered 2-quart baking dish. Sprinkle the top with a few crushed almonds or with sesame seeds or poppyseeds. Bake in the preheated oven for 1 hour or until the top is well browned. Cool the pudding at room temperature overnight. Cut it into slices to provide 8 to 10 servings.

Date Meringue Pudding

1 cup chopped walnuts
1 cup chopped pitted dates
2 cups sugar
1 tsp flour
1 tsp baking powder
3 egg whites
Whipped cream

Preheat oven to 300 degrees. In a mixing bowl combine the nuts, dates, and 1⅔ cups of the sugar sifted with the flour and baking powder. Beat the egg whites to the soft-peak stage. Add the remaining sugar, a little at a time, continuing to beat until the whites are stiff. Fold them into the prepared mixture. Spread the batter evenly in a buttered, 8-inch square baking pan and bake in the preheated oven for 45 minutes, or until the pudding is firm. Serve cooled, with whipped cream, to provide 4 to 6 servings.

Baked Indian Pudding

1 quart milk
½ cup sugar
½ cup yellow cornmeal
3 eggs, slightly beaten
1 tsp grated orange rind
½ tsp cinnamon
1 tsp ginger
1 tsp salt
1 cup dark molasses
Vanilla Ice Cream (page 160)

Preheat oven to 450 degrees. In a saucepan scald the milk. Add ¼ cup sugar. Add the cornmeal gradually, cooking the mixture over low heat and stirring it constantly until it is thick and smooth. Vigorously beat in the eggs, a little at a time. Combine and add to the cornmeal mixture the grated rind, cinnamon, ginger, salt, molasses, and remaining sugar. Stir to blend. Spread the batter evenly in a buttered 8-inch square baking pan and cover it with a square of buttered foil. Immerse the pan in water poured to a depth of ½-inch in a larger pan, and bake the pudding so in the preheated oven for 1 hour. Serve the pudding hot, apportioned to provide 6 servings with accompaniments of vanilla ice cream.

A Pudding with Lemon Bread

¼ cup butter	¼ cup milk
1 cup sugar	Juice of 1 lemon
4 eggs	¾ cup heavy cream
Grated rind of ½ lemon	¼ cup milk
¾ cup flour	¼ tsp orange extract
1 tsp baking powder	⅛ tsp nutmeg
⅛ tsp salt	Heavy cream, liquid or whipped
2 Tbl finely chopped almonds	

Preheat oven to 350 degrees. In a mixing bowl thoroughly cream together the butter and ½ cup of the sugar. Vigorously beat in 1 of the eggs and the lemon rind. Sift the flour with the baking powder and salt, and stir it into the creamed mixture, a little at a time, along with the almonds, alternating those additions with small quantities of the milk. Butter a 7 x 3½ x 2-inch loaf pan, cover the bottom with waxed paper, and butter the paper. Transfer the prepared batter to the pan and bake it in the preheated oven for 45 minutes or until a cake tester inserted in the center of the loaf can be withdrawn clean. In a saucepan heat together the lemon juice and ¼ cup of the sugar, stirring until the sugar dissolves. Remove the loaf pan from the oven and brush the bread with the lemon syrup, continuing until all of the syrup has been absorbed. Let the loaf cool in the pan. Remove it and cut it into slices ½-inch thick. Reduce oven heat to 300 degrees.

Arrange ½ the bread slices in a buttered, 9-inch, deep pie pan. In a mixing bowl beat together the remaining eggs, the cream, milk, orange flavoring, and nutmeg. Add the remaining ¼ cup of sugar and stir until it dissolves. Pour ½ the mixture over the bread slices in the pie pan. Cover with the remaining slices and pour the remaining egg mixture over them. Bake in the oven at the reduced heat for 30 minutes or until a table knife inserted in the center of the custard can be withdrawn clean. Serve warm or cooled, with liquid or whipped cream.

Pashka | Russian Easter Pudding

4 egg yolks	**1 tsp vanilla extract**
1 cup sugar	**¾ cup chopped blanched almonds**
1 cup heavy cream	**¾ cup seedless raisins, chopped**
3 cups dry pot cheese	**½ cup chopped mixed glazed fruit**
1 cup butter, softened	**Jelly eggs (jelly beans),**
¼ cup sour cream	**for decorating**

In the top pan of a double boiler beat together the egg yolks, sugar, and heavy cream. Set the pan over simmering water and cook the mixture, stirring constantly, until it thickly coats the spoon. Remove the pan from over the water and let the custard cool completely. Force the pot cheese through a sieve into a mixing bowl, and beat into it the softened butter, the sour cream, and the vanilla. Stir in the nuts and the fruit, and blend in the cooled custard.

Traditionally the mixture is molded into a pyramid shape in a pashka mold. If such a container is not available, line a large flower pot (one with a hole in the center of the bottom) with a heavy cloth and pack the cheese mixture into it. The flower pot may be overfilled. It will settle as the mixture drains. Fold the overhang of the cloth over the filling, and set the pot in the refrigerator on a rack fitted over a shallow baking pan. Place a small chopping board or a saucer on top of the filling and weight it heavily. Let the pashka drain for 24 hours. Unmold it onto a chilled serving platter and decorate with a cross of little jelly eggs pressed into 1 side. A pashka this size provides about 8 servings.

Mansion Fruit Pudding

1 recipe Sponge Cake (page 14)
⅓ cup cognac
1 recipe Pastry Cream (page 58)
2 Poached Pears (page 243)
1 cup drained & pitted canned
   black cherries
2 drained canned figs

1 or 2 slices drained
   canned pineapple
6 large fresh strawberries,
   hulled & washed
2 drained canned greengage plums
1 cup (double recipe) Apricot
   Glaze (page 70)

Prepare the cake batter as directed in the recipe and bake it in two 9-inch cake pans at the temperature and for the length of time indicated. Cool the layers, sprinkle them equally with the cognac, and arrange them as a 2-layer cake thickly filled with the pastry cream. Arrange the fruits randomly over the top and pour over them the apricot glaze, coating the pieces well and allowing some of the glaze to flow down over the sides of the sponge layers. Chill the pudding and serve it, apportioning cake, filling, and fruit to provide 8 servings with, if desired, lightly sweetened whipped cream.

NOTE: Mansion Fruit Pudding is pictured on the covering jacket of this volume.

Plum Pudding

1 cup seedless raisins
1 cup currants
½ cup diced citron
2 cups bread crumbs
1 cup chopped suet
1 cup molasses
1 cup sugar
1 cup flour

1 tsp cinnamon
1 tsp nutmeg
1 tsp ground cloves
1 tsp salt
3 eggs, well beaten
1 tsp baking soda
1 cup milk
½ cup cognac

Prepare the pudding well in advance of the day it is to be served. Traditionalists consider one year in advance to be about right. However, a few days may be sufficient.

In a mixing bowl combine the fruit, bread crumbs, suet, molasses, and sugar, and blend into the mixture the flour sifted with the spices and salt. Stir in the beaten eggs and the soda, dissolved in the milk. Transfer the mixture to a buttered, 2-quart pudding mold and cover it securely. Set the mold on a rack in a deep pot and pour in enough boiling-hot water to immerse the mold halfway. Cover the pot, set it over low heat, and let the pudding steam for 4 hours. Replenish the water as needed to maintain the depth. Unmold the pudding, wrap it in foil, and store it in the refrigerator until needed. Before serving it, steam the pudding again for 1 hour, or until it is heated through. Place it on a heat-proof serving platter. Gently heat the cognac, set it ablaze, and pour it over the pudding. Cut the pudding to provide 8 to 10 servings with accompaniments of Hard Sauce (page 283) or Foamy Sauce (page 278).

Heavenly Rice Pudding

⅔ cup currants

¼ cup orange juice

1 tsp lemon juice

⅓ cup rice

2½ cups light cream

¼ tsp salt

2 Tbl butter

1 tsp grated orange rind

3 eggs, separated

½ cup sugar

In a glass bowl steep the currants in the citrus juices for several hours. Combine the rice, cream, and salt in the top pan of a double boiler and cook over simmering water, stirring frequently, for 1½ hours or until the grains of rice are soft. Remove the pan from over the water and stir in the butter and orange rind. Add the currants, along with any remaining juice. Let the rice mixture cool. Add the egg yolks 1 at a time, beating each in vigorously. In a bowl beat the egg whites until they begin to stiffen. Add the sugar, ⅓ at a time, continuing to beat until the whites are stiff. Fold them into the rice mixture. Spread the mixture in a 6-cup baking dish and bake in a preheated 325-degree oven for 45 minutes, or until the top of the pudding is delicately browned. Cool the pudding, chill it, and apportion it to provide 6 servings with, if desired, whipped cream.

Raisin Pudding

1 cup sifted flour	1 cup firmly packed brown sugar
2 tsp baking powder	1¾ cups water
1 cup sugar	1 Tbl butter
½ cup milk	2 Tbl lemon juice
1 cup seedless raisins	1 Tbl grated lemon rind

Preheat oven to 350 degrees. Into a mixing bowl sift together the flour, baking powder, and sugar. Stir in the milk and blend in the raisins. Spread the mixture in a buttered, 9-inch cake pan. In a saucepan over low heat dissolve the brown sugar in the water. Add the butter and, when it melts, remove the pan from the heat. Stir in the lemon juice and rind. Pour this syrup over the mixture in the pan and bake in the preheated oven for 50 minutes, or until the pudding is puffed and nicely browned. This recipe provides 6 servings to be accompanied, if desired, with whipped cream.

Almond Rice

1 cup heavy cream	2 cups cold, cooked rice
¼ cup fine granulated sugar	Cherry liqueur
⅔ cup slivered & toasted blanched almonds	

In a mixing bowl stiffly whip the cream with the granulated sugar. In another bowl stir the almonds into the rice, and fold in the whipped cream. Chill the rice thoroughly and apportion it among sherbet glasses to provide 6 to 8 servings; pour a little cherry liqueur over each.

Shaker Christmas Pudding

2 pounds raisins	4 cups flour
4 cups white wine	1½ tsp salt
12 eggs, separated	1 tsp mace

½ cup maple syrup   1 Tbl cinnamon
2 cups milk   1 Tbl ginger
1 pound suet, finely chopped

In a glass bowl plump the raisins overnight in 2 cups of the wine. In a mixing bowl beat together the egg yolks, maple syrup, and milk. Add the suet and the raisins, along with any remaining liquid. Blend in the flour sifted with the salt and spices, and fold in the egg whites, stiffly beaten. Thoroughly dampen a pudding bag and coat it well with flour. Fill it with the pudding mixture and tie loosely but sufficiently to keep the contents entirely enclosed. If the pudding is too tightly enclosed it may burst the bag as the mixture expands during cooking. Place the bag on a rack in a deep pan and pour around it the remaining wine and enough water to immerse the bag completely. Cook the pudding at a slow boil for 3 hours, replenishing the water as it evaporates. If preferred, the pudding may simply be steamed in the remaining wine, adding water as needed. Unmold the pudding hot onto a serving dish and apportion to provide 10 to 12 servings with, as desired, Hard Sauce (page 283) or Foamy Sauce (page 278).

Tapioca Cream Pudding

¼ cup pearl tapioca

Warm water

2 cups milk

⅓ cup sugar

¼ tsp salt

2 eggs, separated

1 tsp vanilla extract

½ cup heavy cream, whipped

In a bowl cover the tapioca with warm water and let it soak for 1 hour. Drain the tapioca and combine it in the top pan of a double boiler with the milk. Set the pan over simmering water and cook until the tapioca is clear. Add ½ the sugar and the salt and stir to dissolve them. In a small bowl beat the egg yolks with the remaining sugar, and add gradually just enough of the hot tapioca mixture to heat the yolks through, beating constantly. Blend the heated yolks into the remaining tapioca mixture, continuing to stir until the custard thickens. Remove the pan from over the water and add the vanilla. Let the custard cool completely and fold into it the whipped cream and the egg whites, stiffly beaten. Chill the pudding and apportion it to provide 4 to 6 servings in chilled sherbet glasses.

Washday Pudding

¾ cup blueberries, or other
   fruit, chopped

3 Tbl sugar

¼ tsp cinnamon

2 eggs

1½ cups milk

1½ cups flour

1½ tsp baking powder

½ tsp salt

2 Tbl butter

Preheat oven to 325 degrees. Pick over the berries, and wash and drain them. In the bottom of each of 6 buttered custard cups place 2 tablespoons of the berries and sprinkle them with sugar, using 1½ tablespoons of sugar in all, and with the cinnamon. In a mixing bowl beat the eggs with the milk. Sift the flour with the baking powder and salt and blend in. Fill each of the cups ¾ full with the batter and bake in the preheated oven until a cake tester inserted in the center of the puddings can be withdrawn clean. Unmold the puddings for individual servings and place 1 teaspoon of the butter on each. Serve the puddings hot with, if desired, light cream to be added to individual preferences.

Boiled Custard

4 egg yolks	2 cups milk, scalded
⅓ cup sugar	1 tsp vanilla extract (see Note)
⅛ tsp salt	

In the top pan of a double boiler beat together the egg yolks, sugar, and salt. Add the hot milk gradually, pouring it in a thin stream and stirring constantly. Set the pan over simmering water and cook the mixture, stirring it constantly until it coats the spoon. Despite the name, a "boiled custard" should never be boiled. Serve it cooled, with the flavoring added, and chilled. This recipe provides about 2½ cups of custard.

NOTE: The custard may be flavored alternatively with 1 tablespoon of rum or sweet sherry, or by scalding the milk with a 2-inch strip of thin lemon peel. Remove the peel before continuing with the preparation.

Crème Caramel

1½ cups sugar	1 tsp vanilla extract
½ cup water	3 cups milk, scalded
7 eggs	

Preheat oven to 350 degrees. In a skillet over low heat cook ½ the sugar with the water until the resulting syrup turns amber in color. Butter 6 ¾-cup-capacity ramekins and pour an equal amount of the syrup into each. In a mixing bowl beat together eggs, remaining sugar, and vanilla. Blend the hot milk into them very slowly, beating constantly. Strain the custard into the ramekins. Bake in a pan of hot water in the preheated oven for 20 minutes, or until a table knife inserted in the center of the custard can be withdrawn clean. Run a sharp knife around the edges of the custards and unmold them onto individual plates for serving. Serve cooled or chilled.

Caramel Custard

¾ cup sugar

3 cups milk, scalded

6 egg yolks

¼ tsp salt

1 tsp vanilla extract

Whipped cream

Preheat oven to 350 degrees. In a skillet over low heat melt ½ cup of the sugar and let it caramelize. Add the hot milk, stirring it in very gradually until the caramel and milk are thoroughly combined. In a mixing bowl beat the egg yolks with the salt, the remaining sugar, and the vanilla. Add enough of the hot caramel milk to heat the egg yolks and then combine the 2 mixtures. Pour into a buttered ring mold and bake in a pan of hot water in the preheated oven for 1 hour, or until a table knife inserted in the center of the custard can be withdrawn clean. Cool the custard, unmold it onto a chilled serving platter, and chill it thoroughly. Fill the center with whipped cream. This custard provides 6 servings.

Orange Nut Flan

1¾ cups sugar

½ cup water

1 cup chopped toasted almonds

4 cups light cream

1 Tbl vanilla extract

8 whole eggs

3 egg yolks

½ cup orange juice

Preheat oven to 350 degrees. In a skillet over low heat cook together 1 cup of the sugar and the water until the resulting syrup caramelizes lightly. Blend in the almonds and remove the pan from the heat. Butter 8 ¾-cup-capacity ramekins and coat them evenly with the caramel-nut mixture. Let them cool.

In a saucepan over medium heat reduce 2 cups of the cream to ½ their volume. Remove the pan from the heat and stir in the remaining cream and the vanilla. Let the mixture cool. In a mixing bowl thoroughly beat together the whole eggs, yolks, orange juice, and the remaining sugar. Blend in the cream. Pour it all equally into the prepared molds. Bake in a pan of hot water in the preheated oven for 30 minutes, or until a table knife inserted in the center of the custards can be withdrawn clean. Unmold the custards onto individual serving plates and chill until ready to serve. If the caramel-and-nut layer in the cups hardens excessively, soften by returning cups to the pan of hot water for a few moments.

Raspberry Custard

5 egg yolks
3 Tbl sugar
1½ cups milk, scalded &
   cooled to lukewarm

2 Tbl sweet sherry
6 Tbl seedless raspberry
   preserves
Whipped cream

Preheat oven to 325 degrees. In a mixing bowl beat the egg yolks and sugar together, and add the milk gradually. Pour the mixture in equal portions into 6 small, buttered soufflé molds. Bake in a pan of hot water in the preheated oven for 30 minutes, or until the custards are set. Float a teaspoon of sherry over each and place a tablespoon of the raspberry preserves on top. Decorate the rim of the custards each with a garland of tiny whipped cream rosettes piped from a pastry bag fitted with a very small star tube.

Crème Brûlée | Broiled Cream

2 recipes (double quantity)
   Basic Custard Cream (page 176)

1 tsp vanilla extract
Dry light brown sugar, sifted

Flavor the custard cream with the vanilla. Pour equal amounts of the cream into 6 shallow, heat-proof dishes for individual servings. Cool and chill the custard cream until the surface is firm. Sift light brown sugar over the surface of each portion of cream, covering it completely with a layer about ⅛-inch thick. Set the dishes on a baking sheet under a hot broiler and let them remain just long enough to caramelize the sugar. Turn the dishes frequently, so that the sugar browns evenly and does not burn. Let the creams cool at room temperature and chill them briefly in the refrigerator. As the caramel coating of the cream cools it becomes brittle. If chilled too long, it will melt.

Chestnut Custard

2 recipes (double quantity)
  Boiled Custard (page 213)

1 recipe Sweet Chestnut Purée
  (page 68)

While it is still warm stir the double recipe of the custard into the purée a little at a time. Pour the mixture into a serving bowl and cool and chill it. Serve, if desired, with chilled whipped cream. This quantity of chestnut custard is sufficient for 8 servings.

Phirni | India Custard

1 cup cream of rice
4 cups milk, scalded
¼ cup ground cardamom
¼ cup sugar

1 tsp rosewater
Pistachios
Slivered blanched almonds

In a saucepan over low heat stir the cream of rice into the hot milk. Add the ground cardamom and cook the mixture, stirring frequently, for 30 minutes. Add the sugar and continue cooking and stirring until the granules dissolve and the phirni is smooth and thick. Stir in the rosewater. Transfer the custard to a serving bowl to be apportioned in 4 to 6 servings. Sprinkle with pistachios and almonds and serve warm or chilled.

Blueberry Grunt

1 pint blueberries
½ cup brown sugar
½ cup water
¼ tsp cinnamon
¼ tsp ginger
1 cup flour

1½ tsp baking powder
½ tsp salt
1 Tbl butter, melted
⅓ cup milk
Additional butter
Heavy cream

Pick over and wash and drain the berries. Combine them in a saucepan with the brown sugar, water, and spices, and cook them very gently. Sift together into a mixing bowl the flour, baking powder, and salt, and

stir in the butter and milk, just until the mixtures are blended. Drop the batter by generous teaspoons onto the berries and cover the pan. Let the dumplings cook so, continuously covered, for 20 minutes. Remove the dumplings with a slotted spoon, and arrange them on a warmed serving platter. Make a slit in each, using 2 forks, and drop a bit of butter into each opening. Pour the berries around the dumplings. Apportion the blueberry grunt to provide 6 servings; provide heavy cream to pour over them.

Viennese Cheese Dumplings

¾ cup butter
5 egg yolks
2 cups farmer cheese

¼ tsp salt
⅔ cup coarse dry bread crumbs
Stewed fruit (plums, cherries,

1½ cups farina

6 egg whites, stiffly beaten

In a mixing bowl soften ½ the butter and work into it the egg yolks, cheese, and farina. Stir in ¼ of the egg whites and fold in the remainder. Let the batter rest for 30 minutes. Drop tablespoons of it into lightly salted simmering water and cook, covered, for 12 to 15 minutes, or just until the dumplings are firm. Sauté the bread crumbs in the remaining butter until they are well browned and crisp. Drain the dumplings and roll them in the crumbs. Apportion them to provide 6 to 8 servings, accompanied by the stewed fruit.

Avocado Cream

3 avocados, peeled & pitted

¼ cup lime juice

1 Tbl confectioners' sugar

¼ cup light rum

½ cup heavy cream, whipped

Mash the avocados in a bowl and sprinkle them with the lime juice. Force them through a sieve or purée them in an electric blender. If prepared in the blender, take care, since the pulp liquefies very quickly. Stir in the sugar and rum, and fold in the whipped cream. Transfer the avocado cream to a glass or china serving bowl, cover it tightly with waxed paper or plastic wrap, and chill it briefly. Serve the cream in sherbet glasses to provide 6 to 8 servings. The cream should not be made too far in advance. Avocado pulp oxidizes and discolors rather quickly.

Coeur à la Crème

2 cups creamed cottage cheese

1 Tbl sugar

⅛ tsp salt

1 cup heavy cream

Fresh strawberries

In a mixing bowl combine the cheese, sugar, and salt, and beat the mixture with a rotary beater until it is very smooth. Beat in the cream, a little at a time. Line a heart-shaped basket (see Note) with several thicknesses of cheesecloth and spread the prepared mixture evenly in it. Set the basket on a cake rack over a plate in the refrigerator and let the cream drain overnight. Unmold the cream onto a chilled serving plate and decorate the plate with small whole strawberries. This quantity of coeur à la crème provides 4 to 6 servings.

NOTE: Heart-shaped baskets traditionally used for this preparation are available at specialty housewares shops. The cream may also be drained in a sieve lined with cheesecloth.

Oeufs à la Neige | Snow Eggs

2 recipes (double quantity)
   Basic Custard Cream (page 176)
1 tsp vanilla extract

4 egg whites
½ cup confectioners' sugar
Caramel Glaze (page 71)

Flavor the custard cream with the vanilla and pour it into a shallow 6-cup-capacity glass bowl. In a mixing bowl partially beat the egg whites. Add the sugar, a little at a time, continuing the beating until the whites are stiff. Using 2 soup spoons, dipped frequently into cold water, shape the egg white to resemble large eggs. Poach the shaped "eggs" in barely simmering water for 2 to 3 minutes, turning them just once. Drain the eggs in a slotted spoon and arrange them in the bowl of custard cream. Decorate each egg with a spiral of caramel glaze, dripped in a thin stream from a teaspoon. Apportion the eggs to provide 6 servings, each with a generous quantity of the custard cream.

Prune Whip

2 cups cooked prune pulp
2 Tbl orange juice
1 tsp lemon juice
1 tsp grated orange rind

3 egg whites
⅛ tsp salt
2 Tbl sugar

In a mixing bowl combine the prune pulp, citrus juices, and rind. In a separate bowl beat the egg whites with the salt to soft-peak stage. Add the sugar and continue beating until the whites are stiff. Fold them into the prune mixture. Transfer lightly to a serving bowl and chill thoroughly before serving with, if desired, Custard Sauce (page 282). This quantity of prune whip is sufficient for 6 servings.

Syllabub

½ cup fine granulated sugar, or to taste	Strained juice of 1½ lemons
1 cup medium-dry white wine	Grated rind of 1½ lemons
½ cup medium-dry sherry	2 cups heavy cream, whipped

In a pitcher dissolve the sugar in the wines, lemon juice, and rind combined. Chill the mixture in the refrigerator overnight. Strain the wine mixture into the whipped cream in a serving bowl, stirring in the liquid gradually. Chill the syllabub for 1 hour before serving it in chilled sherbet glasses to provide 6 servings.

Trifle

½ recipe (1 layer) Sponge Cake (page 14)	2 Tbl cognac
Strawberry (or seedless raspberry) preserves	2 recipes (double quantity) Boiled Custard (page 213)
⅓ cup sweet sherry	1 cup heavy cream, whipped
	Slivered toasted blanched almonds

Bake the cake in an 8-inch pan at the temperature indicated in the recipe for 40 minutes, or until a cake tester inserted in the center of the cake can be withdrawn clean. Cool the cake as directed and split it into 2 layers. Spread them with a thin coating of preserves and reassemble them with the filling enclosed. Cut the 2 together into small squares and arrange them in a glass serving bowl. Sprinkle the squares with just enough of the combined sherry and cognac to moisten them; they should not be drenched. Strain the prepared custard over them. Chill in the refrigerator for 3 hours, or until the custard is set. Using a pastry bag, pipe the whipped cream in a decorative layer over the custard and stud it with the almonds. Serve the trifle from the bowl to provide 6 to 8 servings.

10|fruit desserts

The most versatile of all dessert ingredients surely must be fruit. It can be served uncooked and unadorned as a complete dessert, unsurpassed for sheer beauty and aesthetic satisfaction. It can be cooked simply and so be made to render up its inherent flavor and aroma. Together with other foods, it permits piquant and surprising marriages of flavor, as when apples are baked with a filling of Roquefort cheese, bananas intriguingly masked with chocolate, or melon perfumed with green Chartreuse. Arranged in the style of a della Robbia composition, fruit becomes an artistic as well as a gastronomic delight.

Along with its versatility, fruit has the advantage of ready availability. It is at hand, in one variety or another, almost everywhere in every season. The following desserts spotlight the fruits themselves. You will find other ways to use fruits among the recipes for cakes, pies, frozen desserts, and sauces. Such classics as Strawberry Shortcake, Blueberry Pie, and Lemon Ice illuminate still further the glorious possibilities of fruit.

Baked Apples

6 medium McIntosh (or Jonathan)
  apples
¾ cup brown (or maple) sugar
Cinnamon

Freshly grated nutmeg
6 Tbl butter
Additional sugar

Preheat oven to 375 degrees. Core the apples through the stem end to within ½-inch of the bottom. Do not pierce the blossom end. Peel a band around the top of each apple about 1 inch wide. Arrange the apples in a baking dish and fill each cavity with 2 tablespoons of sugar, $\frac{1}{16}$ teaspoon each of cinnamon and nutmeg, and 1 tablespoon butter. Pour hot water around the apples to a depth of about 1 inch and bake them in the preheated oven for 30 minutes, or until they are soft. Sprinkle them with a little additional sugar and continue the baking for a few minutes longer, until the sugar melts and glazes the apples. Serve the apples warm, 1 to a serving, with, if desired, Vanilla Ice Cream (page 160); or serve them cooled or chilled, plain or with a sauce.

Variations:

Augment the filling for the apples with finely chopped preserved ginger, raisins, nuts, chopped dates or figs, or currant jelly, singly or in combination.

Ginger Apple Betty

½ cup butter
4 cups soft bread crumbs
6 apples, peeled, cored & diced
  (about 4 cups)
1 cup sugar

¼ cup preserved ginger, finely
  chopped
¼ tsp salt
2 tsp preserved ginger syrup
Heavy cream

Preheat oven to 375 degrees. In a skillet over moderate heat melt the butter and in it sauté the crumbs until they are lightly browned and crisp. Sprinkle ½ of them over the bottom of a baking dish, and spread over them the apples, sugar, ginger, salt, and syrup combined. Cover them with the remaining crumbs. Bake, covered, in the preheated oven for 30 minutes, or until the apples are tender. Remove the cover and continue the baking for 10 minutes longer, or until the crumb topping is well browned. Serve warm with cream. This recipe makes 6 servings.

Apple Crunch

6 medium-size tart apples	**½ cup butter**
1 cup flour	**Freshly grated nutmeg**
½ cup sugar	

Preheat oven to 375 degrees. Peel, core, and cut the apples into thin slices. Arrange them in even layers in a buttered baking dish. In a mixing bowl work the combined flour and sugar into the butter to produce a smooth, soft paste, and spread it over the apples. Grate a little nutmeg over the top. Bake in the preheated oven for 30 minutes, or until the topping is crunchily crisp. Serve hot with, as desired, Hard Sauce (page 283) or whipped cream.

Apple Fritters with Vanilla Sauce

2¼ cups flour	**6 apples**
2 Tbl sugar	**Fat for deep frying**
¼ tsp salt	**Additional flour**
1 cup light beer	**Cinnamon Sugar (page 70)**
4 egg whites	**Vanilla Sauce (page 287)**

Into a mixing bowl sift the flour with the sugar and salt. Stir in the beer, blending it in well. Fold in the egg whites, stiffly beaten, and let the batter rest in a warm place for several hours before using it.

Peel and core the apples, and cut them into thick, round slices. In a fryer or deep saucepan heat fat for deep frying to 375 degrees. Dredge the apples in the flour and coat them with the batter. Fry them in the heated fat—as many at a time as the pan can accommodate—for 8 minutes, or until they are golden brown. Drain them on absorbent paper. While they are still hot, roll them in cinnamon sugar and serve them with vanilla sauce. This quantity is sufficient for 8 servings.

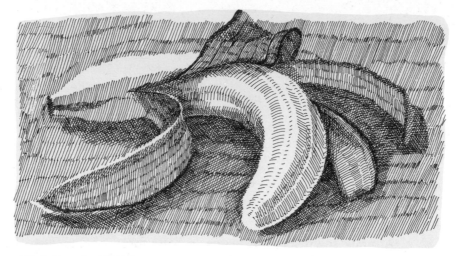

Icy Hot Apple Meringue

12 Ladyfingers (page 24)	**3 egg whites**
4 cups Applesauce (page 227), very cold	**3 Tbl confectioners' sugar**

Preheat oven to 450 degrees. Butter the bottom and sides of a shallow baking dish and line the dish completely with ladyfingers split into halves. Pour in the ice-cold applesauce. In a mixing bowl beat the egg whites to soft-peak consistency. Add the sugar, 1 tablespoon at a time, continuing to beat until the whites are very stiff. Spread the meringue over the applesauce and ladyfingers, covering them completely, right to the edges of the dish. Bake in the preheated oven for 5 minutes, or just until the meringue is lightly browned. Serve immediately, apportioned for 6 to 8 servings.

Roquefort-Filled Baked Apples

6 medium-size firm tart apples	**4 ounces Roquefort cheese**
4 Tbl butter	**¼ cup ground walnuts**
4 Tbl sugar	**1 Tbl cognac**

Preheat oven to 375 degrees. Wash the apples, dry them well, and peel them about 1 inch down from the stem end. Scoop out the cores, leaving a cavity in each apple about 1 inch in diameter cut to within 1 inch of the bottom. Coat the peeled surfaces of the apples each with 1 teaspoon of the butter and 2 teaspoons of the sugar. Arrange the apples in a baking pan and pour hot water around them to a depth of about ¼-inch. Cover the pan and bake in the preheated oven for 30 minutes or until the apples are tender. Cool the apples slightly. In a mixing bowl work to a smooth paste the remaining butter, the cheese, walnuts, and cognac, and fill the apples equally with the mixture. Serve the apples while they are still warm. This recipe provides 6 servings.

Pommes Normande

6 sweet apples
4 Tbl butter
½ cup sugar
¼ cup Cinnamon Sugar (page 70)

⅓ cup Calvados (French apple
  brandy)
Whipped cream

Peel, core, and slice the apples, and pat the slices dry on sheets of paper toweling. In a skillet melt the butter over moderate heat. Add the apples and cook them until they begin to take on a little color. Sprinkle the sugar over them. Turn the slices—carefully, so as not to break them—coating them well with the sugar. When the sugar has melted, sprinkle the apples with the cinnamon sugar. Cover the pan and let the apples cook gently for a few moments, until they are tender. Reserve 1 tablespoon of the Calvados. Gently warm the remainder in a small saucepan and set it ablaze. Pour it over the apples and shake the pan until the flame subsides. Serve the apples hot, apportioned for 6 servings, with chilled whipped cream flavored with the reserved apple brandy.

Applesauce

8 tart cooking apples
1 cup water
¼ tsp salt

Sugar to taste
¼ tsp cinnamon or freshly
  ground nutmeg

Wash the apples, cut them into quarters, and core them. Combine them in a saucepan with the water and salt. Cook them covered, over low heat, until they are soft, 20 to 30 minutes. Purée the apples by forcing them through a food mill back into the saucepan. Discard the skins. Add sugar to taste and the spice, and stir over low heat until the sugar dissolves. Serve the applesauce warm or cooled. This quantity is sufficient for 6 servings.

Spun-Silk Apples

3 apples
1 cup flour
½ cup water
1 egg

Vegetable oil for deep frying
¾ cup sugar
⅓ cup water

Peel the apples, core them, and cut them into wedges about ½-inch thick. In a mixing bowl beat together the flour, water, and egg to produce a smooth batter. Dip the apple wedges in the batter, coating them thinly but completely. Reserve 1 tablespoon of oil. Heat the remainder in a fryer or deep saucepan to 375 degrees, and in it fry the apple wedges a few at a time until they are crisp and brown. Arrange the apples in a single layer on a warmed serving platter.

In a saucepan combine the sugar, the ⅓ cup of water, and the reserved oil. Bring the liquid to a boil and cook the resulting syrup to the hard-ball stage (250 degrees on a candy thermometer). Pour the syrup over the apple wedges in the platter and serve at once. Place a bowl of ice-cold water (with ice) in the center of the table. Each guest serves himself, using his table fork (or chopsticks) to immerse a syrup-coated wedge of apple in the cold water. The syrup will immediately become brittle and form silk-like threads. This recipe provides 6 servings of still-warm apple with a chilled brittle coating, a classic Chinese dessert.

Apple Soufflé

6–8 McIntosh apples (see Note)
Lemon juice
2 cups Applesauce (page 227)

½ tsp cinnamon
2 Tbl Calvados (French apple
   brandy) or applejack

1½ tsp cornstarch 3 egg whites
¼ cup cool water

Preheat oven to 350 degrees. Cut a thick slice from the top of each apple. Scoop out the pulp of the apples, leaving shells about ⅜-inch thick. Sprinkle the shells with lemon juice to retard discoloring and set them aside for the moment. In a saucepan cook the applesauce over moderate heat, stirring frequently, until it is reduced to 1 cup. Dissolve cornstarch in the water and add with the cinnamon. Continue cooking and stirring for a few moments longer to thicken the sauce a little more. Remove the pan from the heat and let the sauce cool completely. Stir in the Calvados. Fold in the egg whites, stiffly beaten, and fill the prepared apples with the mixture. Bake in the preheated oven for 25 minutes, or until the filling is well puffed and lightly browned. Serve the dessert hot, 1 filled apple to a serving.
NOTE: Use the pulp scooped from the apples to prepare applesauce for future use. It is insufficient for this recipe.

Chocolate-Coated Baked Bananas

6 firm ripe bananas 2 Tbl cognac
2 Tbl butter 6 squares (6 ounces) semisweet
2 Tbl brown sugar   chocolate
1 tsp grated lemon rind ⅓ cup strong-brewed coffee
1 tsp grated orange rind Whipped cream

Preheat oven to 350 degrees. Peel the bananas and pierce them in several places with the tines of a fork. In a mixing bowl thoroughly combine the butter, brown sugar, and the grated lemon and orange rind. Coat the bananas equally with the mixture and seal each in an 8 x 12-inch sheet of foil. Set the wrapped bananas on a lightly buttered baking sheet and bake in the preheated oven for 15 minutes. Remove the bananas from the oven and open the wrappings, leaving the fruit still partially enclosed. In a small saucepan gently heat the cognac, set it ablaze, and pour equal amounts over the bananas. Let the bananas cool in the foil. Drain and unwrap them, and pat them dry with paper toweling. Chill them well.

In the top pan of a double boiler over simmering water melt the chocolate with the coffee. Arrange the bananas on a cake rack over a sheet of waxed paper (to catch the chocolate drippings) and pour the melted chocolate over them. If the bananas are properly chilled the chocolate will begin to harden almost immediately. Chill the bananas to harden the chocolate completely. Serve them on 6 individual serving plates and, using a pastry bag fitted with a star tube, pipe a fluted border of the whipped cream around the base of each.

Bananas Flambées

6 firm ripe bananas	**2 Tbl orange juice**
¼ cup butter, softened	**1 Tbl grated orange rind**
½ cup brown sugar	**⅓ cup dark rum**

Preheat oven to 400 degrees. Peel the bananas and coat them equally with the butter, brown sugar, orange juice and rind, creamed together. Wrap the bananas separately in buttered foil and arrange them on a lightly buttered baking sheet. Bake in the preheated oven for 15 minutes. Unwrap the bananas, reserving the cooking liquid. Place each on a heat-proof serving dish. In a saucepan combine cooking liquid and rum and heat the mixture very gently (too much heat will vaporize the alcohol and there will be no flame). Set the warmed mixture ablaze and pour a little of it over each banana. Serve flaming, 1 to a serving.

Fresh Blueberries with Lemon Ice

1 pint fresh blueberries	**2 tsp lemon juice**
1 cup fresh raspberries	**⅛ tsp salt**
3 Tbl sugar	**6 scoops Lemon Ice (page 162)**

Pick over and wash the blueberries and apportion them among 6 sherbet glasses. Wash the raspberries and force them through a sieve. You should have about ¾ cup of purée. Sweeten the purée in a mixing bowl with the sugar, and stir in the lemon juice and salt. Place a scoop of lemon ice in each glass. Mask each of the 6 servings of berries and ice with the prepared purée.

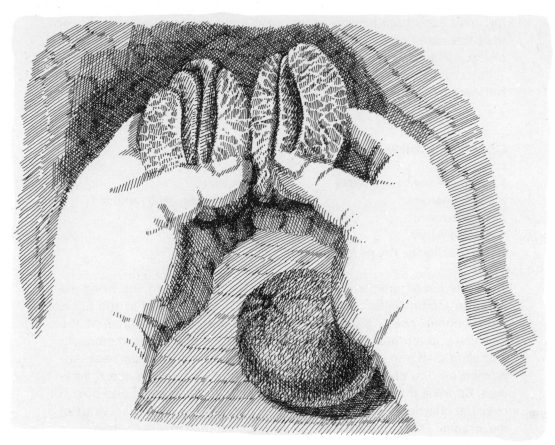

Citrus Fruit in Syrup

6 large navel oranges
   (or 3 medium grapefruit)
1 cup sugar
½ cup water

2 Tbl cognac (or rum,
   orange-flavored liqueur,
   or crème de menthe)

Cut enough of the fruit zest (the tissue-thin peel, free of white pulp) into needle-thin shreds to provide 2 tablespoons. Completely pare the fruit, separate the segments, and peel them. In a saucepan over very low heat cook together the sugar, water, and prepared shreds of zest until the resulting syrup thickens somewhat. Stir in the desired spirit or liqueur and add the fruit segments. Let the fruit cool in the syrup. Transfer it to a serving bowl, pour the syrup over it, and chill it in the refrigerator. This quantity of fruit and syrup provides 6 servings.

Cherries Jubilee

1 1-pound, 4-ounce can pitted
  black cherries
1 Tbl cornstarch
1 Tbl cool water
1 quart Vanilla Ice Cream (page
  160)

2 tsp sugar
¼ cup cognac, gently warmed
  in a small pan

Drain the juice from the canned cherries into a saucepan and bring the liquid to a boil. Dissolve the cornstarch in the water, add to the juice, and continue cooking until the juice thickens and is clear. Add the cherries and let them heat through. Transfer the cherries and sauce to a chafing-dish pan at the table and keep them warm over low heat. Apportion the ice cream in heat-proof serving dishes to provide 6 servings. Sprinkle the cherries with the sugar. Ignite the cognac and pour it over the cherries. Pour the flaming fruit and sauce over the servings of ice cream. The sugar is less for sweetening than to help produce a spectacular blaze and to prolong it.

Cranberry Crisp

1 cup oatmeal flakes
½ cup flour
1 cup brown sugar

½ cup butter
2 cups cranberry sauce

Preheat oven to 350 degrees. In a mixing bowl combine the oatmeal flakes, flour, and sugar, and rub in the butter until it is completely incorporated. Butter an 8-inch square baking pan and spread ½ the prepared mixture over the bottom. Cover with the cranberry sauce, and spread it with the remaining oatmeal mixture. Bake in the preheated oven for 45 minutes, or until the topping is firm and crisp. Cut into squares to provide 6 portions and serve them hot with a sauce of choice or with Vanilla Ice Cream (page 160).

Flaming Figs

1 large can Kadota figs
1 tsp cornstarch
2 thin slices lemon

⅓ cup cognac
2 tsp sugar

Drain the syrup from the figs into a chafing-dish pan. Dissolve the corn-starch in a little of the syrup and stir the mixture into the remainder. Set the pan over gentle heat and cook the syrup, stirring constantly, until it thickens. Add the figs, lemon slices, and 2 tablespoons of the cognac, and let the figs heat through. Sprinkle them with the sugar. Warm the remaining cognac slightly in a small saucepan and set the spirit ablaze. Pour it over the figs and shake the pan to prolong the flaming. Serve the figs, apportioned for 6 servings in heat-proof dishes, with some of the still-flaming sauce poured over them.

Stewed Fruit with Lemon Rice

1½ cups water
⅓ cup sugar
Juice of 3 lemons
Grated rind of 1 lemon

⅛ tsp salt
¾ cup rice
Fruit of choice, stewed

In a saucepan combine all ingredients except rice and fruit. Bring the liquid to a boil and add the rice a little at a time, so as not to stop the boiling. Cover the pan and cook over very low heat until all of the liquid has been absorbed and the grains are tender (about 25 minutes). Rinse a ring mold with cool water and pack the rice in it. Chill it in the refrigerator thoroughly. Invert the rice ring out onto a serving platter and fill the center with the stewed fruit to provide 6 servings.

Brandied Fruit Salad

3 apples, peeled, cored & thinly
    sliced
3 pears, peeled, cored & thinly
    sliced
1 cup pitted black cherries

1 cup melon balls
    (watermelon or cantaloupe)
½ cup sugar
2 cups moderately dry white wine
½ cup cognac

Combine the prepared fruits in a large bowl and sprinkle them with the sugar. Pour over them the wine and cognac combined, and stir gently to blend. Chill this salad dessert thoroughly in the refrigerator. Serve in chilled compote dishes apportioned to provide 6 servings.

Fruit Compote

"Compote" refers specifically to cooked fruit, prepared whole or cut, singly or in combination, always in a syrup but not always flavored. The fruit may be fresh or dried (if the latter, it must be presoaked), and it may be poached or baked. It is occasionally served warm, but should, properly, be cooled. For a compote of combined fruits, the cooking time required by each should be taken into account. Raspberries, for example, should not be cooked over direct heat at all; they need only to have boiling syrup poured over them in a heat-proof bowl (as in the recipe which follows).

Syrup-Poached Fruit Compote

3 cups Simple Syrup (page 278)
1 small fresh pineapple
2 pints fresh raspberries

2 cups black currants
¼ cup kirsch

In a saucepan heat the syrup to boiling hot. Peel and core the pineapple and cut it into small cubes. There should be about 2 cups. Gently wash the raspberries and drain them. Separate the currants from the stems and wash the berries lightly. Place the pineapple in a heat-proof bowl and pour 1 cup of the boiling syrup over it. Let it cool completely. Drain off the syrup and recombine it with the remaining 2 cups in the saucepan. Reheat it. Add the currants to the pineapple and pour 2 cups of the boiling syrup over them. Again let the mixture cool. Once more drain the syrup and recombine it with the remainder. Reheat. Add the raspberries to the currants and pineapple, and pour all of the boiling hot syrup over the combined fruits. Add the kirsch and let the fruits and syrup cool completely. Drain off half the syrup and reserve it for other poaching. Chill the compote if desired. Serve the fruit with the syrup apportioned to provide 6 to 8 servings.

Quince Compote

6 medium quince	**2 cups sugar**
1 small tart apple	**1-inch length cinnamon stick**
7 cups cool water	

Thoroughly wash the quince, peel them, and cut them into halves. Core them and reserve the peel, cores, and seeds. Wash, peel, core, and dice the apple, and combine it in a saucepan with the quince halves, peels, cores, and seeds. Pour 6 cups of the water over them. Bring the liquid to a boil, cover the pan, and cook the quince at simmer for 10 minutes. In a small saucepan over low heat dissolve the sugar in the remaining water. Add the liquid and the cinnamon stick to the quince and continue cooking for 10 minutes longer or until the fruit turns pink and is tender. Remove the halves carefully and place them in a serving bowl. Strain some of the cooking liquid over them and let them cool. Chill them in the refrigerator. Serve the quince, apportioned to provide 6 servings; if desired, pour over them a little of the syrup and some liquid heavy cream.

Green Grapes with Cointreau

3 cups stemmed seedless green grapes	**¼ cup light brown sugar**
1½ cups sour cream	**¼ tsp cinnamon**
	Cointreau

Wash the grapes and drain them well. Place them in a bowl and stir into them the sour cream combined with the sugar and cinnamon. Chill in the refrigerator for at least 1 hour. Serve the grapes in the cream in sherbet glasses to provide 6 servings, with accompaniments of small individual decanters of Cointreau to be poured over the grapes.

Green Grapes in Sour Cream

2 pounds seedless green grapes (about 6 cups stemmed grapes)

¼ cup brown sugar
2 cups sour cream

Wash the grapes and remove them from the stems. Drain them well and place in a mixing bowl. Sprinkle the sugar over them, turning the grapes to coat them evenly. Let them stand for several minutes, until the sugar dissolves, and gently blend in the sour cream. Chill for several hours. Serve in sherbet glasses to provide 8 servings.

Della Robbia Fruit with Cheese

2 small bunches seedless green grapes
2 small bunches red grapes
2 small bunches purple (Concord) grapes
2 egg whites
Fine granulated sugar
4 apricots
2 russet pears

2 Golden Delicious apples
2 Red Delicious apples
Lemon juice
1 large round of cheese, about 2 pounds, at room temperature (Brie, Camembert, Gruyère, Bel Paese, Roquefort, Cheddar, etc.)
Crusty French bread
Butter

Wash the grapes and wrap them gently in paper toweling to dry them well. In a mixing bowl beat the egg whites to a froth and dip the bunches of grapes in the whites, coating them well. Shake off the excess and roll the bunches in the sugar. Arrange the grape bunches on a plate and chill them for 15 minutes in the refrigerator. Dip them again in the egg whites and once more coat them with the sugar. Chill them again thoroughly. Wash and dry the remaining fruit. Cut the pears and apples into halves and brush the cut sides with lemon juice to retard

Versatile fruit, the ultimate dessert, is used as main ingredient and flavoring or served simply alone.

discoloring. On a large circular platter, preferably one of wood, arrange the fruit around the edge, alternating the whole and halves of fruit with the now frosty-looking grapes to simulate a della Robbia design. Place the round of cheese in the center. Serve with crusty French bread and butter. This quantity of fruit and cheese provides 16 servings.

Chilled Fruit Soup

3 ripe pears
4 greengage plums
2 cups tart cherries
¼ cup blanched almonds
4 cups claret-type red wine
4 cups water

1½ cups sugar, more or less to taste
1 Tbl cornstarch
½ cup heavy cream
¼ cup sour cream

Wash the fruit. Cut the pears and plums into halves and remove the stones. Pit the cherries. Combine the fruit and nuts in a large enamel-coated or stainless-steel saucepan and pour over them the wine and water. Stir in and dissolve the sugar. Set the pan over moderate heat, cover it, and cook for 30 minutes or until the fruit is all very soft. Drain off about ¼ cup of the liquid, let it cool, and dissolve the cornstarch in it. Strain the remaining liquid into another saucepan and force the fruit pulp through the strainer. Discard the residue. Stir in the dissolved cornstarch and cook over gentle heat, stirring constantly until the fruit mixture thickens slightly. Remove the pan from the heat and let the soup cool. Chill it thoroughly in the refrigerator. Apportion the soup to provide 6 to 8 servings, each garnished with 2 tablespoons of the heavy cream and sour cream whipped together until stiff.

Grapefruit with Rum-Flavored Avocado

3 seedless grapefruit
2 medium-size ripe avocados
Juice of 1 lime

3 Tbl rum
3 Tbl confectioners' sugar

Peel the grapefruit and separate and peel the segments. Apportion the

Distinctive flavors of lemon, strawberries, macaroons, framboise, and Grand Marnier blend in Strawberries Flambées (page 247).

segments equally among 6 individual serving plates, arranging the segments in a ring slightly overlapped. Peel and pit the avocados. Mash the pulp smoothly in a bowl and blend in the lime juice, rum, and confectioners' sugar. Place equal amounts of the avocado in the center of the 6 servings of grapefruit segments and serve at once.

Melon with Green Chartreuse

3 melons (honeydew, cantaloupe,   1½ cups green Chartreuse
   cavallon, or small Spanish type)

Cut the melons into halves and remove the seeds. Pour ¼ cup of the Chartreuse into each half and chill them thoroughly. Each melon half is a serving. Do not drain them.

Ambrosia

5 navel oranges   Sugar
¼ cup light rum   ⅓ cup flaked coconut, toasted

Peel the oranges and separate and peel the segments. Arrange in a serving bowl and sprinkle the rum over them. Sprinkle them with sugar to taste. Chill the oranges in the bowl under normal refrigeration, stirring the segments gently from time to time to season and sweeten them uniformly. Sprinkle the coconut over them just before serving. Apportion to provide 6 servings.

Almond Peaches

6 peaches   ½ cup coarsely chopped
1½ cups sugar   unblanched almonds
2 cups water   Whipped cream (optional)
⅛ tsp salt   ½ tsp vanilla extract

Loosen the peel of the peaches by blanching them in boiling-hot water, then plunging them into ice-cold water. The peaches can then be peeled easily without bruising the pulp. In a saucepan combine the sugar, water, and salt, and cook over low heat until the resulting syrup thickens slightly. Add the almonds and continue cooking for 10 minutes longer. Strain out the almonds. They may, if desired, be cooled and combined with slightly sweetened whipped cream to accompany the peaches. Return the syrup to the pan, reheat it, and add the peeled peaches. Poach them in the syrup for 15 minutes. Remove the pan from the heat. Stir in the vanilla and let the peaches cool in the syrup. Chill, as desired, and serve, 1 peach to a serving, with a little of the syrup or the combined almonds and cream.

Guava Peaches

6 whole freestone peaches   **¾ cup guava jelly**
3 egg whites

Blanch the peaches briefly in boiling water, then immerse in ice-cold water. Drain them and peel them. Cut the peaches into halves and remove the stones. In a mixing bowl partially beat the egg whites. Add the jelly, a little at a time, continuing to beat until the jelly whip is stiff. Arrange the peaches in a chilled serving bowl and spread the guava whip over them. This recipe provides 6 servings.

Brandied Spiced Peaches

6 firm ripe peaches   **2 1-inch pieces stick cinnamon**
1 cup brown sugar   **2 Tbl peach liqueur**
½ cup honey   **½ cup cognac**
½ cup water
½ cup unflavored white wine
   vinegar

Blanch the peaches in boiling water for 1 minute, then immerse in ice-cold water. Drain and peel them. Cut them into halves and remove the stones. In a saucepan combine the sugar, honey, water, vinegar, and spice, and cook over moderate heat for a few moments until the sugar dissolves and the ingredients are well blended. Add the peaches and continue cooking for 10 minutes longer, basting the fruit frequently with the syrup. Remove the pan from the heat and add the liqueur and cognac. Let the peaches cool in the syrup. Chill, if desired. Serve the peaches, 1 to a serving, with a little of the syrup strained over them.

Poached Pears

Firm ripe pears   **Flavoring (see Note)**
Simple Syrup (page 278)

Peel as many pears as required, leaving the stems intact, or wash and leave them unpeeled. Arrange the pears in a saucepan large enough to accommodate them in a single layer. Heat as much syrup as required to cover the pears completely, add flavoring if desired, and pour the syrup over them. Poach the pears, uncovered, over gentle heat for 15 minutes or until they are tender but still firm. Cool them in the syrup. Core the pears, if required, when they are cool, and use as directed. NOTE: Flavor to taste with almond or vanilla extract or a liqueur.

Pears Armenonville

2 cups boiling water   **2 packages frozen raspberries,**
1 cup sugar   **thawed**
¼ cup lemon juice   **¼ cup port wine**
2 Tbl butter   **½ cup sour cream**
6 firm ripe pears   **½ cup heavy cream, whipped**

Preheat oven to 350 degrees. In a saucepan cook the water, sugar, lemon juice, and butter together over moderate heat for 5 minutes. Peel the pears, leaving the stems intact, and arrange them in a heat-proof casserole. Pour the prepared syrup over them and bake, covered, in the preheated oven for 45 minutes, or until the pears are tender. Let them cool in the syrup and drain them. Transfer them to a bowl. Force the raspberries through a sieve, or purée them in an electric blender and strain out the seeds. Stir in the port wine. Pour the purée over the pears and chill them in the refrigerator for several hours, basting them with the purée frequently. Serve the pears, 1 to a serving, with some of the purée and separate servings of the sour cream and whipped sweet cream combined.

Poached Pears with Chocolate Cream

6 firm ripe pears
3 cups Simple Syrup (1½ recipes, page 278)
½ cup syrup drained from preserved ginger

Paper-thin peel of ½ orange
1 cup heavy cream
2 squares (2 ounces) semisweet chocolate, melted & cooled
1 Tbl cognac

Peel the pears, leaving the stems intact, and place them in a saucepan large enough to accommodate them in a single layer. Pour over them the simple syrup and ginger syrup combined, and add the orange peel. The fruit should be completely immersed in the liquid. Cook them over gentle heat for 15 minutes or just until they are tender but still firm. Drain the pears and cool and chill them. Scoop out the cores through the bottoms of the pears. In a mixing bowl partially whip the cream. Add the melted and cooled chocolate and the cognac and continue beating until the cream is stiff. To serve, apportion the cream among 6 sherbet glasses and set a chilled pear upright in each.

Filled Pears Milanese

6 large firm ripe pears
¾ cup toasted blanched almonds, ground
¼ tsp almond extract

3 Tbl confectioners' sugar
4 maraschino cherries, finely chopped
½ cup medium-dry sherry

Preheat oven to 350 degrees. Wash the pears and, with a sharp knife, ream out the cores through the blossom ends. Leave the stems intact. In a saucepan, with a wooden spoon, work the almonds, flavoring, sugar, and cherries to a smooth paste. Fill the pears equally with the mixture. Arrange them in a baking dish and pour the sherry around them.

Cover the dish and bake the pears in the preheated oven for 20 minutes, or until they are tender but still firm. Serve the pears hot or cooled, 1 to a serving, with a little of the cooking liquid sprinkled over them.

Filled Pineapple

2 medium-size ripe pineapples	1 cup raspberries
1 cup ball-cut cantaloupe	1 cup blackberries
1 cup ball-cut honeydew melon	⅓ cup pear brandy

Cut off the top of each pineapple about 2 inches down from the stem; reserve top. Hollow out the inside and remove and discard the core. Dice the tender pulp and combine in a mixing bowl with the melon balls and berries, picked over, washed, and drained. Pour the pear brandy over the fruit. Cover bowl with waxed paper or plastic wrap, and let the mixed fruit chill in the refrigerator for 2 hours. Fill the prepared pineapples with the fruit and pour in the juice. Replace the tops for presentation at table. Each filled pineapple provides about 4 servings.

Purée of Prunes with Port

36 large prunes	¾ cup heavy cream, whipped
3 cups ruby port wine	2 Tbl sugar
1 cup Praline Powder (page 71)	⅛ tsp almond extract
½ cup orange juice	

Wash the prunes, drain them well, and place them in a bowl. Pour 2 cups of the port over them and let them steep in it at room temperature overnight. Transfer the prunes and all remaining wine to an enamel or stainless-steel saucepan and add the additional 1 cup of port, the praline powder, and orange juice. Cook the prunes, covered, over moderate heat for 30 minutes or until they are very soft. Cool the prunes and remove the pits. Reserve any remaining cooking liquid. Force the prunes with the liquid through a sieve or purée them in an electric blender. Chill the purée in a serving bowl in the refrigerator for several

hours or overnight. Serve the purée, apportioned for 6 servings, with the whipped cream to which the sugar and flavoring have been added.

Raspberry Whip

2 pints raspberries   **2 egg whites**
1 cup confectioners' sugar

Gently wash the berries and drain them. Force ½ of them through a sieve. Reserve the remaining berries in a bowl and sift over them ½ the sugar. In a separate bowl beat the egg whites to the consistency of lightly whipped cream. Add the remaining sugar, a little at a time, alternating those additions with small quantities of the raspberry purée and beating constantly until the mixture has almost tripled in volume. Turn the reserved whole berries gently to blend them with the sugar. Take care not to crush them. Fold them into the whipped purée. Chill the whip thoroughly and serve it in chilled sherbet cups to provide 6 servings.

Strawberries Flambées

¾ cup butter, melted & cooled
1 Tbl fine granulated sugar
2 Tbl Grand Marnier liqueur
1 Tbl lemon juice
36 large firm ripe strawberries
3 Tbl regular granulated sugar

⅓ cup framboise (see Note),
   gently warmed
⅔ cup heavy cream, whipped
2 Macaroons (page 90), dried &
   crumbled

In a mixing bowl thoroughly combine the butter, fine granulated sugar, Grand Marnier, and lemon juice. Set the mixture aside for the moment. Hull the strawberries, wash them, and drain them thoroughly. At the table in a chafing-dish pan over gentle heat melt the regular granulated sugar. Immediately add the strawberries and, holding the pan above the heat, swirl the berries around in the syrup, coating them well. Set the pan down on the heat again and stir in the butter mixture, carefully so as not to crush the berries. In a small saucepan set ablaze the warmed framboise and pour it over the berries, shaking the chafing-dish pan until the flame expires. Apportion the strawberries and sauce among 6 individual dishes and serve them with a topping of the whipped cream and a sprinkling of the macaroons. *(See photograph, page 238.)*
NOTE: Framboise, a colorless brandy, is a distillate of fresh raspberries and is available in liquor shops.

Sugar-Dipped Strawberries

3 pints firm ripe strawberries
Cointreau

Confectioners' sugar

Wash the berries lightly and drain them well. Do not remove the hulls; they must serve as handles. Apportion the strawberries to provide 6 individual servings, each with separate servings of about ¼ cup of Cointreau and a little mound of sifted confectioners' sugar. For eating, they are held by the hull, dipped first in the Cointreau, then in the sugar.

Glazed Strawberries

24 large strawberries   **⅓ cup water**
2 cups sugar   **⅛ tsp cream of tartar**

Use only firm, fresh strawberries with stems. Do not wash the berries. Clean them by rolling them gently in paper toweling. In a saucepan combine the sugar, water, and cream of tartar dissolved in a little of the water. Cook the mixture over moderate heat until the resulting syrup spins a long, brittle thread when dripped from a spoon (310 degrees on a candy thermometer). Holding the strawberries by the stems, dip them, 1 at a time and for just a split second, in the syrup. Let the excess syrup drip back into the pan. Place the coated berries on a lightly oiled baking sheet and let them cool and dry. Strawberries may be prepared in this way about 2 hours (but not much more than that) before they are to be served. They should be made only on cool, dry days. Serve the berries 4 to 6 to a serving.

Berry Glacier Flambé

1½ cups Orange Butter (page 68)   **¼ cup kirsch**
Thin whole peel of 1 lemon   **¼ cup orange juice**
⅔ cup Bar-le-Duc   **6 scoops Vanilla Ice Cream**
1 pint fresh strawberries   **(page 160)**

Prepare this at the table in a chafing dish. In the chafing-dish pan combine the butter and lemon peel. Set the pan over gentle heat and let the butter melt and become flavored with the peel. Add the Bar-le-Duc and let it reduce and caramelize slightly. Remove and discard the lemon peel. Gently stir in the berries and cook them for 2 minutes. Sprinkle a teaspoon or so of the kirsch, slightly warmed, over the berries. Set the remaining warmed kirsch ablaze and pour it over the berries. Let the flame burn out, and stir in the orange juice. Place a scoop of the ice cream in each of 6 serving dishes and pour equal quantities of the berries and sauce over each.

Stewed Rhubarb and Strawberries

3 cups washed rhubarb, cut in
   1-inch lengths
1½ cups sugar

6 Tbl water
3 cups strawberries, hulled &
   washed

In a covered saucepan, over low heat, cook the rhubarb with the sugar and water until it is tender, about 20 minutes. Add the strawberries during the final 5 minutes. Serve warm or cooled to provide 6 servings.

Fruit-Filled Watermelon

½ ripe watermelon
Pulp of 1 honeydew melon, seeded
   & diced
Pulp of 1 cantaloupe, seeded &
   diced
3 cups stemmed seedless green
   grapes, washed
2 pints strawberries, hulled,
   washed & halved

6 unpeeled apples, washed, cored
   & diced
3 firm ripe bananas, peeled &
   sliced
4 unpeeled ripe pears, washed,
   cored & diced
1 cup cognac
¼ cup granulated sugar

Hollow out the watermelon half, leaving a sturdy shell. Chill the shell thoroughly. Remove the seeds from the watermelon pulp and cut pulp into cubes. In a large bowl (you'll need one the size of a large punch bowl) combine the cubes of watermelon with all of the remaining fruit, except 1 cup of the grapes, prepared as indicated; reserve the grapes. Pour the cognac over the fruit in the bowl and stir the pieces gently. Cover the bowl and chill the fruit well. Spread the reserved grapes on a plate and sift the sugar over them; do not stir. Let them chill undisturbed in the refrigerator. At serving time heap the combined fruit in the watermelon shell and sprinkle the reserved grapes (which by then will be sugar frosted) over the top. This is a fine dessert for a buffet or outdoor party. The quantity is sufficient for 18 to 20 servings.

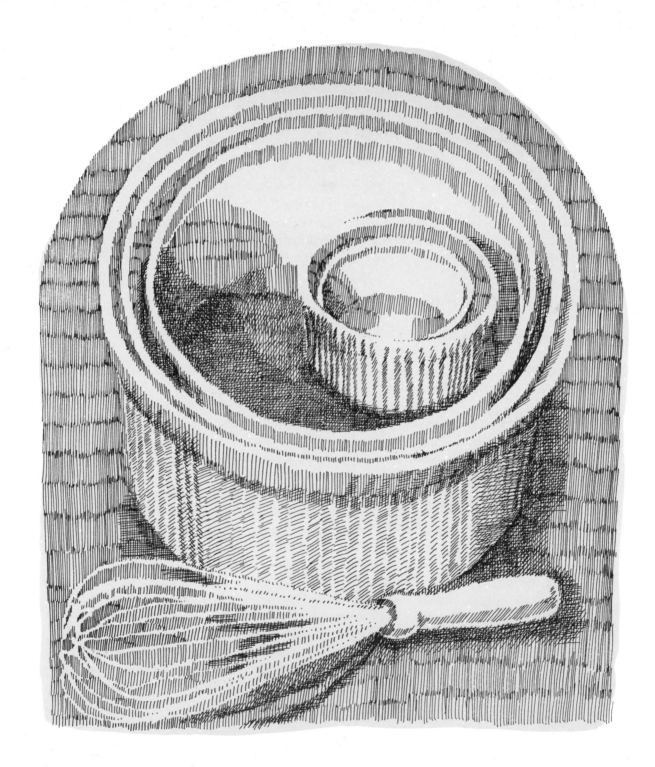

11 | soufflés and omelettes

You cannot rush the cooking of a soufflé and it is impossible to retard it, but it is possible to delay baking prepared soufflé batter, as you will see in the note appended to the recipe for Basic Dessert Soufflé on the next page. Soufflés are not quite so fragile as they are reputed to be. A cooked soufflé will not keep its airiness for very long but, still, it is not necessary to rush it to the table as if seconds counted. The sudden change of temperature caused by the speed may do as much to deflate a soufflé as an over-long delay in serving it. For a soufflé with as much height as possible, use this trick: Moisten a few bread crumbs or zwieback crumbs with cognac and distribute them over the bottom of the baking dish before you pour in the batter.

The soufflé omelette differs from the soufflé mainly in the method of cooking. Soufflé omelettes are cooked partially on top of the stove and completed in the oven. American-style omelettes (rarely served as dessert) and French-style regular omelettes have little in common except the eggs. The Gallic presentation (of which our Rum Omelette is a classic example) is stirred over the heat, cooked without browning on one side only, and rolled into a lozenge shape onto the serving plate. The American version is cooked without stirring, browned on both sides, and served pancake style.

How to Season A Skillet

Reserve a heavy aluminum or cast-iron skillet exclusively for cooking pancakes and omelettes. If it is properly "seasoned" for this use, the cooked crêpes, pancakes, and omelettes will not stick to the pan.

Scour the pan with a steel-wool soap pad, wash it with warm, soapy water, rinse it, and dry it thoroughly. Fill the pan to a depth of ½-inch with bland cooking oil (do not use olive oil). Set the pan over the lowest possible heat and let it remain until the oil begins to smoke. Properly heated, this should take at least 45 minutes. Remove the pan from the heat and let the oil cool completely. This may take several hours. Don't hurry it. Drain off the cooled oil. (Don't discard it. The oil is still usable.) Wipe the pan with paper toweling, wrap it in foil or plastic wrap. *Never wash it again!* Simply rub it clean with salt. If the pan is inadvertently washed, it may have to be seasoned again.

Basic Dessert Soufflé

4 Tbl butter
4 Tbl flour
1½ cups milk, scalded
½ cup sugar

6 egg yolks
Flavoring (see Note)
8 egg whites

Preheat oven to 375 degrees. In a saucepan melt the butter over low heat. Blend in the flour and cook this roux, without letting it take on color, for 1 minute. Gradually add the hot milk, stirring constantly, to produce a smooth sauce. Remove the pan from the heat and add ⅓ cup of the sugar, stirring until it dissolves. Beat in the egg yolks. Add the flavoring and let the sauce cool. In a mixing bowl, beat the egg whites to soft-peak consistency. Add the remaining sugar and continue to beat until the whites are stiff. Stir ¼ of them into the yolk mixture. Fold in the remainder carefully but completely. Butter a 9-cup soufflé dish and coat it lightly with sugar. Transfer the prepared batter to it and bake in a pan of hot water in the preheated oven for 30 minutes, or until the soufflé is well puffed and nicely browned. Serve at once, apportioned for 6 servings.

NOTE: Flavor the soufflé as directed in specific recipes, or as desired. Bake the soufflé in the size baking dish indicated in the specific recipe. If baked in too small a receptacle the batter will steam and ultimately fall before it is completely cooked. A soufflé cooked in a pan of hot water, as directed in the recipe above, will be soft (as this one should be); for crisper, crustier soufflés, bake without the pan of hot water. When desirable, a soufflé will rise to greater height if baked in an ungreased soufflé dish. When so baked, it is best to tie a 2- or 3-inch collar of baking liner paper or cooking parchment around the rim of the dish to prevent overflowing. Cooked soufflés should be served as soon as they are removed from the oven, but uncooked soufflé batter, with the beaten egg white already contained, can be held in the soufflé dish for about 1 hour before baking, if it is kept at room temperature and completely covered under an inverted bowl.

Dessert Soufflé Omelette

8 eggs, separated	¼ tsp salt
1 cup sugar	2 Tbl Clarified Butter (page 23)
Flavoring (see Note)	

Preheat oven to 425 degrees. In a mixing bowl beat the egg yolks with ½ cup of the sugar and the flavoring until the mixture is light in color, smooth, and very thick. In a separate bowl beat the egg whites with the salt to soft-peak consistency. Add the remaining sugar, 2 tablespoons at a time, continuing to beat until the whites are stiff and glossy. Pour the yolk mixture over them and carefully but thoroughly fold it in. In a deep skillet, about 10 inches in diameter and with a heat-proof handle, melt the butter over low heat. Remove the pan from the heat and spread ¾ of the batter into it, smoothing the top with a spatula. Using a pastry bag fitted with a star tube, decorate the top with rosettes and fluted swirls of the remaining batter. Set the pan over low heat and cook the omelette for 3 minutes, or until the bottom is set. Transfer the pan to the preheated oven, and continue the cooking for 8 minutes, or until the omelette is firm and the top is golden brown. Serve the omelette from the pan, cut to provide 6 servings. *(See photograph, page 255.)*

NOTE: Suggested flavorings include nut, fruit, or spice extracts or liqueurs to taste.

Fluffy Dessert Omelette

4 eggs, separated
¼ cup milk
1 Tbl sugar
¼ tsp salt

2 egg whites
2 Tbl Clarified Butter (page 23)
Jelly or preserves
Confectioners' sugar

Preheat oven to 350 degrees. In a mixing bowl beat together the egg yolks, milk, sugar, and salt. Separately beat all 6 egg whites until they are stiff, but not dry, and fold them into the yolk mixture. Melt the butter in an 8-inch skillet over low heat. Spread the batter evenly in the pan and cook for 3 minutes, or until the underside of the omelette is lightly browned. Transfer the pan to the preheated oven and continue the cooking for 10 minutes longer, or until the omelette is firm and the top is golden brown. Spread ½ of it with jelly or preserves and fold in half to enclose the filling. Dust the omelette with confectioners' sugar and cut it in wedges to provide 4 to 6 servings. *(See photograph, page 255.)*

Omelette Grande Époque | Gay Nineties Omelette

⅓ cup coarsely chopped glazed
    chestnuts
⅓ cup chopped mixed candied
    fruit
¼ cup orange-flavored liqueur
    (Cointreau, Curaçao, Grand
    Marnier, or such)
2 egg yolks
7 whole eggs
⅓ cup sugar

⅓ cup flour
½ tsp salt
1 cup warm milk
1 tsp vanilla extract
6 Tbl butter
12 Macaroons (page 90), dried &
    pulverized (see Note)
¼ cup heavy cream, stiffly whipped
¼ cup chopped angelica

In a small bowl combine the chestnuts and fruit and pour the liqueur over them. Let them steep so for several hours.

Dessert Soufflé Omelette (page 253)
swirled with rosettes and Fluffy Dessert Omelette
filled with plum preserves.

In the top pan of a double boiler combine the egg yolks, 1 of the whole eggs, and ¼ cup of the sugar. Beat the mixture until the sugar is completely incorporated and blend in the flour and ¼ teaspoon of the salt. Stir in the warm milk gradually and cook over simmering water, stirring constantly until the mixture is thick and smooth. Add the vanilla and blend in 2 tablespoons of the butter and ⅓ of the powdered macaroons. Remove the water pan from the heat, but leave the top pan in place to keep the sauce warm. Stir it occasionally. Drain the steeped fruit and nuts and warm them gently in a small saucepan. Keep them warm.

Separate the remaining eggs into 2 mixing bowls. Beat the yolks with the remaining sugar until they are very thick. Beat the egg whites with the remaining salt until they are stiff but not dry. Stir the whipped cream into the yolks and carefully but thoroughly fold in the whites. Melt 1 tablespoon of the remaining butter in each of two 8-inch omelette pans over low heat and let the butter foam. Immediately the foaming subsides spread ½ the egg mixture in each of the pans and cook until the puffy omelettes are well browned on the undersides. Brown the tops under a medium-hot broiler. Turn 1 of the omelettes out onto a warmed flame-proof serving platter and spread the warmed fruit and nuts over it. Place the second omelette on top and pour the prepared sauce over the entire 2-layer omelette. Flow the remaining butter, melted, over the top and sprinkle with the chopped angelica and the remaining powdered macaroons. Brown the top lightly under the broiler and serve at once, apportioned to provide 6 servings.
NOTE: To dry macaroons, heat them in a slow oven (225 degrees). Turn off the heat and let the macaroons cool and dry in the oven overnight. Roll them to a powder between sheets of waxed paper or pulverize them in an electric blender.

Rum Omelette

12 eggs	¼ tsp salt
1 Tbl cool water	6 Tbl butter
¼ cup sugar	⅓ cup light rum

Particolored Harlequin Soufflé (page 262)
—half flavored with vanilla, half with chocolate—
is surprising dessert variation.

Using a whisk, beat the eggs in a mixing bowl with the water, sugar, and salt, until the mixture flows in a thin thread from the whisk. Do not over-beat. The eggs should not be frothy. For each of the 6 omelettes which this recipe provides, heat 1 tablespoon of the butter in a seasoned 5-inch pan (page 252). Let the butter foam and immediately the foaming sub-sides, pour in about ½ cup of the egg mixture (approximately the equivalent of 2 eggs). Holding the handle of the pan in your left hand, shake the pan back and forth over the heat and, at the same time, with your right hand stir the eggs vigorously in a circle with a table fork held flat on the bottom of the pan. Let the omelette cook for a moment or two until the eggs are cooked to the preferred consistency. Using the fork, fold 1 edge of the omelette to the center and bring the other edge over to meet the fold. Transfer the pan to your right hand and, holding the pan over a warmed serving dish, tilt the pan so that the handle is up and the opposite side is at the level of the dish. Slide the omelette out onto the plate in such a way that the underside comes out on top. Sprinkle the omelette with a little of the rum and keep it warm. Prepare the remaining 5 omelettes in the same way. Each omelette should take less than 1½ minutes to prepare. In a small saucepan gently heat the remaining rum and set it ablaze. Pour a little of the flaming spirit over each omelette and serve them at once.

Soufflé Omelette with Strawberries

1 pint strawberries	⅛ tsp vanilla extract
⅓ cup cognac	2 egg whites
3 egg yolks	⅛ tsp salt
1 whole egg	Confectioners' sugar
3 Tbl sugar	2 Tbl butter
2 Tbl milk	

Wash and hull the strawberries and cut them into halves. Place them in a bowl, pour the cognac over them, and let them steep for 30 minutes. In another bowl thoroughly beat together the egg yolks, whole egg, 2 tablespoons of the sugar, the milk, and the vanilla. Fold in the egg whites beaten with the salt until stiff. Drain the berries and roll them in

the confectioners' sugar, coating them well. In a heavy 9-inch skillet
melt the butter over medium heat and spread ½ the prepared batter
over it. Cook for 2 minutes, or until the layer of batter begins to set and
the underside is lightly browned. Cover with the prepared berries and
spread the remaining batter over them. Sprinkle with the remaining
sugar. Transfer the pan to a moderately hot broiler and let it remain
until the omelette is well puffed and brown. Serve immediately apportioned for 6 servings.

Omelette Stephanie

1 pint strawberries	**1 cup sugar**
¼ cup seedless raspberry	**2 Tbl flour**
preserves	**1 Tbl kirsch**
6 eggs, separated	**⅛ tsp salt**

Preheat oven to 400 degrees. Hull and wash the strawberries, cut them
into halves, and combine them in a mixing bowl with the preserves.
Place equal amounts of the mixture in 6 buttered gratin or shallow baking dishes. In a mixing bowl beat the egg yolks with ½ the sugar until
they are very thick. Blend in the flour, and stir in the kirsch. Separately
beat the egg whites with the salt to soft-peak consistency. Add the
remaining sugar, a little at a time, continuing to beat until the whites
are stiff and glossy. Fold them into the yolks. Spread the mixture equally over the strawberries in the baking dishes. Bake in the preheated
oven for 15 minutes, or until the soufflé topping is well puffed and nicely
browned. Serve the omelettes in the baking dishes. Flame, if desired,
with a small quantity of additional kirsch.

Apricot Froth Soufflé

2 eggs	**5 egg whites, stiffly beaten**
¾ cup sugar	**⅓ cup pulverized almonds**
½ cup apricot preserves	

Preheat oven to 325 degrees. In a mixing bowl thoroughly beat together

the eggs, sugar, and preserves. The mixture should be very thick. Fold in the egg whites. Spread the mixture in a buttered and lightly sugared 6-cup soufflé dish and sprinkle the top with the almonds. Bake in the preheated oven for 1 hour, or until the soufflé is firm. Serve immediately, apportioned for 6 servings with, if desired, cognac-flavored whipped cream.

Papos de Anjo | Brazilian Poached Soufflés

12 egg yolks	**3½ cups cool water**
2 cups sugar	**1 tsp vanilla extract**
2 egg whites	

Preheat oven to 325 degrees. In a mixing bowl beat together the egg yolks and ¼ cup of the sugar until the mixture is thick. Fold in the egg whites, stiffly beaten. Butter 8 to 12 small custard cups and place 2 tablespoons of the batter in each (the number depends upon the size of the egg yolks and whites). Set the cups in a pan of hot water in the pre-heated oven and bake for 30 minutes, or until the little soufflés are puffed and nicely browned. While the soufflés bake, prepare the poaching liquid.

In a saucepan dissolve the remaining sugar in the water and cook the resulting syrup at simmer for 5 minutes. Stir in the vanilla, and re-move the pan from the heat. Unmold the baked soufflés a few at a time into the hot syrup, turning them once or twice to coat them evenly.

Arrange them on a shallow serving dish and let them cool. Chill them in the refrigerator. Chill the remaining syrup separately. Serve the soufflés, 2 to a serving, with a little of the chilled syrup poured over them.

Variations:

1. Substitute maple syrup for the vanilla syrup. Sprinkle with chopped pecans.
2. Serve with Hard Sauce (page 283).
3. Serve with Custard Sauce (page 282) and toasted, shredded coconut.

Chocolate Soufflé

1 recipe Basic Dessert Soufflé (page 252)

3 squares (3 ounces) unsweetened chocolate, melted

1 square (1 ounce) semisweet chocolate, melted

½ tsp vanilla extract

Whipped cream

Preheat oven to 375 degrees. Prepare basic soufflé batter as directed in the recipe, reducing the flour to 2 tablespoons. Blend in all of the melted chocolate and the vanilla, and let the mixture cool. Continue as directed, baking the soufflé in the preheated oven for 30 minutes, or until the soufflé is well puffed and browned. Serve with well-chilled whipped cream. This recipe provides 6 to 8 servings.

Date Soufflé

1 recipe Basic Dessert Soufflé (page 252)

2 cups pitted fresh dates, finely ground

1 tsp grated orange rind

Preheat oven to 350 degrees. Prepare basic soufflé batter as directed in the recipe and blend into it the ground dates and grated orange rind. Continue as directed in the soufflé recipe. Bake in the preheated oven for 45 minutes, or until the soufflé is well puffed and browned. Serve the soufflé apportioned for 6 to 8 servings with, if desired, Orange Sauce (page 285).

Grand Marnier Soufflé

1 recipe Basic Dessert Soufflé
(page 252)

⅓ **cup Grand Marnier liqueur**

Preheat oven to 375 degrees. Prepare the basic soufflé batter as directed in the recipe, adding the liqueur as flavoring. Continue and bake as directed. Serve immediately apportioned for 6 to 8 servings.

Harlequin Soufflé

1 recipe Basic Dessert Soufflé
(page 252)
1 square (1 ounce) semisweet
chocolate, melted

1½ tsp vanilla extract

Preheat oven to 375 degrees. Divide the yolk mixture of the basic souf-

flé equally between 2 mixing bowls. Blend the melted chocolate into the mixture in 1 bowl and the vanilla into the other. Fold ½ the stiffly beaten egg whites into each. Butter and lightly sugar a 9-cup soufflé dish. Cut a piece of cardboard to fit exactly the inside diameter of the dish and cover the cardboard with foil. Butter it. Fit the cardboard upright into the dish, dividing the receptacle into halves. Pour the chocolate soufflé batter on 1 side of the divider and the vanilla-flavored on the other. Remove the dividing cardboard. Bake in the preheated oven for 30 minutes, or until the soufflé is well puffed and well browned. This soufflé provides 6 servings. *(See photograph, page 256.)*

Délices à l'Orange | Orange Soufflé Delights

½ recipe Basic Dessert Soufflé (page 252)

¼ cup orange-flavored liqueur
6 navel oranges

Preheat oven to 425 degrees. Prepare ½ recipe as directed, using orange sugar (see below) for the basic soufflé batter instead of the indicated amount of regular granulated sugar. Stir the orange-flavored liqueur into the cooled batter and continue as directed in the recipe. Trim a 1-inch slice from the top of each orange and carefully, so as not to damage the shell, scoop out the pulp of the oranges. (Use the pulp for juice, or as desired; it is not required for this recipe.) Divide the prepared soufflé batter equally among the 6 orange shells, filling them ¾ full. Arrange the filled shells on a baking sheet and bake in the preheated oven for 10 minutes or until the soufflés are well puffed and browned. Serve immediately, 1 to a serving.

Orange Sugar:

Thoroughly rub thin peel of ½ orange into ⅓ cup sugar, suffusing the sugar with the zest. Remove and discard the peel.

Praline Soufflé

1 recipe Basic Dessert Soufflé (page 252)

1 cup Praline Powder (page 71)

Preheat oven to 375 degrees. Prepare the basic soufflé batter, omitting the ½ cup of sugar. Stir the praline powder, indicated above, into the hot batter. Continue and bake as directed in the preheated oven. This recipe provides 6 to 8 servings. Serve, if desired, with Chocolate Sauce (page 281).

Variation:

Prepare soufflé as in the recipe above, substituting 1 cup pulverized peanut brittle for the praline powder.

Sybarites' Lemon Soufflé

6 egg yolks
½ cup sugar
Grated rind of 2 lemons

Juice of 2 lemons
7 egg whites
Confectioners' sugar

Preheat oven to 375 degrees. In a mixing bowl beat the egg yolks with the sugar, lemon rind, and juice until they are very thick. Separately beat the egg whites until they are stiff but not dry, and fold them carefully but thoroughly into the yolks. Butter and lightly sugar an 8-cup soufflé dish and transfer the batter to it. Set the dish in a deep roasting pan in the preheated oven and pour boiling-hot water around it to a depth of about 1 inch. Bake for 30 minutes, or until the soufflé is well puffed and browned. Dust the soufflé with confectioners' sugar and serve it at once, apportioned for 6 servings with, if desired, chilled, lightly sweetened and vanilla-flavored whipped cream.

NOTE: This soufflé is not only for the pleasure-loving, but for the lazy as well. It is by far the most easily prepared and wonderfully delicious soufflé ever.

Salzburger Nockerln | Salzburg-Style Soufflés

5 egg yolks
3 Tbl Vanilla Sugar (page 70)
4 tsp flour
7 egg whites

6 Tbl butter, melted
Vanilla confectioners' sugar
**   (see Note)**

Preheat oven to 425 degrees. In a mixing bowl beat the egg yolks with 2 tablespoons of the vanilla sugar until they are very thick. Blend in the flour. In a separate bowl beat the egg whites to soft-peak consistency. Add the remaining vanilla sugar and continue to beat until the whites are very, very stiff. Fold them carefully but thoroughly into the beaten yolks. Coat each of 6 individual shallow baking dishes with 1 table-spoon of the melted butter and heap onto each an equal quantity of the prepared batter, rounding the tops. Bake in the preheated oven for 5 minutes, or until the soufflés are golden brown and creamily soft with-in. Dust them with vanilla confectioners' sugar and serve at once in the baking dishes.
NOTE: Vanilla confectioners' sugar and vanilla granulated sugar (page 70) are made in the same way.

Tapioca Soufflé à la Brésilienne

1¼ cups sugar	1 Tbl cornstarch
⅓ cup water	1 tsp vanilla extract
2 cups milk	5 egg whites
2 Tbl butter	Rum Caramel Sauce (page 279)
½ cup quick-cooking tapioca	

In a saucepan over medium heat dissolve ¾ cup of the sugar in the water. Cook the resulting syrup until it caramelizes to a rich brown. Pour the caramel into a 6-cup soufflé dish and swirl the syrup around to coat the dish evenly. In the top pan of a double boiler, over direct heat, scald the milk. Add the remaining sugar, the butter, tapioca, and cornstarch, and stir to blend. Set the pan over simmering water and cook the mixture for 10 minutes, stirring constantly until it thickens. Remove the pan from over the heat and stir in the vanilla. Cool the mixture and fold in the egg whites, stiffly beaten. Spread the batter in the prepared soufflé dish. Set the dish in a pan of hot water in the pre-heated oven and bake it for 30 minutes, or until it is well puffed and lightly browned. Remove the dish from the oven and let the soufflé cool and fall. Unmold it onto a serving platter to be apportioned for 6 servings with the rum caramel sauce.

12 | crêpes and pancakes

Pancakes are a universal pleasure, appearing one way or another in almost every country of the world. From the basic pancake recipe—a combination of flour, sugar, eggs, and milk—each country has evolved its own distinctive preparations. To the basic four ingredients, France has added water, bland cooking oil, and liqueur, and so has created Crêpes. Sweden added an accompaniment of luscious lingonberries and produced its famous Tunna Plättar. Hungary's Palacsinta were achieved by combining the basic ingredients with walnuts, raisins, and grated orange rind. Germany had only to stir into the base a few raisins to produce Kaiserschmarrn, while another country, probably one of the Slavic group, created heroic-sized Yogurt Pancakes by incorporating baking powder and yogurt into the batter and omitting the eggs and milk. America's flapjacks hew close to the line, generally using just the basic four ingredients bolstered on occasion with a little baking powder and melted butter. They have yet to charm their way into the special company of desserts, however.

Crêpes

3 whole eggs
3 egg yolks
2¼ cups milk
½ cup cool water
¼ cup Grand Marnier liqueur
¼ cup bland cooking oil

1½ cups sifted flour
1 Tbl sugar
¼ tsp salt
Additional milk
Additional cool water

In a mixing bowl combine the whole eggs, egg yolks, milk, water, liqueur, and oil. Beat well. Sift together the flour, sugar, and salt, and blend the mixture into the combined liquids. Beat the batter with a rotary beater until it is very smooth. Chill for at least 1 hour. The batter will thicken somewhat as it chills. Before using it, thin it to the consistency of light cream with equal quantities of milk and cool water. Cook the pancakes in a 6- to 7-inch crêpe pan or heavy skillet. Heat the pan and grease it lightly with butter. Pour in ¼ cup of the batter and tilt the pan immediately, swirling the batter evenly over the bottom. Cook the crêpe over moderate heat, browning it lightly on both sides. Proceed in the same way with the remaining batter. This recipe provides about 30 crêpes. They may be served with syrup or preserves, or as required in specific recipes. Cooled and separated with sheets of waxed paper, they will keep in the refrigerator for 1 week to 10 days, or in the freezer for a month or longer.

Crêpes with Ginger and Ice Cream

¾ cup orange juice
¼ cup grapefruit juice
½ cup syrup drained from
   preserved ginger
¼ cup butter

¾ cup finely chopped preserved
   ginger
1 recipe Crêpes (above)
1 tsp sugar
¼ cup dark rum, gently warmed

In a skillet heat together the orange and grapefruit juice, and stir in the ginger syrup. Add the butter, stirring until it is melted. Spread 1½ teaspoons of the chopped ginger over each of the prepared crêpes, and fold the crêpes over it into quarters. Transfer the prepared sauce to the pan of a chafing dish over moderate heat, and arrange in it the filled crêpes, overlapping them slightly. Sprinkle them with the sugar. Set the warmed rum ablaze and pour it over the crêpes. Shake the pan until the flame expires. Serve the crêpes apportioned for 6 servings with, if desired, Vanilla Ice Cream (page 160).

Crêpes with Maple Icing

½ recipe Crêpes (page 268)   **Maple Icing (page 62)**
1½ cups Pastry Cream
  (page 58)

On each of the cooled prepared pancakes place 2 tablespoons of the pastry cream. Roll the pancakes, tucking in the sides, to enclose the fillings completely. Set them on a baking sheet lined with waxed paper and coat them evenly with the icing. Serve the crêpes cooled, but not chilled, apportioned to provide 6 servings.

Crêpes Suzette

¾ cup sugar   **⅓ cup Grand Marnier liqueur**
Thin whole peel of 2 oranges   **2 Tbl finely shredded orange peel**
Thin whole peel of 1 lemon   **1 recipe Crêpes (page 268)**
Juice of 4 oranges   **¼ cup cognac, gently warmed**
Juice of 1 lemon

Reserve 2 teaspoons of the sugar and set them aside. In a mixing bowl rub into the remaining sugar the orange and lemon peels, thoroughly suffusing the sugar with the zest. Remove and discard the peels. In the pan of a chafing dish at the table dissolve the flavored sugar in the juice of the oranges and lemon. Set the pan over moderate heat and cook the syrup until it is reduced somewhat and slightly thickened. Add the liqueur and the shredded peel. Coat 1 side of each of the prepared crêpes with a little of the sauce. Fold the pancakes into wedge-shaped quarters and arrange them, overlapping slightly, in the sauce in the pan. Baste the pancakes with the sauce until they are heated through. Sprinkle them with the reserved sugar. Set the warmed cognac ablaze and pour the flaming spirit over the crêpes. Shake the pan until the flame expires. Serve the crêpes, 3 or 4 to each of 6 or 8 servings, with a little of the sauce poured over them.

Viennese Pancakes in Custard

1 cup toasted blanched almonds, grated
⅔ cup sugar
3 Tbl seedless raisins, chopped

1 recipe Crêpes (page 268)
4 egg yolks
2 cups milk
½ tsp vanilla extract

Preheat oven to 350 degrees. In a mixing bowl combine the almonds, ½ cup of the sugar, and the raisins. Spread the crêpes evenly with the mixture and roll them, tucking in the sides, to enclose the mixture securely. Arrange the rolled pancakes in a buttered baking pan. In another bowl thoroughly beat together the egg yolks, milk, and remaining sugar. Stir in the vanilla. Pour the mixture over the pancakes and bake in the preheated oven for 30 minutes. Serve the pancakes, apportioned for 6 to 8 servings, with a quantity of the custard.

Kaiserschmarrn | Emperor Omelette Pancakes

4 eggs, separated
1¼ cups milk
1½ tsp sugar
¼ tsp salt

1 cup flour
⅓ cup seedless white raisins
¼ cup butter
Confectioners' sugar

In a mixing bowl thoroughly beat together the egg yolks, milk, sugar, and salt. Combine the flour and raisins and stir the mixture into the egg yolks and milk. Fold in the egg whites, stiffly beaten. In each of two 8- or 9-inch skillets heat 2 tablespoons of the butter. Pour into each pan ½ of the prepared batter. Cook over moderate heat, browning the pancakes nicely on both sides. Turn them, carefully, just once. Place the pancakes on a warmed serving platter and, using 2 forks, separate them into random-size pieces. Sift confectioners' sugar over them and serve at once. These omelette pancakes provide 6 servings.

Chocolate-Filled Crêpes

1½ pints very firm Chocolate Ice Cream (page 159)

½ recipe Crêpes (page 268)

Liqueur Chocolate Sauce (page 280), heated

Slivers of thin orange peel

Place ¼ cup of the ice cream in the center of each of the prepared cooled crêpes. Fold the crêpes envelope-fashion over the cream, enclosing it completely. Store the filled crêpes in the freezer until serving time. Serve them, 2 to a serving, with a quantity of the hot liqueur chocolate sauce poured over them and a sprinkling of the slivered orange peel. This recipe provides 6 to 8 servings.

Apple Pancakes

3 large apples
½ cup lemon juice
4 eggs
1½ cups milk
1 cup sifted flour

2 tsp sugar
¼ tsp salt
Cinnamon Sugar (page 70) or
  honey

Peel and core the apples and cut them into very small, fine julienne. Place them in a glass bowl and pour the lemon juice over them. Turn the apples frequently, so they are uniformly seasoned with the juice. In a mixing bowl thoroughly beat together the eggs and milk. Sift the flour with the sugar and salt, and blend the mixture into the eggs and milk. Stir in the apples. Cook the batter, ¼ cup at a time, on a buttered hot griddle or in a heavy skillet, browning the pancakes well on both sides. Serve the pancakes, apportioned for 6 servings, with the cinnamon sugar or honey.

Palacsinta | Hungarian Pancakes

2 cups ground walnuts
¾ cup sugar
½ cup milk
¼ cup rum
⅓ cup seedless raisins

Grated rind of 1 orange
½ recipe Crêpes (page 268)
Butter
Liqueur Chocolate Sauce (page
  280), heated

In a mixing bowl work together into a smooth paste the nuts, sugar, milk, and rum. Blend into it the raisins and grated rind. Spread the prepared crêpes equally with the paste and fold them over the fillings, envelope-fashion. In a skillet over moderate heat, sauté the filled crêpes in a small quantity of butter, browning them very lightly. Apportion the crêpes among 6 individual serving plates and pour hot liqueur chocolate sauce over them. Serve, if desired, also with rum-flavored ice cream.

Szentgyorgyi Palacsinta:

Fill the crêpes as directed above in the recipe for Hungarian Pancakes, but do not sauté them. Cut the filled crêpes in halves and arrange them in a baking dish. Pour over them 6 tablespoons browned butter and cover with a meringue of 4 egg whites, stiffly beaten with ¼ cup sugar. Bake in a preheated 400-degree oven for 10 minutes or until the meringue is delicately browned. Apportion to provide 6 servings.

Rice Pancakes

1½ cups cooked rice	1 cup flour
1 cup milk	2 tsp baking powder
2 eggs	½ tsp salt
2 Tbl butter, melted & cooled	Lemon Sauce (page 281)

In a mixing bowl blend into the rice the milk and eggs thoroughly beaten together. Stir in the melted butter. Sift together the flour, baking powder, and salt, and stir the mixture into the rice. Bake the pancakes, 1 tablespoon of batter to each, on a very hot buttered griddle or in a skillet, browning them well on both sides. This recipe provides about 48 small pancakes, sufficient for 6 to 8 servings with lemon sauce.

Tunna Plättar | Swedish Pancakes

2 eggs	1½ tsp sugar
2 cups milk	¼ tsp salt
2 cups flour	Lingonberry preserves

In a mixing bowl beat the eggs with ¼ cup of the milk until they are well blended. Beat in the remaining milk. Sift the flour with the sugar and salt, and blend the mixture into the combined eggs and milk. Let the batter season at room temperature for about 2 hours.

Bake the pancakes on top of the stove in a *plättpanna,* a special pan with small shallow depressions just large enough to accommodate the proper amount of batter for each pancake. Heat the pan, butter the depressions lightly, and spread about 2 tablespoons of the batter in each. Bake the pancakes, browning them nicely on both sides, turning them only once. The amount of batter in this recipe will provide 6 generous servings. Serve the pancakes hot with lingonberry preserves.

Yogurt Pancakes

2 cups yogurt   1 tsp baking powder
2 eggs   Honey
1 cup flour

In a mixing bowl thoroughly beat together the yogurt and eggs and blend in the flour sifted with the baking powder. Butter a hot griddle or skillet and on it bake the pancakes, using ½ cup of the batter for each of 6 pancakes. Brown them well on both sides. Pancakes will be large and thick. Serve 1 to a serving, with honey.

Waffles

4 eggs, separated   2 Tbl sugar
2¼ cups milk   ½ tsp salt
1 Tbl cool water   1 tsp vanilla extract
3 cups sifted flour   ⅔ cup butter, melted & cooled
4 tsp baking powder

In a mixing bowl beat together the egg yolks, milk, and water, combining them thoroughly. Sift together the flour, baking powder, sugar, and salt, and blend in. Stir in the vanilla and the melted butter. Fold in the egg whites, beaten until stiff but not dry.

Heat the waffle iron. If the iron has no heat indicator, test for correct baking temperature with a drop of water on the iron. If the water simmers and takes a second or two to evaporate, the iron is at proper temperature. If the drop bounces about and evaporates almost immediately, the iron is too hot; allow it to cool. When it is at the proper temperature, pour in a quantity of the batter. Fill the iron only ⅞ full and then spread the batter to fill it completely. Close the iron and bake the waffle until the steaming subsides, about 4 minutes, or until the indicator signals the completion of the baking. Do not open the iron until the waffles are completely baked. Remove the waffle, and continue baking the remaining batter. This recipe provides 6 large, 4-section waffles. Serve them, as desired, with butter and syrup or preserves.

Variations:

1. Add ½ cup finely chopped nuts to the batter. Serve the waffles with ice cream and/or Chocolate Sauce (page 281).

2. Add 1 cup grated cheddar cheese to the batter. Serve the waffles with stewed fruit and/or sour cream.

3. Add ½ cup chopped seedless raisins, or ¾ cup shredded coconut, to the batter. Serve with Hard Sauce (page 283).

4. Add to the batter ¾ cup thoroughly drained cooked apricots or prunes and 1 additional tablespoon sugar. Serve with Vanilla Sauce (page 287).

5. Add to the batter just before baking ¾ cup blueberries, washed and thoroughly drained. In a saucepan over moderate heat cook heavy cream, slightly sweetened, until it is very thick. Serve hot with the waffles.

6. Blend into the batter 2½ squares (2½ ounces) semisweet chocolate. Serve hot or cold with whipped cream, flavored with cognac and slightly sweetened.

Waffled French Toast

3 eggs	⅛ tsp salt
1½ cups milk	18 slices white bread, trimmed &
1 Tbl sugar	cut to fit the sections of the
½ tsp vanilla extract	waffle iron
¼ tsp nutmeg	

In a mixing bowl thoroughly beat together the eggs, milk, and sugar. Stir in the vanilla, nutmeg, and salt. Place the slices of bread in the prepared batter and let them absorb it. Drain them slightly. Bake as for waffles, in a heated and buttered iron, each slice of bread fitted into a waffle section. This recipe provides 6 servings of 3 slices each. Serve with a sauce of choice, puréed berries, or cooked fruit.

13 | sauces

Unlike the multitude of basic sauces for main courses, those for desserts are of only two kinds: the custard type, which also serves as the basis for other dessert sauces, and the fruit variety, using either the purée or juice of the fruits. Both types of sauces are sweetened, but only the juice sauces are thickened, usually with cornstarch or arrowroot powder.

Dessert sauces have much the same function in cooking as those for entrées. They may be used to add flavor (as does caramel sauce to plain custard), to give a compatible contrast (as between orange sauce and chocolate bread pudding), or to supply a flaming flourish (as for Cherries Jubilee). Of all the dessert sauces, Boiled Custard—seemingly the simplest to prepare—is the most difficult. Given as little as half a degree too much heat, or cooked a split second too long, boiled custard becomes what one neophyte *saucier* described as "Disgruntled Eggs."

Try to learn a full repertoire of dessert sauces. They permit imaginative combinations and show attention to detail, the mark of every inspired (and aspiring) chef.

Simple Syrup

1 cup sugar   **2 cups water**

In a saucepan combine the sugar and water. Bring the liquid to a boil and cook the resulting syrup for 5 minutes. Cool it, store it in a well-sealed container, and use as required.

Caramel Syrup

1 cup sugar   **½ cup boiling-hot water**

In a skillet over low heat melt and lightly caramelize the sugar. Stir in the water slowly and by small additions, to avoid spattering. Continue cooking until the caramel is dissolved and the resulting syrup is quite dark in color. Cool the syrup and store it in a securely covered container. This recipe provides about 1 cup of caramel syrup.

Foamy Sauce

3 eggs, separated   **¼ cup cognac**
½ cup confectioners' sugar   **3 egg whites**
⅛ tsp salt

In the top pan of a double boiler over simmering water beat together the egg yolks, sugar, and salt until the mixture is thick. Stir in the cognac. Remove the pan from over the water and let the mixture cool. Fold in the egg whites, stiffly beaten. This recipe provides 1½ cups of sauce; it should not be stored, but should be made fresh for each use and served immediately.

Butterscotch Sauce

¾ cup firmly packed brown sugar   **¼ cup butter**
1 cup light corn syrup   **1 cup heavy cream**

In a saucepan over low heat dissolve the sugar in the syrup. Add the butter and, when it melts, blend in the cream. Bring the mixture to a boil and let it simmer for about 3 minutes, or until it thickens slightly. Remove the pan from the heat and let the sauce cool; there will be about 2½ cups of sauce. Stored in a tightly covered jar in the refrigerator, it can be kept for 4 to 5 days.

Caramel Sauce

1 recipe Caramel Syrup (page 278)   **¼ tsp vanilla extract**
⅛ tsp salt   **1½ cups light cream, well chilled**

Cool the syrup and add to it the salt and vanilla. In a mixing bowl stir the syrup into the chilled cream. This recipe provides about 2½ cups of sauce.

Rum Caramel Sauce

1 recipe Caramel Syrup (page 278)   **2 Tbl dark rum**
½ cup boiling-hot milk
1 pint Vanilla Ice Cream (page
   160), softened

Into hot caramel syrup in a saucepan stir the hot milk, a little at a time, blending the 2 completely. Cool to warm, add the ice cream, and beat the mixture to the consistency of lightly whipped cream. Stir in the rum. There will be about 3½ cups of sauce. It may be served warm or chilled.

Chestnut Sauce

¾ cup unsweetened chestnut purée   **½ cup heavy cream**
   (see below)   **¼ tsp lemon extract**
½ cup Vanilla Sauce (page 287)

Prepare chestnut purée as directed in the recipe for Polish Chestnut Cake (page 41). In a mixing bowl combine the chestnut purée, vanilla sauce, and cream and beat the mixture until it is very smooth. Stir in

the lemon flavoring. Use with chocolate mousse or chocolate soufflé, or as required. This recipe provides about 1½ cups of sauce.

Liqueur Chocolate Sauce

⅓ cup butter
3 Tbl sugar
Grated rind of 2 oranges
Juice of 2 lemons
¼ cup rum
¼ cup orange-flavored liqueur

¼ cup cognac
6 squares (6 ounces) unsweetened
   chocolate, melted
½ cup finely chopped walnuts
   (optional)

In a saucepan over low heat melt the butter. Add the sugar and let it just begin to caramelize. Stir in the orange rind and lemon juice. Add the rum, liqueur, and cognac, and set them ablaze. Let the flame burn for just a few seconds and extinguish it by covering the pan. Remove the pan from the heat, stir in the melted chocolate, and let the sauce cool. Stir in the nuts, if desired. Use the sauce as required. This recipe provides about 2 cups of sauce.

Chocolate Sauce

6 squares (6 ounces) semisweet
  chocolate
1 square (1 ounce) unsweetened
  chocolate

¾ cup heavy cream

Melt the chocolate in the top pan of a double boiler over simmering water. Blend in the cream. This recipe provides about 1½ cups of sauce.

Chocolate Peppermint Sauce

1 recipe Chocolate Sauce
  (above)

¼ tsp peppermint extract

Let the sauce cool and stir into it the peppermint flavoring. This recipe provides about 1½ cups of sauce.

Coconut Sauce

2 cups shredded coconut
2 cups milk, scalded
1 recipe Basic Custard Cream
  (page 176)

¼ tsp vanilla extract

In a heat-proof bowl steep the coconut in the hot milk for 30 minutes. Strain the milk through several thicknesses of cheesecloth, squeezing coconut to extract as much liquid as possible. Prepare the custard cream as directed, substituting the prepared coconut milk for the milk indicated in recipe. Stir in the vanilla. This makes about 2 cups of sauce.

Lemon Sauce

1 recipe Basic Custard Cream
  (page 176)

Grated rind of 1 lemon
Juice of 1½ lemons

Prepare custard cream as directed in the recipe, adding the lemon rind and juice while the cream is still hot. Let the sauce cool and use it as required. This is a very lemony sauce. If a less tart one is desired, reduce the quantity of lemon juice or increase the sugar content of the cream. This recipe provides slightly more than 2 cups.

Maple Sauce

2 cups maple syrup
1 Tbl butter

¼ cup chopped pecans (optional)

Pour the syrup into the top pan of a double boiler set over simmering water and beat it with a rotary beater until the syrup becomes opaque and creamy. Stir into it the butter and, if desired, the chopped nuts. This recipe provides about 1½ cups of sauce.

Custard Sauce

3 egg yolks
1 whole egg
2 Tbl sugar

⅛ tsp salt
1½ cups milk, scalded
1 tsp vanilla extract

In the top pan of a double boiler beat together the egg yolks, whole egg, sugar, and salt. Add the milk, a little at a time, pouring it in a thin stream and beating constantly. Set the pan over simmering water and cook the mixture, continuing to stir, until it coats the spoon. Remove the pan from over the water and let the custard sauce cool. Flavor it with the vanilla, or as required. This recipe provides about 2 cups of sauce.

Glazed Fruit Sauce

1 cup Basic Custard Cream
  (page 176)
¼ tsp vanilla extract

1 Tbl apple jelly, melted
½ cup finely chopped mixed
  glazed fruit

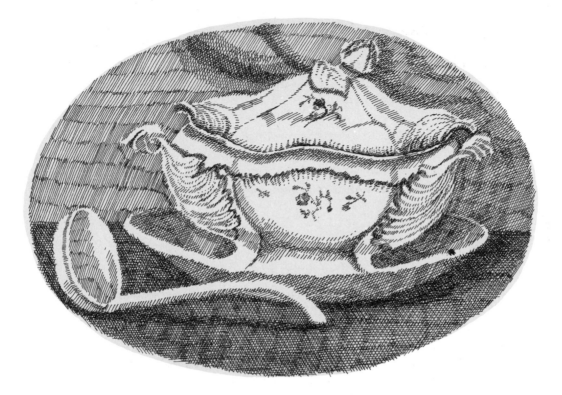

Into the cooled custard cream stir the vanilla extract and the melted jelly. Fold in the glazed fruit. This recipe provides about 1½ cups of sauce.

Hard Sauce

½ cup butter, softened
1¼ cups confectioners' sugar
¼ tsp vanilla extract
⅛ tsp salt
1 Tbl bourbon (or rye whiskey or cognac)

In a mixing bowl beat into the butter the confectioners' sugar, a little at a time, until the mixture is very fluffy. Stir into it the vanilla and salt. Blend in the spirit. Chill the sauce in the refrigerator until it is firm but (despite its name) not hard. There will be about 1½ cups.

Ice Cream Sauce

1 pint Vanilla Ice Cream (page 160), softened
½ recipe Basic Custard Cream (page 176)

¼ tsp vanilla extract

In a mixing bowl beat the ice cream with a whisk until it is the consistency of lightly whipped cream. Stir into it the cooled custard cream and the vanilla. Serve with steamed puddings, or as required. This recipe provides about 3 cups of sauce, sufficient for 6 to 8 servings.

Sauce Laura

4 egg yolks
½ cup sugar
¼ tsp salt

¼ cup cognac
1 tsp orange-flower water
¾ cup heavy cream, whipped

In the top pan of a double boiler beat together the egg yolks, sugar, salt, and cognac. Set the pan over simmering water and beat the mixture with a rotary beater until it thickens and increases in volume. Remove the pan from over the water and let the mixture cool. Stir in the orange-flower water and fold in the whipped cream. This recipe provides about 2 cups of sauce.

Melba Sauce

1 pint fresh ripe strawberries
1 pint fresh ripe raspberries

¾ cup sugar

Purée the strawberries and raspberries together either by forcing them through a sieve or reducing them in an electric blender. Combine the purée in a saucepan with the sugar and cook the mixture over very low heat for 4 to 5 minutes, or just until the sugar dissolves and the purée begins to foam. Remove the pan from the heat and let the sauce cool. If the purée becomes too thick, it may be thinned with a little dry white wine. This recipe provides about 2 cups of sauce.

Dessert Mint Sauce

**1 recipe Basic Custard Cream
(page 176)**

**3 Tbl crème de menthe liqueur,
green or white**

Cool the custard cream completely and stir into it the crème de menthe.
The recipe provides 2 cups of sauce. Use as required.

Orange Sauce

**1 recipe Basic Custard Cream
(page 176)**
1 cup light cream

1 Tbl grated orange rind
½ cup orange juice
1 Tbl Grand Marnier liqueur

Prepare custard cream as directed in the recipe, omitting the milk and
substituting the cream, orange rind, and juice. Cool the sauce and
strain out the rind. Add the liqueur. This recipe provides about 2 cups
of sauce.

Peppermint Candy Sauce

**1 recipe Basic Custard Cream
(page 176)**
**⅓ cup medium-finely crushed
peppermint stick candy**

1 or 2 drops red food coloring

While the custard cream is still hot, dissolve in it 2 tablespoons of the
crushed peppermint stick. Stir in the food coloring and let the custard
cream cool. Fold in remaining candy. Recipe yields about 2 cups of
sauce.

Pineapple Sauce

**2 cups cooked fresh
(or canned drained) pineapple**
½ cup Simple Syrup (page 278)

2 tsp cornstarch
1 tsp cool water
¼ tsp vanilla extract

Force the pineapple pulp through a fine sieve and combine it in a sauce-

pan with the syrup (or purée the pineapple in an electric blender, adding the syrup to facilitate the blending). Stir in the cornstarch dissolved in the water and heat the purée, stirring constantly until it thickens somewhat. Stir in the vanilla. Cool the sauce and use as required.

Mocha Sauce

4 egg yolks	**1 Tbl cocoa**
½ cup sugar	**2 Tbl boiling-hot water**
2 cups light cream	**¼ tsp vanilla extract**
3 Tbl instant coffee powder	**¼ cup whipped cream (optional)**

In the top pan of a double boiler beat together the egg yolks, sugar, and cream. Set the pan over simmering water and cook the mixture, stirring constantly, until it becomes syrupy. Combine the coffee powder and the cocoa and dissolve them in the hot water. Stir the mixture into the hot yolk syrup. Let the sauce cool and stir in the vanilla. Fold in the whipped cream, if desired. This recipe makes 2 cups of sauce without the whipped cream. When the whipped cream is used, the recipe yields about 2½ cups of sauce.

Pineapple Mint Sauce

1½ cups cubed cooked fresh
  pineapple with cooking liquid,
  or canned pineapple with syrup

½ tsp cornstarch
1 Tbl cool water
⅓ cup green crème de menthe

Make purée by forcing pineapple through a coarse sieve, or by whirling it in a blender together with ½ cup of liquid to facilitate blending; this may be liquid in which pineapple was cooked, or syrup from canned pineapple augmented if necessary by Simple Syrup (page 278). Transfer the purée to a saucepan and stir into it the cornstarch dissolved in the cool water. Cook purée over low heat, stirring constantly, until it thickens slightly. Remove pan from heat. Cool the purée and stir into it the green crème de menthe. Use over lemon ice, or as required. This recipe provides 2¼ cups of sauce.

White Rum Sauce

1 pint Vanilla Ice Cream
  (page 160), softened

¼ cup white rum
⅛ tsp almond extract

In a mixing bowl beat the ice cream to the consistency of lightly whipped heavy cream. Stir in the rum and the almond flavoring, and chill thoroughly. This recipe provides 6 to 8 servings, about 2 cups of sauce.

Vanilla Sauce

1½ cups light cream
1 2-inch length vanilla bean, slit

1 recipe Basic Custard Cream
  (page 176)

In a saucepan scald the cream with the vanilla bean. Let the cream cool and discard the bean. Prepare basic custard cream as directed in the recipe, substituting the scalded vanilla cream for the milk. About 2 cups of sauce will result.

Hot Red-Wine Sauce

2 cups full-bodied red wine   2 or 3 whole cloves
½ cup sugar   2 tsp cornstarch
2-inch stick cinnamon   1 Tbl cool water

In a saucepan combine the wine, sugar, and spices, and cook the mixture at bare simmer for 10 minutes. Remove and discard the spices. Stir in the cornstarch dissolved in the water and continue cooking for a few seconds longer, stirring constantly until the sauce thickens slightly. Strain the sauce and serve it hot or cooled as required. This quantity is sufficient for 6 servings as an accompaniment to a fruit pudding or similar dish.

Whipped Cream

Use the required amount of heavy cream (it will double in bulk when whipped) and thoroughly chill it, the bowl in which it is to be whipped, and the beater. If the bowl and beater are not chilled, the cream may be churned to butter before it thickens properly. If the cream is stored 1 or 2 days before it is used, it can be whipped more easily and to greater volume. It can be whipped with any kind of beater, but best results are obtained with a whisk or a rotary beater. Beat at a steady rate of about 150 strokes with a whisk (or turns of a rotary beater) per minute for the first minute or so, retarding as the cream begins to thicken. It should be completely whipped in 2 to 3 minutes. Sweeten fully whipped cream with confectioners' sugar (1 tablespoon or more to each cup) and blend in the desired flavoring; or add confectioners' or fine granulated sugar and flavoring when the cream begins to thicken, and continue beating until the cream is properly whipped. Some cooks in-

sist that the latter method allows for stiffer whipping and less chance of churning the cream to butter.

Whipped cream will hold under refrigeration for several hours. Sweetened and flavored whipped cream may render a little of its water content after a time. It should be drained. Better still, store the cream in a collander set over a bowl in the refrigerator and the liquid will drain off by itself. For soft-frozen whipped cream, which is occasionally called for in specific recipes, place whipped cream in the freezing compartment of the refrigerator until it reaches the desired frozen consistency.

As accompaniment, ⅓ cup of whipped cream provides an average serving. For other requirements, use as directed in specific recipes.

glossary

Almond paste Finely ground blanched almonds worked to a smooth paste for use in making pastries and other desserts. Almond paste, unsweetened or with sugar added, is available commercially.

Bar-le-Duc A preserve of seeded currants, so named for the French town where it was originally made.

Beat To turn a mass over and over rapidly with a fork, whisk, or rotary beater in order to aerate it (as is done to produce whipped cream and stiffly beaten egg whites), or to blend ingredients or to thicken them.

Blanch To immerse uncooked foods briefly in boiling-hot water. Nut skins and fruit peel are frequently softened by this process to make them easier to remove.

Blend To work one ingredient or mixture thoroughly into another; also the process of reducing an ingredient or mixture to a finer texture in an electric blender.

Boiling point The temperature at which a liquid subjected to heat begins to bubble.

Caramelize To heat sugar in a pan until it melts and turns amber or darker brown, as required.

Charlotte A dessert in which a Bavarian cream is encased in slices of sponge cake. A charlotte may also be a preparation of fruit enveloped in overlapping slices of buttered bread. The two are related only by the mold in which they are made, which should be round, deep, and straight-sided.

Cream To work a firm ingredient, such as butter or cream cheese (often in combination with sugar or flour), to the consistency of lightly whipped cream by beating with a spoon or spatula against the side of the bowl.

Crimp To score uncooked pastry, specifically the rim of a pie, by pressing down on it with the tines of a fork or similar implement in order to secure the pastry to the pan and provide a decorative edge.

Cut in To blend solid shortening into one or more ingredients; this can be done with a special cutter, with two forks or two knives, or with the fingers.

Dredge To coat with a dry, powdery ingredient such as flour or sugar.

Dust To sprinkle lightly with a dry, powdery ingredient such as flour or sugar.

Filo (phyllo) pastry Tissue-thin pastry, similar to strudel dough but made without eggs. Sheets of filo are available commercially in shops specializing in Greek food products.

Flambé To "flame," that is, to pour a gently warmed spirit (such as brandy, whisky, gin, or liqueur) over food and set it ablaze. The alcohol is thereby volatilized, leaving only the true flavor of the spirit with which to imbue the food.

Flute — To provide a decorative edge to an uncooked pie pastry shell by pressing it between the fingers into a succession of scallops.

Fold — The method of blending an aerated ingredient, such as stiffly beaten egg whites or whipped cream, into a heavier substance, such as a cake batter. This is done by spreading the aerated material over the other and then cutting down through to the bottom of the mass at one side and bringing a part of the two ingredients together over the top. This is repeated, always gently, as many times as needed to complete the blending.

Frost — To coat a cake or pastry with sweetened paste which contains unincorporated solids, such as nuts, but is of spreading consistency.

Glaze — To ice a cake or pastry thinly; also, to provide it with a coating of fruit preserve preliminary to frosting or icing it.

Ice — To coat a cake or pastry with a smooth, sweet paste of spreading consistency.

Knead — To work dough with the hands by pressing, folding, and turning it until it becomes cohesive and smooth or of whatever texture is required by a recipe. This can also be accomplished in an electric mixer fitted with a dough hook.

Poach — To cook in a liquid at a simmer.

Purée — To reduce a food to a moderately thick, partially liquefied consistency by use of a sieve, blender, grinder, or food mill.

Scald — To heat a liquid slightly below its boiling point until very small bubbles just begin to rise to the surface.

Semolina — Fine flour milled from durum or other hard wheat. It is generally available at shops specializing in products used in Middle European cooking.

Sift — To shake a dry ingredient, such as flour or sugar, through a sifter or a fine sieve to aerate it or to remove any lumps or extraneous material.

Simmer — To cook at just below the boiling point; bubbles come gently to the surface.

Steep — To soak a food so that it becomes softened and infused with the soaking liquid.

Strudel dough — A tissue-thin, almost transparent pastry made with flour, eggs, bland cooking oil, salt, and warm water kneaded together and stretched with the hands.

Whip — To beat briskly with a whisk or fine-bladed rotary beater; usually applied to liquids, especially cream.

Zest — The outer peel of citrus fruit; when pressed, twisted, or grated it yields a small amount of aromatic oil, which is also sometimes called zest.

index

Caption references in italics

a

Allemande pudding, 201
Almond
    Bavarian cream, 180
    -paste icing, 61
    pastry cream, 59
    pear mousse, 189
    peaches, 241
    pretzels, 99, *103*
    rice, 210
Ambrosia, 241
Amor frío, 176
Angel food cake, 16
Anise drop cookies, 103
Apple(s)
    applesauce cake, 31
    baked, 224
    brown betty, 200
    crunch, 225
    Danish apple cake, 31
    dumplings, Shaker, 143
    fritters with vanilla sauce, 225
    ginger betty, 224
    icy hot apple meringue, 226
    pancakes, 272
    pie, 108
        deep-dish pie, 108
    (pommes) Normande, 227
    quick pudding, 200
    Roquefort-filled baked, 226
    sauce, 227
    soufflé, 228
    spun-silk, 228
    strudel, 141
Applejack pound cake, 15
Apricot(s)
    froth soufflé, 259
    glaze, 70
    ice, 161
    ring, 176
    tart, 117
Avocado(s)
    Bavarian cream, 181
    cream, 219
    rum-flavored, with grapefruit, 239

b

Baba au rhum, 24
Baci di dama, 95
Baked Alaska, 168
Baked apples, 224
Baked Indian pudding, 204
Baklava, 154
Banana(s)
    chocolate-coated baked, 229
    flambées, 230
Banbury tarts, 121
Basic custard cream, 176
Basic dessert soufflé, 252
Basic ice cream, 158
Basler lebkuchen, 20
Bavarians
    almond cream, 180
    avocado cream, 181
    chocolate cream pie, 182
    coconut cream, 182
Berliner balls, 144
Berry glacier flambé, 248
Birthday cake, 40, *82*
Bisquit tortoni, 168
Blackberry charlotte, 178
Black bottom pie, 122
Black-walnut wafers, 90
Blanc mange, *189,* 201
Blueberry(ies)
    cake, 35
    grunt, 217
    pie, 113
    with lemon ice, 230
Boiled custard, 213
Boston cream pie, 37
Boule de neige, 171
Brandied fruit salad, 234
Brandied spiced peaches, 242
Brandy snaps, *103,* 104
Brazilian poached soufflés, 260